THE RIGHT TO KNOW

THE RIGHT TO KNOW
Media and the Common Good

by William H. Marnell

A CONTINUUM BOOK
The Seabury Press · New York

First Edition

Library of Congress Cataloging in Publication Data

Marnell, William H
  The right to know.

  1. Liberty of the press—United States.
2. Security classification (Government documents)
—United States. I. Title.
KF4774.M35   342'.73'085   72-10373
ISBN 0-8164-9139-9

To
Charles and Helen Martell
and
Reverend Joseph Deacon

CONTENTS

INTRODUCTION

On June 13, 1971, an event began to unfold that was without precedent in American history. *The New York Times* began to publish a series of excerpts from a history of the American role in Indochina which had been prepared by a staff of writers in the employ of the United States government at the direction of Secretary of Defense Robert S. McNamara. Other newspapers, notably the Washington *Post,* later joined in the act of publication. It was clear from the start that these documents, which came to be known as the Pentagon Papers, were not formally released by the United States government. It became clear later that they came into the possession of one Robert Ellsberg and passed from him to *The New York Times* and so to other newspapers. A temporary injunction on their publication was obtained by the government, but a permanent injunction was denied by a six to three decision of the Supreme Court.

The public reaction to the newspaper publication of the Pentagon Papers may not have been what the newspapers expected. For one thing, the papers dealt with events that had occurred at least three years before the date of publication, and so had lost the force of immediacy. More important, they concerned a chapter in American history about which the American people by and large had made up their mind: the Vietnam War had been an act of tragic and mistaken folly, and very few Americans wished anything more of it than a speedy but honorable conclusion. It was the announced policy of President Nixon to bring American participation in the war to such a conclusion, and many Americans obviously concurred in both his decision and his methods. Furthermore, few in a nation heartsick over the whole miserable business could have their curiosity easily whetted about the details of the war or the allocation of responsibility among the several administrations under which it was waged. History is the judgment of the future on the past, not the judgment of the present on the present. There would be time enough for history later.

The public was obviously far less concerned about what the papers contained than it was about how they came to be published in the first place. The one obvious, conceded, incontestable point was that the publication was not officially authorized by the government. It seemed clear that one individual, possibly with advice and help from others, made himself the arbiter of the national well being and decided that it was to the public interest that the papers should be published. Then the participating newspapers assumed responsibility as the public conscience and undertook publication. It was the judgment of the Nixon administration, which was in no way involved in the series of decisions revealed in the Pentagon Papers, a series that terminated in May, 1968, that by continued publication "the national defense interests of the United States and the nation's security will suffer immediate and irreparable harm." This was the contention deemed insufficient by the Supreme Court in a set of opinions so varied in nature and so diversified in philosophy as to comprise seven different intellectual paths to one of two conclusions. Of these seven intellectual paths only the one taken jointly by Justices Black and Douglas could be considered a full justification of the viewpoint of Ellsberg and the newspapers.

One solid object stuck in the public crop: first an individual and then a group of newspapers made a decision about the publication of official government documents. How could this be? Why should it be? These were the questions that the publication of the Pentagon Papers really raised. However the question of possible criminality might be resolved, there was only one resolution possible to the question of principle. No individual and no group of corporations has the right to say, "We, the people of the United States. . . ."

It sometimes happens, however, that the very impropriety of an act reveals a crying need for proper action. Had the government kept the American people in the dark about matters of the first magnitude, issues that struck into the very heart of the American home as this son and that father were sent to fight and die in a war that a minority of Americans understood, a war fought over rice paddies and mountain trails half a world away? Had the government been derelict in its solemn duty to the principles on which the nation rests: first, that an informed electorate be kept steadily aware of basic decisions made by its government, the reasons for them, the alternatives that have been rejected and the reasons for their rejection; and second, that the electorate periodically express an informed verdict on the management of public affairs by the electoral process? All the questions the public really asked by no means reflected on the propriety of the newspaper action. Some questioned the integrity of the government itself in its dealings with the people, and to question the integrity of the government is a far graver matter than to question the integrity of a newspaper.

One conclusion the American people did reach: there must never again be a Pentagon Papers case. This imperative, however, rests just as heavily upon the government as it does upon the newspaper industry. There must be a formalized, regularized method by which the administration in power can give the American people the pertinent information it needs to make up its mind about public affairs. Twentieth-century problems are too massive to be dramatized by newspaper scoops. On the other hand, diplomacy cannot be conducted under arc lights. A national administration not only must be worthy of trust but it must be trusted. The government has quite as solemn a duty to subject to prior restraint the publication of information that would harm the national security as it has to publish the information that can do no harm. Every element in American society must accept that as a fact of national life.

Thus we come to a basic truth about the press and its position in the life of the nation. It exists to serve the truth, but that means to serve the truth to the citizens. Their rights as individuals, their corporate rights as a nation, their functioning rights as a government furnish the framework within which the press functions and set the limits by which its freedom is defined. Freedom of the press is not an absolute, nor is it a philosophic abstraction. A free press is one functioning aspect of the life of a free nation, a necessary and vital aspect, but an aspect that cannot be viewed apart from the framework within which it operates and the limits by which it is defined.

The citizen in a free society accepts as an axiom that a free press is an integral part of his society, a jealously guarded part, an indispensable part. It is guarded in its freedom, not for its own sake but for the welfare of the citizen whom it serves. A free press has no other philosophic justification. The truth does not exist for its own sake, but to make men free. Since the viewpoint we assume is that of the citizen, not that of the government through which his society functions nor that of any of its instrumentalities such as the press, it might be well to attempt a classification of the relationships the citizen has in which the press is a factor.

The first and obvious one is the relationship of the citizen to his government. He expects certain services from the government he supports, and one of these services is keeping him properly informed on matters on which he must pass judgment. He expects the normal and natural avenue through which he will get most of this information to be the press. This implies cooperation between the government and the press, but it implies competition as well. A proper

relationship between government and press would include cooperation in the release of such documents as the Pentagon Papers. There
would be ample room for competition where their interpretation is
concerned. The citizen is thoroughly aware that another time some
self-appointed custodian of the public welfare might publish material about the perilous nature of which there could be no argument.
He has every right to insist that prior restraint on the publication of
information that might recoil to his peril be properly and judiciously
exercised by those who represent him through the electoral process,
and that they cooperate in this regard with the ordinary media of
communication of his society.

The second relationship between the citizen and his government
finds them arrayed against each other. The citizen has come into
conflict with the law. He may be innocent and he may be guilty, but
he is presumed innocent until he is found guilty. Presumed innocent
by whom? He has the right to be presumed innocent by every force
in society in a position to influence courtroom thinking, however
obliquely and externally. The citizen can find himself in no sharper
conflict with the press than this: *Free Press v. Fair Trial.* The issue is
second in importance only to the issue of prior restraint, and the
waters in what should be the serene pool of justice are never more
muddied than when that blast of conflict blows across them.

The third relationship involves the citizen in his own community
and among his neighbors. Everyone has a right to his personal
reputation and a right to a proper degree of personal privacy. The
issue of one's reputation may be involved in our second relationship
and so be an issue before the courts. The right of a free press does
not include the right to rush into print before facts are verified that
may be gravely injurious to the reputation of an individual. Neither
does the right of a free press include the right to violate the normal
sanctions of decent conduct in the invasion of personal privacy. The
principles of good citizenship are precisely as incumbent upon the
press as they are upon the citizen, and the sanctions of the law
should protect the citizen in his right to reputation and to privacy
quite as truly as they protect the press in its right to discover and to
publish.

The fourth relationship is one in which the citizen is involved with
both his government and the press. Every society has a certain moral
climate, one that shifts and changes as the times change, with
imperatives that grow sharper or lose their point as attitudes shift

and vary. It is a mistake to think that because one set of imperatives loses much of its force the total moral climate is taking on a South Sea island languor. There is a latitude in speech now that would have been unthinkable a generation ago. But this is a latitude only in certain aspects of speech. A generation ago the whole black race was an unfailing source of merriment on stage, radio, and screen, and no one else gave it a second thought. We have, and should have, a moral climate that is quite arctic today toward this sort of speech. The point is that although the moral climate itself changes, the fact of a moral climate does not change. People of sound judgment and values have the right to insist that the press curb its freedom to violate what they consider the moral climate in which they choose to live.

These are the rights of the citizen which are at least tangent to the rights of the free press: his right to protection against the disclosure of information perilous to the public safety, his right to a fair trial, his right to his reputation, his right to his privacy, and his right to live in the moral climate of his choice. These are the rights by which the rights of a free press are bounded in a free society, and they comprise the natural divisions of a study of the citizen in his relationship to the press.

Part I

PRIOR RESTRAINT

The first issue in the relationship between the citizen and the press, first in time, first in importance, first in gravity, is the issue of prior restraint. One may consider the issue of prior restraint from the viewpoint of the newspaper. Most books on the subject do precisely that. One may consider it from the viewpoint of the government, and a few books do so in theory. One book treats it in pragmatic form, the memoirs of the public figure who has had to "confirm or deny" rumors and reports, to borrow the title of one of the best contemporary books of the sort, and always have in mind the national interest as he does so. What is not so easily come by is the book that views the issue of prior restraint from the viewpoint of the citizen. We may start with the oldest form in the history of prior restraint, the licensed press, and one of the most famous citizens in the republic of letters, John Milton.

THE LICENSED PRESS

John Milton plunged his quill into his ink horn. He could see one of the worst of tyrannies stalking the land; the spirit of the Papacy and the Inquisition was abroad. Milton wrote, "Give me the liberty to know, to utter, and to argue freely, according to conscience, above all liberties." Parliament had decreed: "no book shall be henceforth printed unless the same be first approved and licensed.... " Milton answered, "Who kills a man kills a reasonable creature, God's image; but he who destroys a good book, kills reason itself, kills the image of God, as it were, in the eye." The very Puritans of London who had fought and died for freedom had become the purblind bigots of London, intent on killing what is deathless in the human spirit. "A good book is the precious life-blood of a master spirit, embalmed and treasured up on purpose to a life beyond life." One defense of intellectual freedom against the licensed press is deathless in English literature, John Milton's *Areopagitica* (1644). The mind thrills and the spirit soars to its eloquence, and quotation is irresistible. Quotation is also misleading.

England had a licensed press before Shakespeare ever killed a deer in Stratford. Before a book or pamphlet could be printed, it had to be registered with the Stationers Company and approved for publication by either the Archbishop of Canterbury or the Bishop of London. The Stationers Company was the guild of printers, and in 1637 the guild itself was licensed when the Star Chamber authorized only twenty printers to comprise the press of England. Indeed a dark year for the English press and for truth itself in England was 1637.

Then the skies brightened with deceptive rapidity in 1641 when the Long Parliament abolished the Star Chamber. The floodgates opened and there poured forth upon an England totally unprepared for what a free press means a flood of pamphlets bitter as only religious debate can be bitter when dogma and the dogmatic blot out religion and the religious. Milton made his own contribution, for his own private purposes, in his divorce tracts. An alarmed Parliament reintroduced licensing, and Milton wrote *Areopagitica*.

Milton argued that under the gospel of Christ individual man achieves Christian liberty, the one right that is absolute, permanently, and totally removed from any licit earthly restraint. It is the right to live a life of virtue according to the law of Christ. But this is law, not license; self-control, wisdom, and responsibility are of its essence. The right to truth is inalienable and Milton based his argument for an unlicensed press upon that as an axiom, but the press itself must be endowed with self-control, wisdom, and responsibility. This quite as truly as the vital necessity of an unlicensed press is the message of *Areopagitica*. This is the part of the message rarely quoted, the part that does not soar with eloquence but that speaks with the measured, grim intensity of the seventeenth century. "I mean not tolerated popery and open superstition, which as it extirpates all religions and civil supremacies, so itself should be extirpate. . . . " And again, "that also which is impious or evil absolutely, either against faith or manners, no law can possibly permit that intends not to unlaw itself." As for books printed without the name of author or printer, "if they be found mischievous and libelous, the fire and the executioner will be the timeliest and most effectual remedy that man's prevention can use." Opposition to censorship is forever associated with the name of John Milton. John Milton was one of Oliver Cromwell's official censors.

What Milton advocated comes down to the elimination of that specific form of prior restraint upon publication which takes the form of licensing. He believed that freedom from licensing brings truth and falsehood into the open, and truth is never beaten by falsehood in an open and fair fight. Thus to Milton an unlicensed press was a means to an end, and the end was the determination of the truth. But Milton was of his own age as well as of the ages. There are some forms of falsehood too horrible to be allowed to enter the lists against truth, even if defeat would be their inevitable lot. One is popery and another is royalty. Milton wrote magnificent prose in the age when the English language was at its supremely flexible, vivid, and colorful best. Consequently *Areopagitica* is imperishable in English literature and, by a misleading if entirely human and understandable process, its message has come to be distorted to fit the patterns of thinking which have prevailed in the three centuries since its composition. It is important to read that message precisely as it was delivered and meant, because *Areopagitica* represents quite accurately what we might term the libertarian position in the seventeenth century. One might add that all Milton's eloquence left his fellow Puritans quite unmoved and the law totally unchanged.

The Licensing Act finally was repealed in 1695 and it was repealed, not because it appeared wrong in principle but because the House of Commons deemed it ineffective in practice and subject to abuse that ranged from petty annoyance to outright blackmail. Prior restraint, however, can take many different forms and the repeal of the Licensing Act merely eliminated a not particularly practical form. The Act was succeeded by a much more subtle form of prior restraint, one impossible to define and excessively difficult to limit, one that is justified in principle and within the bounds of prudence, justice, and sound public policy justified in practice, but also one susceptible to the gravest of abuse. It was prior restraint by means of laws that punished criminal and civil libel.

THE RESPONSIBLE PRESS

John Milton wrote with high poetic intensity of those brave pioneers of freedom "who by their unlicensed books, to the contempt of an Imprimatur, first broke that triple ice clung about our hearts, and taught the people to see day." Sir William Blackstone, over a century later, wrote in earth-clinging dogged prose: "The liberty of the press is indeed essential to the nature of a free state, but this consists in laying no previous restraints upon publications; and not in freedom from censure for criminal matter when published." Yet there is a significant advance in freedom embodied in Blackstone and perpetuated in that great, organic structure of English common law erected by Blackstone in his *Commentaries*. A century and a half after Blackstone the Blackstone principle was still honored, as the

foremost liberal of the twentieth-century American bench, Justice
Oliver Wendell Holmes, wrote in *Patterson v. Colorado*,[1] "The main
purpose of such constitutional provisions [i.e., the freedom-of-the-
press clause in the First Amendment] is to prevent all such previous
restraints upon publications as had been practiced by other governments, and they do not prevent the subsequent punishment of such
as may be deemed contrary to the public welfare." The concept of
the licensed press gave way to the concept of the responsible press,
and as it did gave rise to the really thorny questions. Responsible in
what sense? Responsible to what degree? Responsible to whom?
There is a prior restraint that is subtle, indirect, even concealed, yet
just as effective as any licensing act or formal censorship. It is the
prior restraint implicit in the threat of legal action. Its most potent
historic form has been action for seditious libel.

A libel creates an unfavorable opinion of a person or an institution. In 1791, when the Bill of Rights was added to the American
Constitution, English common law recognized four kinds of libel:
defamatory, seditious, blasphemous, and obscene. A libel which
created an unfavorable opinion of an individual was considered
defamatory. One which denigrated the government or a government
official was seditious. A blasphemous libel was an offense against the
Christian religion, an obscene libel one against accepted standards of
morality. One sought remedy for a defamatory libel by a civil suit;
the other libels were cause for criminal prosecution. The truth or
falsity of a publication had no bearing in a criminal prosecution and,
indeed, "The greater the truth the greater the libel" was the prevailing philosophy. Since truth was not the point at issue in a libel suit,
it followed in the suits for seditious libel, the ones that really mattered to the prevailing order, that the more a libel tended to move
people to change the prevailing order, the more "licentious" it was.
The moral need hardly be spelled out: the more effective criticism of
the government was and the more the truth of the criticism might
move the people to act, the more liable the writer and publisher
were to punishment. A licenser or a formal censor could hardly
exercise prior restraint more effectively than the concept that it is
the bad tendency of a piece of writing which determines its libelous
character. "Let him have his say, and then knock him over the
head" is not freedom of speech.

[1] 205 U.S. 454

The pertinent question where the issue of prior restraint is concerned now becomes this: in 1791 did the bad tendency principle prevail in the thinking of the Founding Fathers? At first the entire matter of freedom of the press was passed over as something for the States to handle; the effort of Charles Pinckney of South Carolina to have a free-speech and freedom-of-the-press clause incorporated in the Constitution was rejected as unnecessary and beyond the competence of Congress. Alexander Hamilton, who later defined freedom of the press in terms that the constitutions of half the states now employ, at first dismissed it as indefinable and something that must depend not on definition for its existence but on the attitude of the people. But state after state incorporated freedom of speech into its constitution and the pressure mounted until the Bill of Rights included a freedom of speech and of the press proviso in its first clause. The only logical conclusion is that the people in general, perhaps more than those who wrote the Constitution, wanted a greater freedom of speech and of the press than was provided by the bad tendency interpretation of the Blackstone principle.

It is important to observe the interrelationship of citizen, government, and press under that principle and interpretation. The true foundation of prosecution for seditious libel was the concept that the government is Big Brother, that the people are the wards of government, and that whatever utterance casts doubt upon the serene wisdom of the rulers of the land is seditious libel. The accepted definition of seditious libel was solidly founded on this concept: the intentional publication, without lawful excuse or justification, of written blame of any public man, or of the law, or of any institution established by law. Since truth was not considered a lawful excuse or justification, and since there is nothing whatever in the definition that even suggests that an utterance must be aimed at causing dissatisfaction among the people before it is a libel, let alone that it be an incitement to rebellion, it followed logically, legally, and historically that in eighteenth-century England and the colonies freedom of the press meant what Blackstone said, freedom from previous restraints upon publication. Experience had proved them unnecessary and had justified the repeal of the Licensing Act as an outmoded and unnecessary instrument of control. Prosecution for seditious libel had proved to be the entirely adequate substitute for a licensing act or formal censorship.

By 1791 the concept of seditious libel as it had been understood in both England and the colonies was under increasingly heavy attack. The First Amendment was one product of that attack, and only a year after the adoption of the American Bill of Rights the passage of Fox's Libel Act by Parliament was another. By this Act an English jury was entitled to pass a general verdict on the matter under contention. The latter concept had already been adopted into Pennsylvania law in 1790 in its freedom of speech and freedom of the press clause. It held that those who spoke or wrote on any subject were to be responsible for the abuse of their constitutional liberty, but then it added, "In prosecutions for the publication of papers investigating the official conduct of officers or men in a public capacity, or where the matter published is proper for public information, the truth thereof may be given in evidence; and in all indictments for libels the jury shall have a right to determine the law and the facts, under the direction of the court, as in other cases." Delaware and Kentucky followed the lead of Pennsylvania in making the truth a defense and a jury the arbiter.

Massachusetts, on the other hand, clung to the Blackstone principle. In a 1791 libel case the Bay State Supreme Judicial Court held that the constitutional guarantee merely protected the press from a system of licensing. Judges in various states continued to apply the old test for seditious libel, on the thesis that the opening words of the First Amendment, "Congress shall make no law..." merely meant that Congress could impose no prior restraints upon the press, again the Blackstone principle. The adoption of the newer concept was gradual, the matter of opening a salient here, a salient there, and slowly the establishment of a new front. The new front was established by 1798, ironically enough in the Sedition Act which so nearly destroyed the freedom of the press. For all the perils that it posed to the free citizen of the new nation, the Act did make the truth a defense in a prosecution for seditious libel and a jury the arbiter.

ALIEN AND SEDITION LAWS

There are two specific statutes in American history known as the Alien and Sedition laws, but the alien-and-sedition-law psychosis may show itself in any national emergency grave enough to conjure it up from the recesses of the national mind. The Alien and Sedition laws were passed in 1798. The former authorized the President to deport aliens he deemed dangerous to the peace and safety of the nation, and the latter punished seditious writings against the President or Congress. Even though the Sedition Law provided that the truth could be a defense and a jury could pass judgment, it simply made the law of the land the old concept of seditious libel as the bad tendency of a piece of writing. The Blackstone principle and its traditional interpretation once more held the field; it was as if the thinking that led to the passage of the First Amendment had never taken place.

One must recall the atmosphere of 1798 to make this explicable. The French Revolution was a bloody, horrifying fact, and war with France seemed imminent. The Western world was terrified by the worst convulsion to tear it since the Thirty Years' War, and it was horrified by the possibility that the Reign of Terror might not be limited to Paris. Might it not indeed be a "Tale of Two Cities," to strike the grim and ominous undertone in the title of Dickens's living evocation of a past horror? Might the other city be London? Or might it be Vienna or Rome or conceivably Philadelphia? It was an austere test of its constitutional principles that America faced, but America passed the test. The hysteria that led to the passage of the acts and the conviction of those allegedly seditious quickly passed. Thomas Jefferson as President freed the prisoners, Congress returned them their fines, and the Federalist party never recovered. As is so often true in human affairs, a legal issue was obliquely settled by a clarification of an issue in people's minds. The real objective of the First Amendment was to permit the free and open discussion of public issues. The principle of a sedition act nullifies that freedom by imposing a prior restraint. The public reaction to the Alien and Sedition acts was an effective repudiation of the principle of a sedition act based on the bad-tendency concept.

That repudiation may itself be repudiated if public hysteria once more arises. It is extremely difficult for one whose memory is based on the national reaction to the Second World War to envisage the national reaction to the First, and one imagines that it must be utterly impossible for one whose memory extends back only to Korea, let alone only to Vietnam. Never in American history, not even in the Civil War, was there such an unstable mixture of dedicated patriotism, admirable self-sacrifice, uncontrolled hysteria, flaming intolerance, and unadulterated nonsense as in 1917. Our concern is with the bad and not the good. There was one universal, dreaded bugaloo, a genie from an empty bottle that eddied up into

terrifying proportions, known as "German propaganda." The result
of the universal dread of German propaganda, a dread all the greater
because such propaganda was impossible to define and ultimately
came to be considered any remark about the conduct of the war of
which one disapproved, was a provision in the Espionage Act of
1917 which provided a fine and imprisonment for "Whoever, when
the United States is at war, shall willfully make or convey false
reports or false statements with intent to interfere with the operation or success of the military or naval forces of the United States or
to promote the success of its enemies." This was further spelled out
in the 1918 amendment, often called the Sedition Act, which extended criminal prosecution to those who said anything detrimental
to the sale of government bonds, who uttered anything that would
subject to scorn or disrepute the American form of government, the
Constitution, the flag, or the military uniform, or anything that
might interfere with the production of whatever was needed to
prosecute the War.

It is both utterly and mercifully beyond our present scope to
follow up the consequences of this act and its amendment into the
realm of prosecution and conviction. To cite a few cases must
suffice. For example, a moving-picture producer did a film called
The Spirit of '76. It depicted Patrick Henry's speech, the signing of
the Declaration of Independence, Valley Forge, but most unfortunately it also showed British soldiers acting deplorably at the Wyo-
ming Massacre. The producer was sentenced to ten years imprisonment for filming an anti-British picture and thus by arousing animos-
ity toward an ally hampering the joint war effort. His sentence later
was commuted to three years. There is unintended irony in the name
of the case: *United States v. Spirit of '76*.

Another such case was *Masses Publishing Co. v. Patten*. *The
Masses* was a revolutionary monthly which cherished a view much
favored by the revolutionary fringe of the period, that World War I
was a sort of business undertaking initiated and perpetuated by Wall
Street for its fiscal enrichment. Patten was the New York postmaster
who barred it from the mails. Judge Learned Hand of the Southern
District of New York held that the Espionage Act of 1917 did not
prohibit all kinds of hostile criticism of the War and that *The
Masses*, which had praised conscientious objectors and persons who
had resisted the draft, had stopped short of urging others to follow
their example. Judge Hand was reversed by the Circuit Court of

Appeals, which held that the Espionage Act of 1917 was broken "if the natural and reasonable effect of what is said is to encourage resistance to law, and the words are used in an endeavor to persuade to resistance." Granted the spirit of the times, the reversal is not surprising however wrong it may appear in retrospect. The essential point is that the old eighteenth-century interpretation of sedition, the bad tendency of something said against government, was once more the law of the land. That it was reestablished is proved by the two thousand or so prosecutions under the Espionage Act, if one has the fortitude to seek out the proof. One who does will be edified to discover that it gave aid and comfort to the enemy to suggest financing the War by heavier taxation rather than by war bonds, to say that war is contrary to the teaching of Christ, to criticize the Red Cross or the Y.M.C.A., and in Minnesota, which had a particularly inspired state espionage act, to say that the soldiers would never see the socks the women were knitting. The citation in the last case, for one who likes the thorny by-paths of the law, is *State v. Freerks,* 140 Minn. 349 (1918).

This is what prior restraint by use of the legal bludgeon can mean in the passion of wartime. Let there be the proper degree of hysteria, and such can be the results when the bad tendency and the presumed intent of the spoken or written word are made the criteria of criminality. The impact of the Espionage Act of 1917 and its 1918 amendment was never felt by what might be termed the standard American press. The press in this sense shared to the full the prevailing dedicated patriotism, admirable self-sacrifice, uncontrolled hysteria, flaming intolerance, and unadulterated nonsense. It was the peripheral press it touched, journals like *The Masses,* the forlorn German language press of the Midwest like the *Missouri Staats-Zeitung* whose editor received a ten-year sentence for questioning the efficacy and constitutionality of the draft, and the zany press of New York which, from its eyrie in the upper stories of a building at Houston and Crosby Streets, showered on the streets below sheets of intellectual manna denouncing the 1918 American expedition to Siberia, thereby earning the young proprietors fifteen and twenty years in jail respectively. Prior restraint can hardly go farther than the passage of the Espionage Act of 1917 and its expanding amendment, accompanied by fanatical interpretation. The madness, to be sure, was transient but the boundaries to which prior restraint over the press is justifiable had to be reestablished. The Schenck and

Gitlow cases largely undid the damage and laid the groundwork for a later rationale of prior restraint entirely unnecessary and quite undreamed of during the World War I period.

THE CLEAR AND PRESENT DANGER TEST

It is part of the irony of legal history that the case which did the most to question the validity of the bad-tendency test of seditious utterance was one in which the Espionage Act was reasonably and properly applied and the guilt of the persons tried under it would appear to have been beyond reasonable doubt. Charles T. Schenck and Elizabeth Baer were under the current radical impression that the First World War was waged as a money-raising device by Wall Street. They mailed pamphlets to draftees urging them to resist the draft, which they regarded as an act of administrative despotism, and to insist upon their constitutional rights. Since Congress has the constitutional power to raise armies and the defendants had urged the young men of America to defy the powers of their Congress during wartime, there would seem to be no reasonable doubt that their action violated the Espionage Act in the most moderate and reasonable interpretation of its provisions. They were tried and found guilty in the lower courts, and ultimately the case reached the Supreme Court. It was the spring of 1919, the War was over, the passions of the wartime period had subsided, and the voice of reason had its chance. Justice Oliver Wendell Holmes spoke for a unanimous Court in sustaining the guilty verdict against Schenck and Miss Baer. The important point is not the legal fate of two allegedly opinionated and perverse-minded persons. The important point is how opinionated and perverse one may be in speech or print where the public welfare is concerned and still be covered by the First Amendment. Justice Holmes laid down a principle that has been tossed about and twisted, wrenched out of context and distorted to alien service in the years since 1919, yet on the whole has stood mistreatment reasonably well:

We admit that in many places and in ordinary times the defendants in saying all that was said in the circular would have been within their constitutional rights. But the character of every act depends upon the circumstances in which it is done. . . . The most stringent protection of free speech would not protect a man in falsely shouting

fire in a theatre and causing a panic. It does not even protect a man
from an injunction against uttering words that may have all the
effect of force. The question in every case is whether the words used
are used in such circumstances and are of such a nature as to create
a clear and present danger that they will bring about the substantive
evils that Congress has a right to prevent. It is a question of proxim-
ity and degree. When a nation is at war many things that might be
said in time of peace are such a hindrance to its effort that their
utterance will not be endured so long as men fight and that no Court
could regard them as protected by any constitutional right.

The principle that Justice Holmes laid down is certainly clear in
theory, however difficult to apply in specific cases. No right is
absolute except the right of the individual to live a virtuous life.
Every other right ultimately is limited by that right. It is part of that
right to live a peaceful life in an orderly society. The peace and
order of society are most gravely threatened in time of war. Hence
the graver the threat to the peace and order of society, the more
rigid the necessary limitation on the exercise of a right which might
endanger that peace and order. Freedom of speech and of the press
are also rights that may contribute to the virtuous life of the individual, and hence they are inalienable rights. But an inalienable right is
not a right in all respects free from legal limitation. A certain
measure of prior legal restraint is always a justified prerogative of
society. Justice Holmes tried to lay down the line at which the right
to freedom of speech and of the press must yield to the right of
society to preserve the peace and order of its existence. His conclusion was that the line is reached when further exercise of the right to
free speech would present "a clear and present danger" to that
peace and order.

The "clear and present danger" test is a perilously difficult one to
apply in practice. The nub of the problem is the distinction between
advocacy and incitement. There is a distinction between the two
and the trend of judicial opinion has been toward the belief that
advocacy of violent change is permissible under the First Amendment but incitement to violent change is not. Such seems also to be
the centrist position of American liberals: unlimited advocacy but no
incitement. Alexander Meiklejohn, once a faculty member of Brown
University, next president of Amherst College, and later a faculty
member of the experimental college at the University of Wisconsin,

so phrased the distinction in his 1955 testimony before the Sub-Committee on Constitutional Rights of the Senate Committee on the Judiciary:

It is, of course, understood that if such persons or groups proceed to forceful or violent action, or even to overt preparation for such action, against the Government, the first amendment offers them, in that respect, no protection. Its interest is limited to the freedom of judgment making, of inquiry and belief and conference and persuasion and planning and advocacy. . . . To advocacy the amendment guarantees freedom, no matter what is advocated. To incitement, on the other hand, the amendment guarantees nothing whatever.

Meiklejohn then proceeded to his definition of incitement. "An incitement, I take it, is an utterance so related to a specific overt act that it may be regarded and treated as a part of the doing of the act itself, if the act is done."

The difficulty with this definition is that it lodges the distinction between advocacy and incitement, not in the mind of the person talking but in the mind of the person listening. If the second party takes no action, it is advocacy; if he acts, it is incitement. The clear-and-present-danger test may be difficult to apply, but there is something distressingly *ex post facto* about Meiklejohn's test. The greatest weakness of liberal thought in contemporary America has been that so much of it has come from universities and colleges, where one has been able to theorize to his heart's content and know that the theories are very unlikely to be put to the test. Of course there can be unlimited advocacy from the ivory tower. It is when the ivory tower is demolished and sleeves are rolled up in the streets outside that advocacy becomes incitement and incitement becomes violence. The academic liberals have been appalled when the academic New Left has turned unlimited freedom of debate into direct incitement to violence, as a new kind of wartime passion was enkindled by the Vietnam war, and showed its supreme contempt for freedom of speech in the process.

Justice Brandeis probably did as much as can be done to put the distinction between advocacy and incitement into the framework of the clear and present danger test when he said in the 1927 case of

Whitney v. California,[1] "But even the advocacy of violence, however reprehensible morally, is not a justification for denying free speech where the advocacy falls short of incitement and there is nothing to indicate that the advocacy would be immediately acted on." In practice, however, in this matter as in all legal matters, the distinction had to be hammered out in case after case. The process which began in the *Schenck* case continued in 1925 in *Gitlow v. New York*.[2]

In 1902 the New York legislature, inflamed by the assassination of President McKinley, passed a law against criminal anarchy, which it defined as "the doctrine that organized government should be overthrown by force or violence, or by assassination of the executive head or of any of the executive officials of government, or by any unlawful means." A doctrine in itself is advocacy; it is in its application that it may become incitement. Had the doctrine which Gitlow advocated become by the act of advocacy an incitement? That was the specific point at issue in the case that bears his name, although it is a quite different issue in the case which gives it its importance.

In 1919 Benjamin Gitlow who was business manager of the *Revolutionary Age*, a publication of the Socialist Party, published in it a Left Wing Manifesto. It should be noted that the left wing in question was the socialistic left wing, and that the left wing separated from the main body of American socialism as a result of this publication. In the course of his duties as author of *Free Speech in the United States*, Zechariah Chafee, Jr., read the thirty-four page Manifesto and commented, "Any agitator who read these thirty-four pages to a mob would not stir them to violence, except possibly against himself." But the year was 1919, there were bolsheviks under every bed, and Gitlow was found guilty in two New York courts and the finding was sustained in the Supreme Court. The Supreme Court was called upon to rule on one specific issue: was the Criminal Anarchy Act of New York constitutional as interpreted by the state courts? The state courts held to the bad-tendency test, rejecting the clear-and-present-danger test, and the Supreme Court upheld it in this respect. Justice Sanford, in ruling for the Court, stated, "A single revolutionary spark may kindle a fire that, smoldering for a time, may burst into sweeping and destructive conflagration. It

[1] 274 U.S. 357
[2] 268 U.S. 652

cannot be said that the state is acting arbitrarily [when] it seeks to extinguish the spark without waiting until it has enkindled the flame or blazed into the conflagration." Justices Holmes and Brandeis dissented from this metaphorical phrasing of the bad-tendency test, adhering to the clear-and-present-danger test. Holmes's dissent casts light on what he considered the distinction between advocacy and incitement which later seemed so important to Meiklejohn:

It is said that this manifesto was more than a theory, that it was an incitement. Every idea is an incitement. It offers itself for belief and if believed it is acted on unless some other belief outweighs it or some failure of energy stifles the movement at its birth. The only difference between the expression of an opinion and an incitement in the narrower sense is the speaker's enthusiasm for the result. Eloquence may set fire to reason. But whatever may be thought of the redundant discourse before us it had no chance of starting a present conflagration.

Obviously this is the clear-and-present-danger test.

The importance of the case does not arise from Court adherence to the ancient bad-tendency test, nor to the adherence of Holmes and Brandeis to the clear-and-present-danger test. It arose from the recognition by the Court that the Fourteenth Amendment did implement the First Amendment on a state basis. The Court stated, "For present purposes we may and do assume that freedom of speech and of the press—which are protected by the First Amendment from abridgment by Congress—are among the fundamental personal rights and liberties protected by the due-process clause of the Fourteenth Amendment from impairment by the States."

The importance of this statement to freedom of the press is paramount. The Fourteenth Amendment reads as follows: "No state shall make or enforce any law which shall abridge the privileges or immunities of citizens of the United States; nor shall any state deprive any person of life, liberty or property without due process of law; nor deny to any person within its jurisdiction the equal protection of the laws." The fundamental purpose of the amendment was to extend to the states the limitations imposed on the Federal government by the Bill of Rights. Its immediate and intended beneficiaries were the freedmen of the former slaveholding states, but the historic development of the amendment has been mainly based on a developing interpretation of its due-process and equal-protection clauses. The development of the due-process clause has been one of extreme intricacy, but the application of the clause in the *Gitlow* case was not and it was a legal necessity that this fact be formally recognized by the Supreme Court. The only real issue between the majority and minority in the *Gitlow* case was how immediate and perilous the danger from injurious utterance must be to the state to bring it under legal sanction, and how perilous it was in this specific instance. As for Gitlow, he was pardoned by Governor Alfred E. Smith. Gitlow himself was supremely unimportant, but the case of *Gitlow* is very important indeed. In it, for the first time, there was enunciated the principle that the freedom of speech and of the press guaranteed by the Bill of Rights is protected by the Fourteenth Amendment from infringement by the states. Henceforth one might suggest in Minnesota that socks knitted for the soldiers might not reach their destination without fear of the constabulary.

One never approaches an understanding of the law until he has come finally, and usually reluctantly, to the understanding that the law in practice is an art and not a science. The clear-and-present-danger test was not new with Justice Holmes; it may be found in Thomas Jefferson. But neither man, nor any other man, can say with scientific certainty how clear and present a danger must be before it is "clear and present." The *Dennis* case, and then the *Yates* case, illustrate this.

The *Dennis* case[1] arose under the Alien Registration Act of 1940, commonly called the Smith Act. Aimed at control of subversion, it was used against various groups, one a set of anti-Stalin Marxists and another a bevy of reputed Nazi sympathizers. To this the Communists took no exception. Then it was used against them. Eleven Communists were indicted on the charge of advocating the desirability and necessity of overthrowing the government of the United States and of banding together to promulgate their doctrine. They were found guilty and ultimately the case reached the Supreme Court.

The Court sustained their conviction, finding that the Smith Act was not an unconstitutional infringement on free speech. It was a six to two decision, Justices Black and Douglas dissenting and Justice Clark not participating. All the justices except Justice Jackson

[1] *Dennis v. United States,* 341 U.S. 494 (1951)

agreed that the clear-and-present-danger test was the test to be used. Chief Justice Vinson gave the Court decision, which was essentially that the government need not wait for the revolution to start before taking action to protect the nation. Rather, Chief Justice Vinson stated, the courts must in each case "ask whether the gravity of the evil, discounted by its improbability, justifies such invasion of free speech as is necessary to avoid the danger." The decision must depend basically on the nature of the danger and the potentialities of the power posing it. When the danger is grave, the element of imminence need not be a factor in a clear and present danger. The dissent of Justice Douglas was based on the contention that Dennis and associates had taught a noxious doctrine but had posed no clear and present danger to society. As truly as the majority, the dissenting justices held to the clear-and-present-danger concept.

Although the concurring opinion of Justice Jackson departs from what had come to be regarded as the accepted test, it was really the reasoning of Justice Jackson which underlay the majority opinion. He held that in a conspiracy like communism the conspirators could be convicted even if they posed no clear and present danger to the government. The clear-and-present-danger test was laid down by Justice Holmes, he said, " ... before the era of World War II revealed the subtlety and efficacy of modernized revolutionary techniques used by totalitarian parties." The test had been used in the past against relatively harmless outbursts against the government; he would use it himself against such. But communism is not a relatively harmless outburst but a carefully laid conspiracy. The principle which Justice Jackson upheld is perfectly clear: the right to national defense is not determined by the arbitrary application of a formula, constitutional or judicial in origin, but by the nature of the peril which confronts the country. When the peril to the citizen is grave enough, the danger is clear and present even in its incipient stages.

Six years later, in a case with an outcome the exact opposite of *Dennis,* this concept was made explicit. The case was *Yates v. United States,*[1] in which fourteen lesser Communists were found guilty by the trial court under the Smith Act. The finding was reversed by the Supreme Court, which dismissed the charges against five of the defendants and ordered retrials for the other nine. The Court declared that to teach the necessity of overthrowing the

[1] 354 U.S. 298 (1957)

government and to advocate it is not illegal unless accompanied by the effort to instigate action. This would seem to sustain the viewpoint Justice Douglas expressed in his *Dennis* dissent. Actually, as Justice Harlan carefully spelled it out in the Court decision, it did nothing of the sort. He explained the *Dennis* opinion as holding that "indoctrination of a group in preparation for future violent action, as well as exhortation to immediate action, by advocacy found to be directed to 'action for the accomplishment' of forcible overthrow, to violence as 'a rule or principle of action,' and employing 'language of incitement' . . . is not constitutionally protected when the group is of sufficient size and cohesiveness, is sufficiently oriented towards action, and other circumstances are such as reasonably to justify apprehension that action will occur."

Justice Clark could find no resemblance between this statement and what had been said in *Dennis*. This may well be, and it may be because Justice Harlan spoke with greater clarity than Chief Justice Vinson. His point is certainly clear. The doctrine of violent overthrow is not in itself punishable because it is too far removed from action. What made advocacy illegal in *Dennis* was "indoctrination preparatory to action." Justice Harlan stated, "The essential distinction is that those to whom the advocacy is addressed must be urged to *do* something, now or in the future, rather than merely to *believe* in something." Yates and company got off because they had expressed their beliefs only in their books, newspapers, and pamphlets. Dennis and company had gone the rest of the way. Justices Black and Douglas were in the minority in holding that the distinction between advocacy of belief and advocacy of action has no validity.

NEAR V. MINNESOTA

The ancient Greeks held to the thesis that history is circular. Once one has shaken off the impact of a terse epigram, it is often possible to see the foundation of truth on which it rests. History does have a way of repeating itself, of coming around again to the point of origin. The licensed press disappeared in 1695, but today we talk of the news media and include radio and television among them. Radio and television are licensed. Censorship faded and died, and the American Bill of Rights and Fox's Libel Act sounded its requiem for the English-speaking world. Then censorship came to life again in the United States in 1931. Again as in the issue of socks for soldiers the case involved a Minnesota statute. To reach it we must imitate history and go back a few years before the *Dennis* and *Yates* cases.

The statute in question authorized the state courts to stop by injunction the publication of any newspaper, magazine, or other periodical which was largely devoted to "malicious, scandalous, and defamatory articles." This was prior restraint in a literal and direct form, not the indirect kind exercised by the punitive threat of the law. The *Saturday Press* came under the ban, the case was appealed to the Supreme Court, and a century and a half after the issue was "settled" the issue came up for settlement.

The *Saturday Press,* which was published in Minneapolis by a man named Near, ran a series of articles in 1927 charging that a Jewish gambler controlled racketeering and bootlegging in the state with the aid of law-enforcement officials, including the county attorney. The attorney sued to have the newspaper suppressed, advancing the claim that not merely the attacks on him but such sentences as the following were typical of the publication as well as malicious, scandalous, and defamatory: "Practically every vendor of vile hooch, every owner of a moonshine still, every snake-faced gambler and embryonic yegg in the Twin Cities is a JEW." The county attorney got an injunction from the lower Minnesota court which was confirmed by the highest court of the state. The injunction later was made permanent on the grounds that the paper was a nuisance and clearly came within the scope of the law. Near appealed to the Supreme Court on the grounds that the Minnesota statute was unconstitutional.

By a five-to-four decision the Supreme Court sustained his contention. Naturally no justice of the Court held that the publication was other than malicious, scandalous, defamatory, and a public nuisance. The real issue concerned the constitutionality of a statute which suppressed such a publication by an act of prior restraint. The viewpoint of the conservative minority of the Court, comprising Justices Butler, McReynolds, Sutherland, and Van Devanter was that such prior restraint was necessary to protect individuals, whether private citizens or public officials, and groups whether their common denominator was race, religion, or something else, from the effects of evil-minded, malicious, public verbal assault. As Justice Butler put it, to hold that such a statute as that of Minnesota was invalid as imposing a prior restraint "exposes the peace and good order of every community and the business and private affairs of every individual to the constant and protracted false and malicious assaults of any insolvent publisher who may have purpose and sufficient capacity to contrive and put into effect a scheme or program for oppression, blackmail, or extortion."

This was the viewpoint rejected by the majority of the Court, comprising Chief Justice Charles Evans Hughes and Justices Brandeis, Holmes, Roberts, and Stone. When the *Gitlow* case was tried before the New York Court of Appeals, in his dissent Judge Pound had said, ". . . the rights of the best of men are secure only as the rights of the vilest and most abhorrent are protected." This was the explicit thesis on which the majority took its stand. Restraint in advance of publication is "of the essence of censorship," in Chief Justice Hughes's phrase and the majority viewpoint held that such control is almost always in violation of the First and Fourteenth amendments. The Chief Justice quoted Blackstone on the important distinction between a restraint and a punishment: "The liberty of the press is indeed essential to the nature of a free state; but this consists in laying no previous restraints upon publications, and not in freedom from censure for criminal matter when published. Every freeman has an undoubted right to lay what sentiments he pleases before the public; to forbid this, is to destroy the freedom of the press; but if he publishes what is improper, mischievous or illegal, he must take the consequences of his own temerity." Minnesota did provide redress for both public officials and private citizens by its libel laws.

As is so often true in cases of the law, the importance of *Near v. Minnesota*[1] immeasurably transcends the despicable action which gave it rise. For the moment we must pass over the libel directed at the Jews. The legal problem of action for group libel is a thorny one, but one that more properly comes under the issue of libel in a free press than under the issue of prior restraint. The matter of libelous criticism of a public official is different. The press certainly must be free to criticize the actions of public officials; as Chief Justice Hughes said, "The conception of the liberty of the press in this country had broadened with the exigencies of the colonial period and with the efforts to secure freedom from oppressive administration. That liberty was especially cherished for the immunity it afforded from previous restraint of the publication of censure of public

[1] 283 U.S. 697 (1931).

officers and charges of official misconduct." The criticism of a public official certainly can be malicious, scandalous, and defamatory whether it is voiced in private utterance or through the printed word. The issue of the right of a public official to recover damages through a libel action also belongs under the issue of libel rather than of prior restraint, and there are some hidden thorns on that issue also. The real danger is that a court subservient to a political machine, or even a single judge who dangles by strings fastened to the fingers of a political puppet master, could declare malicious, scandalous, and defamatory disclosures about a public official and therefore issue an injunction against a newspaper although the disclosures were the truth and nothing but the truth. The majority was certainly right in holding that the Minnesota law was a gag law and therefore unconstitutional.

There is, however, another aspect to the majority opinion that deserves attention every bit as close. Chief Justice Hughes considered whether prior restraint is always illegal, and spoke for the majority in stating that it is not. He held that the issue of prior restraint is particularly involved with the issue of national security.

No one would question but that a government might prevent actual obstruction to its recruiting service or the publication of the sailing dates of transports or the number and location of troops. On similar grounds, the primary requirements of decency may be enforced against obscene publications. The security of the community life may be protected against incitement to acts of violence and the overthrow by force of orderly government. The constitutional guarantee of free speech does not protect a man from an injunction against uttering words that may have all the effect of force.

But limitations of this sort obviously were not involved in the *Near* case, and therefore not prior restraint but legal recourse was the proper action for those libeled to take. "The fact that the liberty of the press may be abused by miscreant purveyors of scandal does not make any the less necessary the immunity of the press from previous restraint in dealing with official misconduct. Subsequent punishment for such abuses as may exist is the appropriate remedy, consistent with constitutional privilege."

The great importance of the *Near* case arises from the fact that for the first time in American legal history it brought under definition the constitutional limitations upon prior restraint. Freedom of the press has never been held to be an absolute by responsible legal opinion in America or indeed anywhere else. Chief Justice Hughes makes it clear that the welfare of the citizen comes before it when his safety, peace, security, and moral well being are at stake. The point is of importance where the press in the strict sense of the term is involved. It is of transcendent importance where the news media in the broader sense are involved. The constitutional limitations which Chief Justice Hughes defined are quite as truly limited as they are limiting. The twentieth century has seen the reinstitution of a "licensed press." Radio is a news medium, as is television. Both radio and television stations are licensed to operate. A "freedom of the press" case involving the license of a radio or television station is far from a remote possibility. Prior restraint could take a form un-dreamed of a half century ago.

In the last analysis, the issue of prior restraint never has been settled, never will be settled, never can be settled. It never can be settled because freedom of the press is not an absolute. There are permanent problems in life, which is merely a way of saying that there are problems which have no permanent solutions.

PRIOR RESTRAINT OF SCIENTIFIC KNOWLEDGE

The fact of fission poses a form of the prior restraint issue which is utterly without precedent in legal history and certainly too profound in its implications for solution by the application of legalisms. The splitting of the atom was made possible only by the resources of an immensely wealthy nation enormously endowed with scientific com-petence of the highest order, imported quite as much as native. The military significance of the achievement, both the part which is history and the part which is apocalyptic prophecy, is totally beyond question. The continuing necessity for prior restraint in the publica-tion of developments where the military application of atomic en-ergy is concerned is so obvious that the foundation on which it rests has never been soberly questioned by those whose questions rest on a foundation of national loyalty, human prudence, and personal responsibility. Neither is the fact questioned that the world is in a state of suspended war and has been since the day Japan invaded Manchuria over a generation ago. Economic, ideological, and racial rivalries have kept the world in a crisis, fluctuating in intensity but permanent in nature, for decade after decade, and will continue to do so as far ahead as prophecy that is less than supernatural can reach. No duty of government is more basic than the duty to protect the citizen from a grave and enduring peril, and no individual or corporate right can impair the freedom of the government in the performance of that duty. The duty of the government to protect comes before the freedom of the press to know and to publish.

That principle, like most theoretic principles, is quite clear and unassailable, but not especially helpful. The real question is, how much of our national safety is vested in secrecy? In 1777 Edmund Burke asked of that restraint upon liberty which is essential for the survival of liberty itself the question that we may well ask, and in his words, today: "It ought to be the constant aim of every wise public council to find out by cautious experiments, and cool rational endeavors, with how little, not how much, of this restraint the community can subsist; for liberty is a good to be improved, and not an evil to be lessened."

This is the basic question we should ask about atomic energy and its military application, and in the answer determine how the prior restraint the public safety requires and the right of the press to know and to publish are to be balanced. In the first place, there is a very important distinction between two kinds of atomic secrets. One type of secret is factual. How many nuclear weapons do we have? Where are they kept? How readily could they be used if the ultimate national emergency that justified their use arose? These are military secrets in the limited and factual sense, admittedly over simplistic as phrased here but the very simplicity illustrates their nature. These are the secrets that every sensible and responsible person knows must be kept, and that no sensible and responsible paper would publish assuming it had access to them. They pose no philosophical problems, whatever the practical problems they pose.

The other type of secret is also factual, but factual in a different way. When we speak of the secrets of atomic energy, we do not mean the secrets illustrated above. We mean the secrets of nature itself, the secrets of that instability in certain elements which permits the instantaneous and cataclysmic transformation of matter into energy. This is the sort of secret that no country can very long keep. What scientific research will unearth in one national laboratory it will unearth in the laboratory that is its national rival. Nature plays no favorites. Her secrets can be ferreted out by all who have the intelligence, perseverance, technical competence, and physical resources to discover them. The secret of nature is very different indeed from the secret of fact.

The secret of nature, however, has its own enormously significant division. It is one thing to know the theory of fission, a very different thing to know how to make an atom bomb. Everyone who studies high school chemistry is taught the theory of the manufacture of steel, but that does not give him the qualifications needed to build United States Steel. Along with the secrets of fact and the secrets of nature we have the secrets of technology. They fall in accessibility somewhere between the other two. They can be partially kept, sometimes totally kept for a period of time, often some aspect of them can be permanently kept although other aspects are discovered or disclosed.

We may have here a clue to the solution of the problem Edmund Burke posed. With how much restraint in the matter of atomic knowledge need we subsist? With how much liberty can we exist? It would seem reasonable that the distinction among the three kinds of secret should provide a clue to the answer. A military secret of fact is a secret in the pure sense and should never be disclosed. How many atom bombs do we have and where are they? Every nation has spies and it is their job to dig out that sort of information. We are certainly under no obligation to help them and under every obligation to frustrate their efforts. History indicates that we shall not be totally successful, but we have every solemn obligation to try to be totally successful and to settle for nothing less.

The issue where the secret of nature is concerned is hardly less involved although very much less obvious. Not to let your left hand know what your right hand is doing certainly lessens the achievement of the left hand. But does it not also lessen the achievement of the right hand? No one scientist, no one laboratory, the entire scientific power of no one nation, is all-sufficient in itself. There must be scientific progress quite as well as scientific secrecy, and no one ever can be certain what seemingly irrelevant discovery, or what inspired guess, will unlock the guarded gates of nature. Gossip has been called the life blood of science, and there is truth in the witticism. One must be very certain indeed that the free flow of scientific information about the secrets of nature, about basic investigation, about "pure" research poses a greater threat to the security of the citizen than a promise to his safety before prior restraint is exercised on its publication. Ignorance and error look just as fashionable in the cloak of secrecy as do knowledge and truth. The principle, at least, is reasonably clear if the application as usual is very much less so. Prior restraint on publication usually does more harm than good where the secrets of nature are concerned. If the secret will be unearthed anyway by the potential enemy, and if publication will aid our scientists more than theirs, or even as much, then prior restraint on such publication cannot be justified in the name of national security. One says this, and one wishes Godspeed to the man whose task it is to apply the principle.

That leaves the secret of technology. The role of technology is the transformation of theory into fact, and there is always to technological knowledge an aspect of both. This makes the problem of the disclosure of technological knowledge theoretically more difficult, although probably simpler in application. To the extent that technology is directly related to the secrets of nature, its secrets cannot be kept anyway and it may often be sound public policy to disclose them. To the extent that technology is related to the secret of fact, or to the trade secret, it may be sound public policy to keep its secrets to the extent that they can be kept. This is merely to apply to atomic technology the regular procedure of industry, and one has at least a rule of thumb whereby technological secrets may be disclosed. Again, one wishes Godspeed to the man whose thumb is used.

This suggests at least the form that the issue of prior restraint has taken in the age of contemporary science. Restraint in advance of publication is always of the essence of censorship, as Chief Justice Hughes said in the *Near* case. There is a continuing, necessary, extremely difficult problem of censorship arising from the fact that atomic research is both so expensive and so extensive that no private agency can undertake it in more than its partial and peripheral aspects. It must be a responsibility of the national government, and one of the most solemn it assumes. Publication, one must always bear in mind, involves an enormous range of publication media. It involves the scientific journal so recondite that only those fully initiated in the science can understand its articles. It involves the intellectual journal intelligently edited for the intelligent and educated citizen who is reasonably informed but not scientifically erudite. It involves the daily press, with its comprehensive spectrum of readers who include those who read the scientific and the intellectual journal as well as those who read little but the daily paper, and those who read only selected items in the daily paper, such as the racing form and the day's number. It involves the popular journals with a flair for adding scent and flavor to a story and making up by sensationalism what they lack in scientific grasp. It involves the lurid sheets to be found on counters in supermarkets, corner stores, and other dispensaries of pabulum, which depart occasionally from the extra-marital achievements of the notorious to essay a venture into scholarship and predict the annihilation through the blessings of science of the entire human race. It also involves the ringing voices of radio, some sonorous enough for the final peal of doom itself, and the grave pundits of television whose jeremiads about science are punctuated but not necessarily relieved by the advertiser's dithyrambs about science and what its additives can do to aspirin. These are the news media, and one can only voice a quiet prayer that their common denominator is truth.

This is a point which must be borne constantly in mind by one who speaks of freedom of the press. The press means far more than *The New York Times* and the Boston *Herald-American,* the Louisville *Courier-Journal* and the St. Louis *Post-Dispatch.* It means the myriad of publications great and small, scholarly, intellectual, popular, sensational, and lurid. It expands to mean the radio and television. It means the medium of publication for those competent to write in the most technical terms for those able to understand them, for those with the gift of translating the technical into terminology within the competence of the intelligent and educated laity, for those with the greater gift of translation into the common tongue, and for those with the dangerous gift of distortion and exaggeration, and those with the perilous gift of utter confusion. It means the media for those who speak with tongues as the gift of the good fairy and the bad fairy as well. We must bear all these in mind when we speak of freedom of the press. When one weighs the welfare of the citizen against the right to express the truth, all these must be put together on one pan of the scales.

PRIOR RESTRAINT IN AN AGE OF CRISIS

There is a further consideration that must be borne in mind as we consider the delicate balance of that scales. To this point we have spoken of what might be termed the static news which may fall into the areas dangerous to the safety of the citizen. The discoveries of science and the developments of technology are static compared to the mad torrent of events which comprises the daily news. There is time to weigh the pros and cons of public revelations about the former, and time to reach a measured judgment about what can safely be published and what cannot. There is no time at all, as the news media operate, for those who must pass judgment on the latter.

One of the most important and informative books about the press and its relationship with the government to be published in these unprecedented days is Phil G. Goulding's *Confirm or Deny.*[1] Mr. Goulding, a newspaperman from Cleveland, became Assistant Secretary of Defense for Public Affairs under President Johnson. It was his job to handle crisis news, to "confirm or deny" reports shot out from the scenes of crisis by those on the scene or envisaging it from afar, to let the people know through the press what was happening in the crisis zone and what the government was doing about it. His book is ten case histories of crises, and one may imagine that for him five or six are scars still tender to the touch. It is unlikely that any reader would ask the author to confirm the accuracy of his case histories, which are accounts not of the crises but of the way the news of crisis was handled. They have the ring of conviction, now and then the ring of righteous anger, occasionally the ring of regret, and once or twice the ring of sorrow. They always have the ring of truth, and from them the reader learns much about crises.

He learns that crisis pays no need to the convenience of geography. When an atom bomb is lost, it is lost in the waters off Spain or better still, on the ice cap of Greenland. The North Koreans capture the *Pueblo* in the waters off North Korea, the Israelis strafe the *Liberty* in the waters off Israel. Crisis has a way of occurring far from facilities of communication, remote from the customary haunts of those who gather news, with no one but those deep in crisis to communicate. The result is inevitable. Bulletins from the crisis zone are brief, fragmentary, disjointed, sometimes incomprehensible. Today's bulletin may contradict and even disprove yesterday's, and at the least tends to make it obscure. This is no one's fault, least of all the fault of those who dispatch the bulletins. Those fishing for atom bombs in waters off Spain or in crevasses in the Greenland ice cap have business on hand more important than the enlightenment of

[1] Phil G. Goulding, *Confirm or Deny: Informing the People on National Security,* New York: Harper & Row, 1970

the listening and reading public back home. Those defending fundamentally non-fighting ships from hostile or mistaken attack have
responsibilities exceedingly prior to the instruction of the public in
the more foreboding aspects of current events. As for those at the
receiving end in Washington, who are receiving tantalizingly little
and that little garbled, distorted, obscure, maddeningly incomplete,
who are beset by the cry to "confirm or deny" what they do not
know enough about to do either, their lot may be physically happier
but certainly it is not emotionally so. Usually it would make them
beatifically happy if they could confirm or deny, because that would
mean they knew the truth themselves.

Competition is and should be the life blood of the news dissemination industry. However, the news media might do well occasionally
to have their blood pressure taken. No one doubts that it is sky high,
and more so than ever in a day in which radio and television can
make the dissemination of printed news at its fastest move by
comparison at a horse-and-buggy pace. Furthermore, speed of dissemination can be so easily translated into drama. "We interrupt this
radio program to announce that. . . ." and there follows the news
flash, in all its garbled, distorted, obscure, maddening incomplete-
ness. It is even more dramatic to break the picture on the television
screen and show some TV pundit who need only exchange his blue
shirt for a flowing robe to be a major prophet Old Testament style as
he reads some bulletin that will be contradicted or even disproved
tomorrow. The presses may be made to whirl at supersonic speed,
and they are, in the hope that greater detail may offset faster
transmission of news, but the greater detail so often masks until
tomorrow the greater breadth of misunderstanding and confusion,
the greater depth of bewilderment and error.

The phrase *prior restraint* can be used in more ways than one. The
right of the press to freedom is constitutionally guaranteed, but the
news media might examine their own moral right to plunge into
speech or print before they have an accurate idea of what they are
talking or writing about. There are occasions when a show of voluntary prior restraint by the media would improve both their public
service and their public image. As Mr. Goulding puts it, "Instant
answers make television news shows more interesting and satisfy
hungry managing editors. . . . However, I wonder whether the people might not prefer to wait a few days for more comprehensive
responses. The United States government cannot avoid responsibility

for its acts; there always will be time for criticism, blame, and fingerpointing. But the government today too often is pressured into shooting from the hip instead of reviewing the situation carefully and speaking more slowly with more fact, knowledge, and logic. I believe leaders of the press might consider reexamining their approach in this respect. Perhaps they would conclude that they should not expect serious government answers to all the serious questions in the first forty-eight or ninety-six hours of a crisis. The government, of course, can do a better job of resisting those pressures, but it needs help. If some of the pressure were eased, as a result of more understanding from the news media, it would be less apt to blurt out answers too quickly and the public would benefit."[1]

There is a point at issue here vastly more important than the speed or the accuracy with which news is transmitted to the public. We have heard in recent years of a "credibility gap," or listened to the less polite phrase, "government lying." Whether such a credibility gap has existed or has deserved to exist is another matter. It obviously serves the purpose of partisan politics to maintain that there is a credibility gap between the party in power and the people, and during the Johnson administration it served the purpose of those who would at least discredit the government, and in some cases undermine it, by planting the seeds of disbelief in its veracity. Perhaps there were grounds for disbelief, perhaps not. This much can be said: the seeds of disbelief easily take root in the soil of confusion, contradiction, and denial. If yesterday's statement is proved false by today's disclosure, it is a short and easy step to the charge that yesterday's statement was a lie. Put together enough discredited yesterdays and the generalization, the government lies to us, can easily be reached. A lie, be it remembered, is an intentional untruth. A government pressured by the news media into premature statements about crises that must later be modified and even denied is a government that is weakening its relationship with the citizen, exposing itself to the charge of dishonesty, making at least potential the danger of a credibility gap. A government so pressured may issue a bushel basket of false press releases, yet not one of them be intentionally false. Every one of them may be actually false, yet no one of them be a lie. Such is not faulty morals, but it certainly is faulty government.

[1] *Op. cit.*, pp. 298-299.

It might be wise, however, for any in the news media who may take a perverse if elaborately concealed delight in the credibility gap to consider who is on the other side of the gap. The people do not necessarily say, the government lies to us. Enough citizens to reckon with say the newspapers or the radio or the television lie to us. There is an old-fashioned phrase little heard today, "newspaper talk." It meant the sort of news reporting that was garbled and distorted, and then made the basis for editorializing equally wrong headed and perverse. The wise use to wag their heads and mutter, "newspaper talk." The phrase may be obsolete, but heads can still wag and heads do.

The matter would not be of perilous importance if it were merely this or that newspaper, radio station, or television network involved, or this or that politician, administration, or political party. But the world in which we live is itself too perilous to let a credibility gap really develop between the citizen and either his government or the news media. There must be faith and trust, and whatever destroys faith and trust undermines a nation. It is well to know the enemy for what he really is. His name is not necessarily falsehood. His name may very seldom be falsehood. His name is very likely to be speed. Speed is the father of misinformation and confusion, the grandfather of contradiction, refutation, and denial. Speed can cleave the perilous gap in which faith and trust sink out of sight and a land that should be strong is weakened, and in the name of nothing more sacred than speed. Truth comes before speed, and in a world beset by global crises and in an atmosphere in which truth emerges slowly, reluctantly, by dribs and drabs, a self-imposed prior restraint by government and news media alike becomes a peremptory virtue. Speed can maim and kill in places even more vital than the highway.

There is another factor involved where faith in the government is concerned. This factor is hard to define, so easy to illustrate that illustration itself becomes meaningless, and yet it is impossible to measure. The writer is convinced that it exists, but that it exists so deep within the American mind that it has become part of the foundation on which thought rests rather than part of thought itself. It is that there is something inevitably incompetent about govern-ment. Newspaper cartoons have been ground out day after day illustrating the same tired old joke about the imbecility of Senator Soandso. Musical comedies, some sprightly and some savage, have had their day and their sport about the venality and the futility of the national government. Radio shows, back in the days when radio was something more than talk shows and weather bulletins, wove their weekly fantasies out of the echoes of fictional sound and fury signifying nothing, emanating from Washington. There are in the comedy two basic characters indistinguishable in their flatulence, pomposity, pretentiousness, and fraud, the Senator and the Bureaucrat. You can tell them apart by their dress. The Senator affects a string tie and the sort of collar that was becoming old fashioned when the Union forces fired on Fort Sumter. The Bureaucrat bears some resemblance to a cartoon favorite of the older generation, Big Business, who used to sport on his hemispheric chest a magnificent vest decorated with $ signs. Put together they personify the pretence, insincerity, and self-seeking shiftiness that might well mask something more sinister, all so characteristic of the national government.

It all rests on what is in itself a sound maxim: you must keep a sharp eye on the politician. But you must also keep a sharp eye on the doctors. You must keep a sharp eye on the teachers. You must keep a sharp eye on the clergy. You must keep a sharp eye on the businessmen. No profession or trade has a monopoly on virtue and an invulnerability to temptation. The danger sets in when the people feel, rather than think, that government and incompetence are inseparable. That is no more true than it is true to feel that medicine and incompetence, teaching and incompetence, religion and incompetence, business and incompetence are inseparable. But no one ever suggests any of the latter, whereas the world of enlightenment and entertainment constantly suggests the latter.

There are incompetents in Congress, to be sure, and there are highly competent, deeply dedicated men and women. Furthermore, they and they alone among the leaders of national thought are chosen by the people. The professional and business leaders are not. What of the benighted Bureaucrat? In many ways his case is the most curious of all. He serves the people, but he is only obliquely selected by them. Let us take a specimen of the kind. There is in a particular business a man in early middle life, finely competent, highly energetic, universally respected, a man of human understanding and humane feeling, able to work with others and to correlate effectively the energies of his associates. The President of the United States needs just such a man to direct the work of a particular governmental agency which the international situation has made sensitive and vital. He appeals to the man's patriotism, and with such a man that appeal prevails. The businessman undertakes the necessary and onerous adjustments: sells a lot of stock he did not mean to sell, cuts a lot of ties he never desired to cut, sells his house, gets less desirable accommodations on the rim above Foggy Bottom, transplants his children to new schools, tells his wife that this is little enough to do for the country that has given them what they have, and boards the plane for Washington. He boards the plane a Businessman; he will leave it a Bureaucrat.

He will work just as hard at Washington as he ever did back home, and probably harder. He will give as much to his country and more than he ever gave to the company. He will learn that the diplomacy within government is at least as subtle and crafty an art as the diplomacy between governments, and he will adapt to it as best he can. What is finest in him will continue to respond to that call from the White House, what is human in his understanding and humane in his feeling will elicit every ounce of service to his country, every ounce of loyalty to that man who called him, who stands so high and so alone in his solemn and inescapable responsibility. For all that he will still be a Bureaucrat, his judgment questioned violently by those who do not even know what he was judging, his integrity slyly gnawed at by those without the courage to slash with bared fang, his competence doubted by the incompetent, his honesty by the dishonest, his courage by the craven and his worth by the worthless. And yet, he will do a reasonably good job. The man in the White House will know that he has done a better job than he realizes, because the President has had vastly more experience in politics than the Bureaucrat and knows the limitations it imposes. There will be parts of his public service that the Bureaucrat will regret but some parts will satisfy him, and he will end life as a Bureaucrat with the 'scutcheon reasonably unblemished.

There is salvation for him. He boards the plane from Washington a Bureaucrat, but he will leave it a businessman again. There is no salvation for the government. The Congress and the bureaus go on being the cartoon stereotype, and the prestige of the government continues to sink at home and to slump alarmingly abroad. There is danger in this, very real danger in a world where the battle for men's minds is universal and constant, and waged with a multiplicity of weapons. Leviathan is fair sport for every harpooner with a lance to hurl and a joy at the gush of blood. Let us remember that we are

Leviathan, and every such wound is self-inflicted. When the prestige
of America is lowered, so is the prestige of every American institution. That includes *The New York Times* and the Columbia Broadcasting System.

And yet, there is a sense in which the fault is really the government's. The government has never begun to make clear its position
on national and international issues. It puts out press releases, it
makes available obliquely phrased statements of administration policy, but it never grapples with the real job of explaining its positions
to the American people and defending their validity. As Mr. Goulding puts it, "The observers who marvel that we succeed in selling
Coca-Colas but fail in explaining government policy have not examined the case. Of course we fail. They overlook the fact that we do
not attempt to explain the policy, that no apparatus for doing so
exists within the federal government, and that any attempt to create
even a tenth-rate apparatus would be greeted with hostility both by
press and by Congress."[1]

WHY NOT A GOVERNMENT JOURNAL?

This brings us close to the heart of the matter. For better or for
worse, and mainly for the latter, we have lived into a day in which
big government is an inevitable, continuing, dominant fact of national and personal life. Everyone agrees that the American people
have a right to know what the government is doing and a duty to
pass judgment on its justice and effectiveness. There remains to be
taken a necessary step. The American people have a right to know
why the government is doing what it is, and the government has the
obligation to explain policy to the American people and to attempt
its justification. It is no longer possible to do this with the press
release, the occasional speech, the semi-periodic press conference,
the managed "leak" of one sort or another. It is entirely possible to
do it in a straightforward, systematic, regularized fashion by running
a government newspaper.

Such a journal would be the official mouthpiece of the administration, explaining government policy, justifying it by revealing what
factual information it is consistent with the welfare of the citizen to
reveal, and frankly and unabashedly arguing for the soundness of the

[1] p. 85

policy. Of course it would be a propaganda medium. It would be worthless if it were not. Two circumstances make propaganda dangerous: when it is disguised as something else and when no one is permitted to attempt its refutation. Every advertisement is propaganda, every exhortation is propaganda. Propaganda is merely the body of doctrines or principles that comprise the objective of some organization. The goals of a national administration become propaganda once they are voiced. So do the goals of every human organization under the sun.

There is available a model for such an administration journal that in broad outlines might provide useful guidance. It is *Osservatore Romano* of Vatican City. This is the official mouthpiece of the Catholic Church, it exists to explain and to advocate the Catholic position on issues important to the Church, and it exists for no other reason. It is propaganda pure, simple, and highly useful. It lets the world know where the Church stands on issues and it is invaluable to the press of the world and the world readership it serves.

Osservatore Romano is totally free from the two circumstances that make propaganda dangerous. There is no secret whatever to its purpose and its mission, and it is published in the atmosphere of a free society in which issues and attitudes can be analyzed and debated without let or hindrance. One may question the church attitude on issues, question it austerely, oppose it bitterly, but there is no excuse for misrepresenting it. The very straightforward nature of *Osservatore Romano* facilitates opposition even as it holds it within legitimate channels.

It is the conviction of Mr. Goulding that any attempt to create an administration journal in Washington would be greeted with hostility by both press and Congress. This might well be so. It would seem clear that in anything so stereotyped and undeviating as American political oratory the shrieks of "propaganda" from the opposition party would pierce the empyrean. That would be quite tolerable, so long as the citizen understood that it was indeed propaganda, knew what propaganda was, and how harmless and even useful it can be when properly employed. Such an organ should not be open to members of Congress. They have the *Congressional Record*. It is unquestionable that government bureaus whose number no man can count, with axes to grind that no man can reckon, would want space in the new medium. Its editor would have to be a man of tungsten steel and he would have to hold rank in the national administration so high that no one short of the President could successfully pull rank on him.

What would really be the attitude of the commercial press? One suspects that this would gradually evolve as the journal itself evolved. Very likely there would be sharp opposition at first. The propaganda ploy could be expected, but it is doubtful if it would be especially effective. There might well be plaintive wails about depending on handouts and about official coloration of the news, but there are handouts now and the constant charge of coloration. The essential saving grace is that an administration journal would be published in the atmosphere of a free society. The private press would be just as free as ever to search out the truth, to question what is officially proclaimed to be the truth, and if anything more nearly free than ever to pass judgment on government policy since it would be more clearly and logically defined than heretofore. In many ways the most important point of all is that the administration could never make the charge that it was being misunderstood or misinterpreted. Citizens all over the country would have copies of its official statements.

The one question that is really basic is the one question that tends not to be asked. What would be the reaction of the people? The tendency to equate oneself with the people is a human tendency. "We the people of England" turned out to be seven little tailors, but they might just as readily have been seven newspaper publishers or television executives. Every now and then something happens that brings home to the news media that they are not "the people of England." The press all but unanimously supported Alf Landon as he swept Maine and Vermont against Roosevelt in 1936. Press and people were almost totally divided in the 1930's. Whether they are divided now and if so to what extent is an open question. Many think there is at least some blue water showing between them.

It does not necessarily follow, then, that the far sighted and wise elements among the news media would view an administration journal as the work of Belial. It would be a device for regularizing the publication of information by the administration and for publicizing the reasons behind government policy. It would furnish a foundation on which responsible editorializing could be based, and just so long as the atmosphere of a free society is maintained and the First Amendment with it, the cause of political truth in America would no more suffer than the cause of religious truth suffers by the publication of *Osservatore Romano.*

All this does come under the head of prior restraint, remote though it may seem from it. In matters of national policy, until there is a press release there is restraint of the news. Until there is a disclosure in a formal speech calculated as the medium for the disclosure, until there is a meticulously couched, carefully prepared answer to the one right question at the press conference, there is prior restraint of the news. This is in no sense wrong. What is wrong is the disordered, unorganized, haphazard way that it is done. Whatever one thinks of the Vietnam war, and the writer shares the widespread belief that it has been the saddest national tragedy since the Civil War, there must have been some reason that the Kennedy and Johnson administrations deemed it a necessity of national policy. Yet the unbelievable fact remains a fact. No single member of the executive branch of the government in either administration had as his sole responsibility the explanation of the national policy involved. That is really inexcusable.

The people do not instinctively distrust their government. The citizen does not instinctively believe everything he reads in print or hears over the air waves. America is a mature nation and a capacity to think has not vanished from it. An administration journal would not be immune to investigation, refutation, and attack. On the other hand, an administration journal could present in an orderly and systematic fashion the information the citizen needs for judgment and the reasons that underlie government policy he must appraise. Finally, an administration journal would be a medium for the systematic publication of declassified documents and records, and help to end the excessively prolonged withholding from public knowledge of information which no longer need be concealed for the sake of the public safety. Properly managed, wisely guided, and dedicated to the principle that there should be no prior restraint on the news unless necessitated by the welfare of the citizen, it could end such unsound and unseemly news raids as led to the publication of the Pentagon Papers.

AGAIN THE PENTAGON PAPERS

Since the phrase *Pentagon Papers* is usually equated with the selection from them printed in *The New York Times* and other papers, it should first be made clear that the equation is far from complete. In 1967 Secretary of Defense McNamara ordered a study of American policy in Vietnam. The study filled 7000 pages in forty-seven volumes, some 4000 pages written by thirty-six different persons over a year and a half, and the rest devoted to photographic reproductions of Defense Department, State Department, and Central Intelligence Agency documents. There are three published versions of the Pentagon Papers. The well-known one is the set of excerpts first published in *The New York Times* and then in book form by Quadrangle Books and Bantam Books. The most nearly complete one was printed in twelve volumes by the Government Printing Office for the use of the House Committee on Armed Services. The other one with a pretence to completeness is the Senator Gravel edition in four volumes and nearly 3000 pages published by Beacon Press. The Defense Department version omits the sections that deal with diplomatic negotiations still pending. The Gravel edition includes certain sections omitted from the Defense Department version, has only about one-quarter of the documents of the Government edition, but does share with *The New York Times* edition certain documents not included in the former. The historian may collate the three massive compilations, and one wishes him Godspeed in the venture. Let the citizen who thinks he has read the Pentagon Papers because he has slogged his way through the 677 pages of the Bantam paperback know that he has barely wet up to his ankles.

The Supreme Court held by a six-to-three decision that it could not sustain an injunction against *The New York Times* and the other papers publishing the excerpts from the Pentagon Papers. The majority reached agreement by very different routes and, as tends to be true in such matters, for the one who is seeking legal principles it is the routes that are important rather than the agreement. Present in this set of opinions, which sometimes converge and sometimes diverge, are the views of the nine justices on the problem of prior restraint in the form most pertinent to American life today, with the right to know and the right to be protected set the one against the other against a background of global conflict in ideology and great power preparation for mutual annihilation.

Justices Black and Douglas took the position that First Amendment protection of a free press is absolute and hence the exercise of prior restraint by the government over the publication of such documents as the Pentagon Papers is by its nature unconstitutional.

Justice Brennan fell a few steps short of the absolutist position, conceding that there can be cases in which a permanent injunction is justified and that in this case a temporary injunction was perhaps necessary.

The three dissenters, Chief Justice Burger and Justices Harlan and Blackmun, denied as valid the absolutist interpretation of the First Amendment freedom and all three stressed what Justice Harlan called the "almost irresponsibly feverish haste" with which the Court handled the case, a haste to be measured in hours and not days although the material in question was at least three years old and *The New York Times* had mulled it over for three months before publishing. The main thrust of their opinions, however, concerned that subtle, difficult, and grave problem of the weighing of comparative values, freedom of expression against the necessity for public protection. As Chief Justice Burger put it,

There is . . . little variation among the members of the Court in terms of resistance to prior restraints against publication. Adherence to this basic constitutional principle, however, does not make this case a simple one. In this case, the imperative of a free and unfettered press comes into collision with another imperative, the effective functioning of a complex modern government and specifically the effective exercise of certain constitutional powers of the Executive. Only those who view the First Amendment as an absolute in all circumstances—a view I respect, but reject—can find such a case as this to be simple and easy.

He then went on to describe why the haste with which the case was forced upon the Court made it impossible for any justice to pass judgment with a full knowledge of the facts, except of course those judges to whom the absolutist position on freedom made a knowledge of the facts unnecessary.

The reasoning of the other three justices who comprised the majority is interesting. Justice Marshall denied that the central issue was whether the "First Amendment bars a court from prohibiting a newspaper from publishing material whose disclosure would pose a grave and immediate danger to the security of the United States." Rather, he stated, "The issue is whether this Court or the Congress has the power to make law." He conceded the power of the Executive to classify information as secret and to safeguard it, but he questioned the power of the Executive branch to invoke the equity jurisdiction of the courts to protect what it considered the national interest. His long opinion can be reduced to a perfectly simple conclusion: the publication of the Pentagon Papers was not illegal because Congress never passed a law that would make it so. There is no evidence in his opinion that he considered the First Amendment protection of a free press the key to the Pentagon Papers case.

Justice White reached the same conclusion as Justice Marshall and by fundamentally the same process of reasoning. There are, however, certain emphases in his opinion that set it apart from his colleague's. He did believe that the publication "will do substantial damage to public interests. Indeed I am confident that their disclosure will have that result." He pointed out pragmatically that publication was actually underway; the cat was out of the bag. He stressed the ancient principle that freedom to publish does not mean freedom from the consequences of publishing. "Prior restraints require an unusually heavy justification under the First Amendment; but failure by the Government to justify prior restraints does not measure its constitutional entitlement to a conviction for criminal publication. That the Government mistakenly chose to proceed by injunction does not mean that it could not successfully proceed in another way." Like Justice Marshall, he stressed the fact that Congress has never authorized the injunctive process against threatened publication. At the heart of Justice White's argument is the thought that a free press is not only a morally responsible press but a legally responsible press as well. Justice Marshall's fundamental argument is that publication was not illegal because Congress never made it so. Justice White was more receptive to the thought that publication might have been in conflict with a criminal statute. His fundamental argument is that the question of legality should be decided by criminal proceedings and not by using the injunctive power of the courts.

Justice Stewart comes directly to grips with the dilemma which lies at the heart of the matter to everyone except those to whom freedom is an absolute—or, presumably, their intellectual kinfolk at the other end of the spectrum to whom governmental authority is an absolute. An informed free press is vital to a free people. So is national security. There must be "an insistence upon avoiding secrecy for its own sake. For when everything is classified, nothing is classified. . . ." Again he stated, "the hallmark of a truly effective internal security system would be the maximum possible disclosure, recognizing that secrecy can best be preserved only when credibility is truly maintained." Since Justice Stewart concurred with Justice White, much of his argumentation is implicit in the argumentation of his colleague. His argument, as made explicit in his concurring opinion, was that the protection of national safety and the conduct of international relations is the responsibility of the Executive and that the role of Congress and the Court is ancillary, the role of Congress being to pass laws punishing violations of proper and constitutional executive safeguards of secrecy and the role of the courts being to pass on the constitutionality and applicability of such laws to the facts of a case at hand. Since he did not believe that there was imminent and irreparable danger to the country in the publication of the Pentagon Papers, his implicit argument was that there can be no proper appeal to an emergency situation that might warrant Court action unless there is an emergency—our old friend, the "clear and present danger test" appearing in a new guise. In the absence of the clear and present danger, his opinion rested on the division of powers and the impropriety of using the injunctive power of the courts to do what properly should be done by the legislative powers of Congress and the administrative powers of the Executive.

The case of the Pentagon Papers at the very least illustrates the argument for an administration journal which would have as one of its functions the regular publication of documents of public concern once the need for their classification has passed. In the absence of that or any other regularized procedure for publication a vacuum was formed and, as always, the vacuum was filled. First, an individual would appear to have made his personal conscience the guide to what official documents should be made public. Then, the board of editors of a privately owned newspaper appointed itself the board of censors as to what it was to the public interest to have published from these documents, and the moral arbiter as to the amount and nature of publication consistent with the public safety. Whether they did their work well or ill, whether they were motivated by the highest ideals of disinterested patriotism or not, whether the net result of the selective publication of the Pentagon Papers by a group of newspapers did a public service or a public disservice, all this is totally beside the point. It is the responsibility of the Executive to preserve the safety of the citizen. As Justice Stewart pointed out, the responsibility of the Congress and the Court is ancillary in this regard, the responsibility of the Congress being to pass laws punishing those who violate executive regulations designed to protect the public safety and the responsibility of the Court being to pass judgment on the applicability and the constitutionality of such laws to cases on hand. It is not the responsibility, nor the prerogative, of any individual or corporation to take over the responsibility of the Executive no matter how exalted may be the motivation nor even how beneficial the interference.

Yet there remains the unsolved problem and the unsatisfied need. The Federal government has no means for the regular publication of statements about government policy, defenses of the reasoning on which they rest, and the publicizing of the documents that illustrate this reasoning and provide the factual foundation for it. Documents dealing with matters of profound national concern should not be reduced to the status of newspaper scoops. The real need, however, is to get rid of the scoop mentality, to get rid of the speed psychosis. Any Supreme Court judge who knew the answer to the Pentagon Papers dilemma in advance would have no trouble reaching a decision. There never is any trouble for those who reach their decisions by a few *a priori* principles. The majority, including three who voted with the majority as well as the three dissenters, do not have that approach to their responsibility. There can be no doubt that the Supreme Court was stampeded into a decision that probably has done no harm, but certainly has done no good unless it has made clear that the issue should never have arisen in the first place. It never would have arisen if the government had a regularized procedure for making public and justifying in the process its policies and objectives, and publishing the information by which those policies and objectives have been determined. The Pentagon Papers would never have become a best seller if published as a series in an executive journal, but this would have been a less disturbed country and a country not the less disturbed because not one American in ten thousand, in all probability, has ever read *The New York Times* series in its entirety. One may only express the pious hope that the newspaper, radio, and television commentators whose views on them were really the foundation of public reaction may have done so. The reader may test the likelihood himself by reading one hundred pages of the finely printed paperback text and seeing how long it takes.

Thus the oldest of the conflicts in terms of which freedom of the press must be defined, the conflict between such freedom and the principle of prior restraint, is just as truly a conflict today as it was when Milton wrote *Areopagitica*. Then the issue involved the licensing of the press. Even that form of the issue could burst into life tomorrow. We still have licensed news media in radio and television, and we must return presently to the problem that fact potentially involves. The threat of prior restraint to the free press usually has taken the form of statutes punishing seditious libel. This was the specific threat the First Amendment freedom was calculated to ward off, and on the whole it has done so superbly. One may seriously question if a major policy of a free nation has ever been so constantly, fundamentally, vehemently, and even violently assailed in print as was the Southeast Asia policy of the Johnson administration. There was never the faintest hint from that beset and unhappy administration that to the most timid of apprehensions could be misinterpreted as a distant threat of action for seditious libel. The First Amendment may have been a weak reed on which to lean during the Civil War and the First World War, but it was certainly a stalwart oak during the Vietnam war.

Yet the issue of prior restraint continues to be very much alive. Its characteristic form now involved the classification of information that might adversely affect the safety of the citizen if published. Here the issue seems simple to no one except the person who affects no belief in any aspect of prior restraint or any reason for prior restraint. Justice after justice in his Pentagon Papers opinion stressed the importance of First Amendment protection against prior restraint and the necessity of keeping it to the minimum genuinely consistent with the national safety, but seven of the nine recognized that that minimum exists. How is the necessary minimum to be determined? The problem is a knotty one, and certainly not one that can be solved by the automatic application of a principle. It is difficult to see how it can be solved except on a pragmatic basis, and then with much soul searching and the probing of many uncertainties. Where scientific information is concerned, it would seem that at least the generalized application of something approaching a principle might be applied: the secret of nature cannot be kept a secret long so it may as well be disclosed, the secret of fact can be kept a secret and should be kept, the secret of technology shares some attributes of the former and some of the latter and should be kept to the extent that its nature makes possible, or indeed desirable. This refers, naturally, to those aspects or pure and applied science directly and ominously concerned with the safety of the citizen.

Where governmental operations in the misty, murky purlieus of international politics are concerned, the problem is at its most acute. It is hard to go with confidence beyond the point that Goulding reaches in *Confirm or Deny:* "In determining what information is to be made public, the government must and does take into account the effect the release of that information will have on sovereign states which are friendly to us, allied with us, neutral about us, potentially hostile or outright enemies. This is a fact of twentieth-century nuclear life."[1]

The achieving of that decision is one of the most solemn and difficult decisions the national administration must make, but it is not a decision it can either evade or share. This is the sort of matter in which a meticulous use of personal pronouns is in order. It is not *our* press in the same sense that it is *our* government. We elect, maintain, support, judge, retain, or dismiss *our* government. We have no such power over *our* press. The press is a vital American institution, but to call the government *America* is a valid employment of that figure of speech in which the part stands for the whole. To call the press *America* is not. Therefore it is not a decision the government can share with the press, and it is most emphatically a decision the press must not preempt.

On the other hand the facts of twentieth-century life demand a more forthright and comprehensive approach to the publicizing and the documenting of governmental policies than has prevailed in the past. There is little place today for such out-moded and inadequate devices as "a government spokesman," "a source close to the White House," "cloak room report," and the like. There may or may not be a place for the televised press conference. That should depend fundamentally on the attitude of the man in the White House. Some men are effective under such circumstances and like the opportunity of visual contact with the people. They certainly should continue the institution. Others might prefer the added time and thoughtfulness made possible by the printed word, and should be free to act upon their preference. In any case the press conference should not be the primary avenue of communication between the President and the citizen, an avenue intermittently opened and one always circum-

[1] p. 20

scribed by the two peremptory categories, time and space. One doubts if an executive journal would be a sprightly sheet, or even a widely read one. One can picture some of the speed drained out of journalism by it, some of the romance grown pallid. The nation can get its speed and its romance other ways. What the citizen must get is a continuing, frank, detailed, intelligible, reasoned exposition of national policy by those fundamentally responsible for it. The lack of that sort of communication is the real curse of the contemporary form of prior restraint.

Part II

FREE PRESS v.
FAIR TRIAL

Among the serried ranks of stately volumes that comprise the Collected Works of Man, few exceed in impressiveness the collection of opinions and decisions issued by the Supreme Court of the United States. Much of the nation's history is written in these volumes, much of the explanation of its present state is to be found within their pages, and the voice of today may be heard giving instruction to tomorrow. In case after case the varied and complex strands of national life are woven into the fabric of our existence, and the direct and simple clauses of the Constitution are made prophetic and admonitory about matters undreamed of when the Fathers framed them. It is one of the great glories, and also one of the great mysteries, of the Constitution that it has proved adaptable to two centuries unimaginably different from the century that saw its birth, and yet seldom in the process of adaptation has the fabric been unduly wrenched and twisted out of shape.

This was made possible only in part by the wisdom of the Founding Fathers. It was also made possible by the fact that the law of the Americans has not been like the law of the Medes and the Persians, which altereth not. No justice of the Supreme Court ever surpassed in professional prestige Judge Learned Hand of the United States Court of Appeals for the Second Circuit. He has been called the "tenth Supreme Court justice," and in the cogency and influence of his lower-court opinions was indeed that from the day Calvin Coolidge appointed him to the bench in 1924 until the day he died in 1961. Judge Hand was a pragmatist in the full philosophic sense, and the natural instinct of the American people is pragmatic. He called the broader provisions of the Constitution moral adjurations. "What," he asked in *A Spirit of Liberty*, "is 'freedom of speech and of the press'; what is the 'establishment of religion and the free exercise thereof'; what are 'unreasonable searches,' 'due process of law,' and 'equal protection of law. . . .' These fundamental canons are not jural concepts at all, in the ordinary sense; and in application they turn out to be no more than admonitions of moderation."[1] He termed the Bill of Rights "merely a counsel of perfection and an ideal of temperance," grounding his thesis on a foundation of philosophic pragmatism: "Once you get people believing that there is an authoritative well of wisdom to which they can turn for absolutes,

[1] Hershel Shanks, ed., *The Arts and Craft of Judging: The Decisions of Judge Learned Hand*, New York: The Macmillan Co., 1968, p. 23.

you have dried up the springs on which they must in the end draw even for the things of this world."[1] If the Warren Court has been roundly assailed in the twentieth century, it has been precisely because its majority sought in the Bill of Rights jural concepts rather than moral adjurations, sought philosophic absolutes and not pragmatic relatives.

There is no provision in the Bill of Rights that is a philosophic absolute. Each provision is relative to other provisions, as is natural in a document which is essentially a counsel of moderation. The prohibition of an establishment of religion is relative to the provision for the free exercise of religion. The entire school prayer hassle has resulted from the treatment of the former prohibition as an absolute. Similarly the free-press provision is relative among other things to the provision for a fair trial. To treat any right guaranteed by the Bill of Rights as an absolute brings it into conflict with another right. The unilateral defense of a single freedom quickly becomes an assault upon another freedom. This is the inescapable fallacy behind the absolutism which certain justices have taken toward specific constitutional provisions and prohibitions, like the provision for a free press and the prohibition of an establishment of religion.

Naturally the justices of the Supreme Court have been aware that the treating of the Bill of Rights provisos as jural concepts has frequently brought about a conflict of rights. Some, like Justices Black and Douglas, have simply held that such rights as freedom of speech and of the press are absolutes, with entire priority to any other rights with which they may conflict. A more philosophic view was taken years ago by Justice Benjamin N. Cardozo in *Palko v. Connecticut*. The case involved double jeopardy. The defendant argued that because of the Fourteenth Amendment a violation of the Bill of Rights committed by the Federal government would be equally unconstitutional if committed by a state. Ruling for the Supreme Court Justice Cardozo drew a distinction between fundamental freedoms and liberties of secondary importance. He placed freedom of thought and speech among the fundamental freedoms. "Of that condition one may say that it is the matrix, the indispensable condition, of nearly every other form of freedom. With rare aberrations a pervasive recognition of that truth can be traced in our history, political and legal. So it has come about that the domain of

[1] *Ibid.*, p. 16

liberty, withdrawn by the Fourteenth Amendment from encroachment by the states, has been enlarged by latter-day judgments to include liberty of the mind as well as liberty of action."[1]

The same thought was further refined by Justice Robert H. Jackson in a school flag salute case, *West Virginia State Board of Education v. Barnett.*[2] The point at issue was the relative superiority under the law of promoting national cohesion by requiring school children to open the day with a salute to the flag and permitting children of Jehovah Witness families to obey the dictates of their creed which forbids such an act as the worshipping of an image, against which there is a stricture in Exodus 20:4-5. The religious freedom of the individual was deemed by the Court higher than the right of the state to exact this show of patriotic allegiance. Justice Jackson said for the Court, "The very purpose of a Bill of Rights was to withdraw certain subjects from the vicissitudes of political controversy, to place them beyond the reach of majorities and officials and to establish them as legal principles to be applied by the courts. One's right to life, liberty, and property, to free speech, a free press, freedom of worship and assembly, and other fundamental rights may not be submitted to vote; they depend on the outcome of no elections." Later, after illustrating the distinction between fundamental and secondary liberties by citing the power of a state to regulate a public utility as a legitimate limitation of a secondary liberty, Justice Jackson stated, "But freedoms of speech and of press, of assembly, and of worship may not be infringed on such slender grounds. They are susceptible of restriction only to prevent grave and immediate danger to interests which the State may lawfully protect."

We are dealing at this point with that doctrine of inalienable rights which is many centuries older than the Declaration of Independence but received its immortal American expression in that document. "Life, liberty, and the pursuit of happiness"; the Declaration states explicitly that the list is not complete, but these are the three signalled out for explicit expression. Justices Cardozo and Jackson wrote only a few years before nuclear science would make it possible for any city in America to be annihilated within minutes by a missile launched half the world away, only a few years before the life and liberty of Americans which the State exists to safeguard

[1] 309 U.S. 319, 326 (1937)
[2] 319 U.S. 624 (1943)

would always be in potentially grave and immediate danger. The right of prior restraint exists to protect life and liberty, and by any tenable set of values they are rights antecedent to freedom of speech and of the press. Yet the real problem is not one of establishing priorities but of adjudicating conflicting claims. The right to life and liberty exists as an axiom of American society. So does the right to free speech and a free press. Even in what seems to be the philosophic ultimates there are no absolutes except the right of the individual to lead a life of virtue. Beyond the Bill of Rights is what the Bill of Rights exists to safeguard, the inalienable right of the individual to life, liberty, and the pursuit of happiness. Freedom of thought, speech, and press are indeed, to borrow Justice Cardozo's metaphor, the matrix in which the other freedoms are formed, but the matrix exists for what is within it and not the other way around.

Nowhere are two rights in more dramatic conflict than in the legal case which has aroused the public interest to the point at which the right of the public to know the truth may be brought into conflict with the right of a defendant to a fair trial. There is no case among the Supreme Court decisions identified as *Free Press v. Fair Trial*, yet that case has been repeatedly reviewed by the Court. It deserves such attention, because no issue between the citizen and the press except the issue of prior restraint on news is of greater importance than the right of a citizen accused of a crime, or indeed implicated in a civil case, to fair treatment before his trial, during it, and during the legal proceedings which may follow it. Just as the courts must be free as well as fair, so the press must be fair as well as free.

Truth is a moral imperative and the search for truth is an inalienable right. But the right to justice is also an inalienable right. One may view the issue in the most serene, unclouded light imaginable, and yet recognize that enthusiasm for the discovery and publishing of the truth may be carried to the point at which it impinges upon the legal processes of justice. It has done so, and that is why the court record contains so many pages devoted to that unheard, untried, unpublished, all pervasive case which finds one moral imperative pitted against another, *Free Press v. Fair Trial*. Let us examine how this comes about.

A PRESIDENT DIES

Two shots ring out in Dallas, and "anarchy is loosed upon the world." Twenty-four hours after President Kennedy was shot, some three hundred newsmen from every corner of America and many a corner of the world were in the Texas city. "A constant battle," a captain of the Dallas police called it, "a constant battle because of the number of newsmen who were there. They would move back into the aisleway that had been cleared. They interfered with the movement of people who had to be there." The Secret Service with a solemn responsibility to meet was overpowered by the human tidal wave; "press and television people just ... took over," said its spokesman. A hundred news and cameramen packed the third floor corridor of police headquarters; television floodlights poured out torrents of unrelenting radiance; wires and cables snaked about the floor and writhed through windows to cars beneath. The guerrilla troops of the world of journalism stalked their prey, armed with still cameras, movie cameras, television cameras, microphones. One witness told the Warren Commission with convincing incoherence that he "tried to get by the reporters, stepping over television cables and you couldn't hardly get by, they would grab you and wanted to know what you were doing down here, even with the detectives one in front and one behind you."

At two o'clock on Friday afternoon Lee Harvey Oswald was brought to police headquarters. The police made a flying wedge and got him through the barricade of reporters and cameramen before the building. At that, several newsmen managed to make the elevator that took Oswald to the third floor. Here another human barricade was faced, another flying wedge was formed, and as it ground its way forward cameras were thrust in Oswald's face, questions shrieked at him, and his incoherent answers shrieked by those who questioned him for the sake of the disadvantaged brethren to the rear. The newsmen demanded a midnight press conference, and got it. The sanhedrin of the news world was at it, and so were some seventy or more unauthorized persons, including one named Jack Ruby. The chief of police made Oswald stand on the floor in front of the stage. Cameras do not photograph well through the one-way nylon screen used to keep suspects from knowing who is in the room. Newsmen bellowed their questions at Oswald, cameramen battled to his side, but the very chaos of the scene was self-destroying. "After Oswald had been in the room only a few minutes, Chief Curry intervened and directed that Oswald be taken back to jail because, he testified, the newsmen 'tried to overrun him.'"

The press was told that Oswald would be moved to the county jail on Sunday morning. The car to take him would be driven into the basement garage at police headquarters. The garage was checked to make sure there was no one in hiding, and then the police let in the flood of newsmen, directing them to stand before the railing on the side of the ramp. They poured down the ramp, and Jack Ruby walked down the same ramp unnoticed and unchallenged. Then Oswald appeared. Some say the newsmen held their place by the railing, and the video tape bears them out. Others say the crowd surged forward. Oswald took several steps forward and was ten feet from the door of the jail. Then Jack Ruby stepped forward and shot him. It was the only killing in human history seen by an entire nation and much of the world.

In the literal sense Jack Ruby killed Lee Harvey Oswald behind news coverage. Nothing but the massing of newsmen in the basement garage made it possible. But in the figurative sense Oswald had been found guilty of a capital crime by the Dallas police and by the press before Jack Ruby made unnecessary the process of a trial. The Dallas police were under positive orders to render whatever aid was feasible to the members of the news media. Implicit in such an order is the obligation not to interfere unduly with the members as they gather news. The Dallas police certainly read into both the explicit and the implicit injunction the command to provide news as well as to expedite its gathering. The Dallas Chief of Police appeared on television and radio at least twelve times during November 22-24. On one occasion, when asked if he had results on the ballistics test conducted on the gun and on Oswald, he replied, "They're going to be favorable. I don't have a formal report yet." "But are you sure at this time they will be favorable?" "Yes." In the context *favorable* hardly requires definition, nor can it be interpreted as other than a finding of guilty. Indeed, the police captain under whom Oswald was interrogated assured the press on Saturday that he was convinced beyond doubt that Oswald had killed the President. So unceasing was the flow of information from the Dallas police to the newsmen, and indeed the flow of garbled information, and outright misinformation as well, that J. Edgar Hoover, whose F.B.I. laboratories were conducting the necessary scientific tests, sent a personal message to the chief of police asking him "not to go on the air any more until this case . . . [is] resolved." But destiny had its own way of resolving the case, and the instrument of destiny, Jack Ruby, stepped out from the massed newsmen and shot Lee Harvey Oswald. This stopped the flow of talk. "Chief Curry made only one more television appearance after the shooting," the Warren commission reported. "At 1:30 P.M., he descended to the assembly room where, tersely and grimly, he announced Oswald's death. He refused to answer any of the questions shouted at him by the persistent reporters, concluding the conference in less than a minute." The Dallas authorities voiced their official apologia the same night when the District Attorney held a long press conference at which he listed, not always accurately, the evidence that had been gathered to prove that Oswald had killed the President.

No one will ever know whether Lee Harvey Oswald would have been convicted of the assassination of President Kennedy. Certainly the news policy of the Dallas authorities would have damaged the prosecution quite as much as the defense. The entire report of the Warren Commission, from which we have liberally quoted, is fascinating, and no part of it more so than Appendix XII, which is entitled "Speculations and Rumors." It extends from page 568 to page 598 and lists 127 publicized speculations that had been refuted in whole or in part by Commission findings. The Commission stated:

Though many of the inaccuracies were subsequently corrected by the police and are negated by findings of the Commission included elsewhere in this report, the publicizing of unchecked information provided much of the basis for the myths and rumors that came into being soon after the President's death. The erroneous disclosures became the basis for distorted reconstructions and interpretations of the assassination. The necessity for the Dallas authorities to correct themselves or to be corrected by other sources gave rise not only to criticism of the police department's competence but also to doubts regarding the veracity of the police. Skeptics sought to cast doubt on much of the correct evidence later developed and to find support for their own theories in these early police statements.

The misinformation and the misleading information steadily broadcast in the hours after the assassination would certainly have cast doubt on the truth of the case assembled by the State. On the other hand, the constant flood of statements about anything so catastrophic as the assassination of a President inevitably made every American to some extent prejudge the guilt of Oswald and make that much more nearly impossible the assembly of an open-minded jury. Similarly much of the evidence gathered by the Dallas authorities might be barred from the courtroom by the rules of law, but it was not barred from the minds of prospective jurors, nor could any juror be kept from bringing it with him to the jury box and the deliberation room. Neither could there be blotted from a juror's mind a knowledge of the public statements by the Chief of Police and the District Attorney expressing the conviction that Oswald shot the President of the United States.

The main onus, no doubt, must rest upon the Dallas authorities. But there would be no such onus to bear if the pressure the newsmen put upon them had not approached the ultimately unbearable. The Warren Commission endeavored to allocate responsibility fairly, but not to minimize the fact that a grave burden of responsibility was to be allocated.

It was therefore proper and desirable that the public know which agencies were participating in the investigation and the rate at which their work was progressing. The public was also entitled to know that Lee Harvey Oswald had been apprehended and that the State had gathered sufficient evidence to arraign him for the murders of the President and Patrolman Tippit, that he was being held pending action of the grand jury, that the investigation was continuing, and that the law enforcement agenices had discovered no evidence which tended to show that any other person was involved in either slaying.

However, neither the press nor the public had a right to be contemporaneously informed by the police or prosecuting authorities of the details of the evidence being accumulated against Oswald. Undoubtedly the public was interested in these disclosures, but its curiosity should not have been satisfied at the expense of the accused's right to a trial by an impartial jury. The courtroom, not the newspaper or television screen, is the appropriate forum in our system for the trial of a man accused of a crime.

Thus the Commission placed the main burden of responsibility upon the Dallas authorities, but it placed an appropriate burden upon the newsmen as well.

The general disorder in the Police and Courts Building during

November 22-24 reveals a regrettable lack of self-discipline by the newsmen. The Commission believes that the news media, as well as the police authorities, who failed to impose conditions more in keeping with the orderly process of justice, must share responsibility for the failure of law enforcement which occurred in connection with the death of Oswald. On previous occasions, public bodies have voiced the need for the exercise of self-restraint by the news media in periods when the demand for information must be tempered by other fundamental requirements of our society.

The conclusion follows logically: "The experience in Dallas during November 22-24 is a dramatic affirmation of the need for steps to bring about a proper balance between the right of the public to be kept informed and the right of the individual to a fair and impartial trial." Thus one moral imperative is pitted against another, in *Free Press v. Fair Trial.* Destiny, a whimsical, sardonic deity, had worked out its own ironic conclusion to the matter. Jack Ruby stepped out of the crowd of newsmen and took care of Lee Harvey Oswald. Later cancer took care of Jack Ruby. But that is not how justice should be administered in a great nation.

THE FORMULAS THAT FASCINATE

History is the systematic account of what is memorable in a nation's past, and the assassination of a President is history. The covering by newsmen of an assassination and its consequences is the recording of history in the making. It is part of the search for truth, and its justification is based on that fact. The intense drama of Dallas was natural drama, a drama that centered about an event of the first magnitude, one that commanded the undivided, fascinated attention of the nation and the world.

Fiction is the creative portrayal of imaginary characters and events. It may be presented to the mind through the medium of words upon the printed page, of pictures upon the illuminated screen, of voices and sounds that impinge upon the ear. Fiction in the making uses the same media as history in the making and if it is "true to life," its methods are similar. The difference, however, is fundamental and profound. The interest in history in the making arises from the identity of the characters and the nature of the events as they are in reality. The interest in fiction arises from their identity and nature as they are creatively imagined and presented by the literary artist.

Certain celebrated cases have had some aspects of both history and fiction. They are grounded in reality, and thus are history in the making, if one may employ *history* with a broad tolerance toward exactitude of meaning. But they are cases that would arouse no interest beyond their immediate neighborhood if the media did not find in them the formulas that fascinate, treat them with creative imagination, and present them with literary artistry.

One formula may be illustrated by "The Sheppard Murder Case." Dr. Samuel H. Sheppard was an osteopath of Cleveland and a member of a prominent local family. Dr. Sam of press, radio, and television was a bone manipulating Jekyll and a homicidal Hyde moving in an atmosphere of society and sex, mystery and violence, a figure brought into being by the creative imagination of newsmen. His actual history is tragically simple: after a decade in jail he was given a fair trial and found not guilty.

The other formula may be illustrated by the case of Leslie Irvin, "the mad dog killer." The record of Leslie Irvin was that of an habitual criminal, the sort of record that is tragically common in the sordid annals of American crime. Out of the creative imagination weaving its pattern of the macabre, the hideous, and the revolting emerges Irvin the mad dog killer. The formula that made the mad dog killer a figure of great local fascination was not the formula that made Dr. Sam a national household word, but the result was much the same.

These would appear to be the two basic formulas. The first is a blend of mystery and violence with society and sex, the formula of Harry K. Thaw, Hall-Mills, Dr. Finch and Carole Tregoff. The other formula uses the dark night of the macabre, the hideous and revolting, the dark night in the shadows of which lurk the semi-fictional Professor Webster, Lizzie Borden, Leopold and Loeb. Their fictional prototype is Edward Hyde, the dark night of the good Dr. Jekyll. Let us examine the details of each.

MYSTERY, VIOLENCE, SOCIETY, AND SEX

Dr. Samuel H. Sheppard maintained that he grappled with the assailant who broke into his house and murdered his wife Marilyn, grappled with him first in the house and later on the beach below his lakeside home. He claimed to have grappled with him in the shadows of a darkened house and in the shadows of the night, and that the assailant never emerged from the shadows. Dr. Sheppard was accused of the murder by the three Cleveland papers, and most violently by the Cleveland *Press* which laid down an unremitting barrage of headlines, editorials, and cartoons berating the slowness of official Cleveland in hauling Sheppard to the bar of justice and excoriating what it called the "protection" of the man it delicately referred to as "the chief suspect." There never was another suspect, unless it was the man who never emerged from the shadows. Finally Sheppard was hauled before the bar of justice, but not before the Roman holiday was opened with a coroner's inquest.

On June 6, 1966, twelve years after Sheppard was found guilty of murdering his wife, the Supreme Court sustained the finding made two years before by the United States District Court that he had not received a fair trial consistent with the due-process clause of the Fourteenth Amendment. Justice Clark delivered the Supreme Court decision, to which only Justice Black dissented, and prefaced his decision with a detailed, factual account of what may well have been the worst travesty of the processes of justice in American legal history. What follows is based on Justice Clark's account.

The coroner's inquest was held in a school gymnasium, a room appropriately large for the overflow audience drummed up by pre-inquest publicity in the Cleveland papers. Sheppard was searched by the police in the presence of several hundred witnesses. The coroner refused to let Sheppard's counsel participate in the inquest. "When Sheppard's chief counsel attempted to place some documents in the record," Justice Clark stated in the Supreme Court decision, "he was forcibly ejected from the room by the Coroner, who received cheers, hugs, and kisses from the ladies in the audience." Justice remained blindfolded, and unmoved.

Before and during the trial the newspapers conducted their own trial of Dr. Sheppard, marshalling their own evidence in blithe oblivion to the rules that govern real evidence in real trials. Having not so much found him guilty as known him to be guilty from the start, one paper quoted by Justice Clark managed an impressive editorial preconviction crescendo: "Now proved under oath to be a liar, still free to go about his business, shielded by his family, protected by a smart lawyer who has made monkeys of the police and authorities, carrying a gun part of the time, left free to do whatever he pleases. . . ." To give *vox populi* a free voice everywhere, the paper published the names and addresses of prospective jurors. Their phone numbers could be found in the Cleveland phone book, by those desirous of instructing them in their duty and the result expected of its performance.

Then the curtain rose. Downstage, inside the bar itself, were facilities for twenty newsmen, the supreme panjandrums of American journalism. Diligent democracy made available to the lesser lights all rooms on the courtroom floor and all seats in the courtroom except one side of the last row. This was reserved for the family of Dr. Sheppard and the family of the late Mrs. Sheppard. The great American public, forced to rely on secondary sources for its titillation, was not neglected. Nothing, and certainly not an edict from the bench, interfered with the flashing of photographer's bulbs during the courtroom proceedings. There were television broadcasts from the courthouse steps. There was a live debate staged by reporters over a local radio station during the progress of the trial. There was the helicopter which hovered above the jury as it assembled at the Sheppard house to view the scene of the killing, along with hundreds of reporters, cameramen, and interested citizens. The bird's-eye view also is valuable. There was the radio broadcast as the trial went on in which a news commentator compared the reported conflict in Sheppard's testimony to the confrontation of Alger Hiss by Whittaker Chambers. There were the tantalizing promises by the press of sensations to come, sensations like the testimony of a cousin of Mrs. Sheppard's to the Jekyll-Hyde character of Dr. Sam, but sensations that never came to pass. There was the epochal discovery by Walter Winchell that a woman on trial in New York for robbery claimed to be the mistress of Dr. Sheppard and mother of his child. There were the heart-rending pleas of the press to remember the dead Marilyn, now sainted by the fourth estate, and to remember as well the Sheppards and what they were. All this, and a burning indictment of the court for its conduct of the trial, is to be found from the pen of Justice Clark in that sober and dignified collection of decisions and opinions of the Supreme Court, under the quiet and unpromising title of *Sheppard v. Maxwell.*[1]

Dr. Sheppard was convicted of second-degree murder. His conviction was upheld by the Ohio courts, his case was carried in 1956 to

[1] 384 U.S. 333 (1966)

the United States Supreme Court, and his writ of certiorari was denied. Ten years later his case was again carried to the Supreme Court and the Court ruled that he had not received a fair trial. Justice Clark concluded the Court decision: "Since the state trial judge did not fulfill his duty to protect Sheppard from the inherently prejudicial publicity which saturated the community and to control disruptive influences in the courtroom, we must reverse the denial of the habeas petition. The case is remanded to the District Court with instructions to issue the writ and order that Sheppard be released from custody unless the State puts him to its charges again within a reasonable time." The State did put him to its charges again, and Dr. Sheppard was found not guilty.

Judge Bell of the Ohio Supreme Court summed it up in a sentence during the 1964 re-hearing of Dr. Sheppard's plea. "Murder and mystery, society, sex, and suspense were combined in this case in such a manner as to intrigue and captivate the public fancy to a degree perhaps unparalleled in recent annals. Throughout the preindictment investigation, the subsequent, legal skirmishes, and the nine-week trial, circulation-conscious editors catered to the insatiable interest of the American public in the bizarre. . . . In this atmosphere of a 'Roman holiday' for the news media, Sam Sheppard stood on trial for his life." Or, one may put it more succinctly in the quoted words of the managing editor of a California paper: "It's been a long time since there's been a murder trial this good." Indeed, this was so. There would not be anything else so good until Dr. Bernard Finch and his reported mistress Carole Tregoff would be tried for murdering Mrs. Finch in 1960. It even stood comparison with the 1922 case of Mrs. Hall and her brothers Henry and Willie Stevens, who were tried for shooting her husband the Reverend Edward Wheeler Hall and the soprano of his New Jersey church choir, Mrs. Eleanor Mills, and then scattering their love letters around the bodies. The Sheppard case was covered by sixty-five out-of-town newsmen; the Chicago *Tribune* alone sent nineteen ladies and gentlemen of the press to cover Hall-Mills.

Both comparison and contrast are possible where the assassination of President Kennedy and the killing of Marilyn Sheppard are concerned. The common denominator, naturally, is something extraneous to the persons involved, to wit, the coverage by the news media. Let us say that both were indeed covered adequately, and let it go at that. It is the fact that comparison is even possible that makes the contrast so important.

The assassination of a President shocks the world. Awe, fascination, horror, and an obliterating absorption that erases everything else from the mind attends an assassination, from the first unbelieving reaction through the tense drama that unfolds in every stage to the rolling drums, the slow paced cortege, the horse without a rider, the prayers by the graveside, and "Taps" with its long drawn note of sorrow, inevitability, and finality. This is the stuff of history, and one reads history, hears history, watches history unfold as a President is killed, his presumptive killer hunted down, then wiped out by an unimaginable act of private retribution in ghastly counterpoint to the solemn closing to a great and admirable life. In covering the assassination of President Kennedy the news media were recording history, and under the circumstances the observance of due process where the suspect was concerned is a counsel of perfection. The inexorable fact remains that the counsel of perfection is precisely that: Be ye perfect. It may not be a counsel achieved, but it cannot be a counsel ignored. It was ignored at Dallas.

Therefore the comparison between two utterly different killings is possible, and the contrast heightened thereby. The killing of Marilyn Sheppard was not a world event of the first magnitude. It was not even a Cleveland event of the first magnitude. Had a tornado cut a swathe of destruction and death through Cleveland the day that Marilyn Sheppard was killed, which event would have received the banner headline in the Cleveland press? But it was made a Cleveland event of the first magnitude by media coverage and then ("It's been a long time since there's been a murder trial this good") it was made a national event of the first magnitude. Rivers of paper flowed from press machines throughout the country as the press associations fed the last detail of the case and many a detail extraneous to it into the maw of transmitting machines in Cleveland. Reporters were sent from big city papers throughout the land to cover the murder trial of a man of whom no one in their city rooms had ever heard until he became the key figure in the best murder trial since Hall-Mills. Readers devoured every word their hometown papers printed, and hungered for more. They had never heard before of Dr. Sam and the dead Marilyn, they were puppets to them in a bloody, thrilling Punch and Judy show, but so long as the masters of the show dangled the puppets, they would watch, wonder, and luxuriate in the adventitious thrill of violence, mystery, sex, and society read in the safety of the printed page, heard in the safety of the bedside radio, watched in the safety of the television screen.

There was something unreal, theatrical, almost fictional about the Sheppard case, as there was years before about the Hall-Mills case, and would be years later in the Finch-Tregoff case. All such cases have in common mystery and violence in high places, and it certainly does not hurt if sex is added. But these are the qualities that make the detective story so popular a form. Such cases are even better than detective stories, because their foundation is real and the man in the street is his own detective. When such cases come along, the media recognize them for what they are and out of the grim foundation of fact which police and district attorneys probe, grand juries assay, where judges preside and juries decide, the media erect dramas of real life and sell them to the public that reads so avidly, listens so intently, watches so fixedly. Out of the inner tragedy that wracks a home until it bursts into overt violence the media erect a piece of merchandise for which there is a market unfailing and never satisfied. The counsel of perfection remains the same, Be ye perfect, but the counsel is properly addressed not to the public officials alone, not to the media alone, but to the people themselves who make such cases possible by their willingness to buy entertainment woven out of what is usually sordid and inevitably is sad domestic tragedy. It is the height of presumption to attempt to justify in the solemn name of truth and man's inalienable right to the truth the perversions of the processes of justice that attended the Sheppard case, or to dignify in the name of the Constitution the exploitation of nothing more admirable than public fascination with violence and mystery in high places (the height of the place may be lowered if enough sex is added) which makes national spectacles of such cases as Hall-Mills and Finch-Tregoff. One can explain the fascination, but one cannot use the explanation to exculpate the denial to the one accused in such cases of his legal rights by due process. When all is said and done, on the foundation of reality the media erected in the Sheppard case a tremendous entertainment. This justifies the comparison with fiction. It is what a consummate novelist or playwright does in the exercise of his craft. What the media did with Dr. Sam and the "assailant in the shadows," Charles Dickens might have done with his tantalizing *Edwin Drood* ("Who is Datchery?") had he lived to finish it. Conan Doyle did it again and again with Sherlock

Holmes. Dickens and Conan Doyle would have viewed with professional admiration and respect, and as Englishmen with amazement and horror, what the media did with the strange case of Dr. Sheppard.

After everything else is stripped away, the fact remains that when Dr. Sheppard was given a trial free from the atmosphere of the trial that found him guilty and sent him to jail for a decade, he was found not guilty. A judge and a jury sent Dr. Sheppard to jail, but no one has ever seriously attempted to deny that the newspapers, the radio stations, and the television found him guilty first, and because they found him guilty, so did the American people. At fault are not the media alone but also the public, who are not satisfied with the titillation honest detective fiction can afford but want its octane rating heightened by an infusion of fact. But that is not the ideal of justice.

THE MACABRE, HIDEOUS, AND REVOLTING

Leslie Irvin of Indiana was called a "mad dog killer." There was more than enough time for the phrase to sink into the consciousness of the people of southern Indiana and the adjacent parts of Kentucky. For six months before his trial the Evansville radio and television stations reinforced the image the Indiana press etched into the public consciousness. A roving reporter had roamed the streets of Evansville, eliciting opinions about his guilt and the punishment he should receive. Virtually every home in Gibson County subscribed to the papers that carried the results of the poll, as well as the banner headlines, the feature stories, and the cartoons about him. The radio and television stations gave every detail they could unearth about his deplorable record, the crimes he committed as a juvenile, his conviction for arson, his record of arrests for burglary. His alleged confession of guilt for six murders was aired, and his alleged attempt to bargain for his life by confessing his guilt. A heroic Kentucky sheriff vowed to devote his life to bringing about his execution if Indiana failed in its solemn duty. One of the alleged murders was committed in Kentucky. Finally he came to trial, and the newspaper headline read: Impartial Jurors Are Hard to Find. That could well have been.

Thus the mad dog killer of Indiana was convicted by the Hoosier press, radio, and television, and awaited the formality of a court trial. He was found guilty, sentenced to death, and his case ultimately made its way to the Supreme Court. Once more Justice Clark wrote the Supreme Court decision which found that the jurors had indeed been prejudiced against Irvin and that pretrial publicity had denied him a fair trial. Once more he outlined what had taken place before the trial, the tidal wave of adverse publicity set in motion by the media which had resulted in two-thirds of the jurors entering the courtroom convinced that Irvin was guilty and, as some of them put it, "it would take evidence to overcome their belief."

Cases in which the macabre, the hideous, and the revolting take the place of the mystery, society, and sex present in the Sheppard sort of case are of tragically common occurrence. Ordinarily a mental aberration is present, but not always. Professor Webster of Harvard owed money to Dr. George Parkman of Boston. He murdered his creditor, dismembered the body, and cremated the segments in his own furnace. Here were the macabre, the hideous, and the revolting in the very highest place that nineteenth-century Boston afforded, and it was worth 100,000 words in each of the Boston papers. A mob broke into a nearby house to watch the execution. Next "Lizzie Borden took an axe and gave her father forty whacks. Then she turned around in fun and gave her mother forty-one." She was found guilty by the Fall River *Globe* and the Boston *Globe,* innocent by the Massachusetts court. Massachusetts was not underprivileged in the nineteenth century where the morbid, hideous, and revolting were concerned.

The child victim is frequently the pathetic central figure in cases of this sort. In 1913 a child was killed in Atlanta. The suspect was a twenty-nine year old New Yorker. A local publication, the *Jeffersonian,* observed by way of pretrial comment, ". . . our little girl—ours by the Eternal God! has been pursued to a hideous death and bloody grave by this filthy, perverted Jew of New York." As the trial progressed the Atlanta *Journal* warned with all solemnity that a verdict of acquittal would cause a riot "such as would shock the country and cause Atlanta's streets to run with innocent blood." That disaster was averted but when the governor commuted Leo Frank's sentence to life imprisonment, a mob effected its own salutary correction. It broke into the jail and lynched Frank.

The stellar case of this sort involved the murder of fourteen-year-old Bobby Franks, of which Nathan F. Leopold, Jr., and Richard A. Loeb were found guilty. Both were brilliant college students in the late teens, both came from wealthy homes, both were killers for the thrill of killing by their own confession and in the defense by Clarence Darrow. Here was the incomparably complete blend of values: the morbid, hideous, and revolting in company with violence in high places and what to the Freudian innocence of the day apparently was some unbelievable, unimaginable aspect of sex distorted and perverted out of conceivable recognition. The press gave total coverage to every aspect of the case before it came to a jury-waived trial, and the Chicago *Tribune* offered as a public service to broadcast the trial over its radio station. In a reassuring display of democracy it put the matter to a public vote. The public rejected the idea 6569 to 4169. Once more the panjandrums of the press occupied the box seats, this time literally in the jury box, while lesser luminaries were seated as close to the judge as possible. The public had its full draught of morbidity, the young men were found guilty and sent to prison for life. Loeb was killed in a prison fight in 1936 and Leopold parolled in 1958.

There are variants on the formula. At the moment of writing, the Boston press is mightily exercised over the case of a man accused of killing a policeman during a bank robbery. The case would be a tragic commonplace were it not that in its background are two young girls accused of being his accomplices, coeds at a local college, thought to have been implicated in a violent revolutionary movement and now vanished from the face of the earth. Thus a tragic commonplace of crime is transmuted into the high tragedy of mystery and violence, quasi-society and sex by the presence in the background of two appropriate characters.

All this does have its bearing on the perennial case, *Free Press v. Fair Trial*. The entire tradition of American journalism encourages the treatment with the techniques of fiction of the sort of case that has the elements of high tragedy or low tragedy, the Sheppard sort of case or the Irvin sort of case. The press did not create the assassination story of President Kennedy. That is true history, a profoundly different sort of thing. It did create what became "The Sheppard Murder Case," as it has created other stories of high and low tragedy out of the raw material of human greed, hatred, passion, and wild violence. The defense of truth by the press has an applicability in the assassination case very different indeed from the same defense in the Sheppard case and the Irvin case. The bare and unadorned facts of the Sheppard and Irvin cases would be good for half a dozen inches on page eighteen. The bare and unadorned facts of the Kennedy case would be blazoned in banner headlines in every newspaper in the world. The difference is precisely there.

Justice Felix Frankfurter, who has been the most vehement advocate of a fair trial in its conflict with a free press in modern Supreme Court history and in all probability the most eloquent, filed a concurring opinion in the Irvin case. "How can fallible men and women," he wanted to know, "reach a disinterested verdict based exclusively on what they heard in court when before they entered the jury box, their minds were saturated by press and radio for months preceding by matter designed to establish the guilt of the accused? A conviction so secured obviously constitutes a denial of due process of law in its most rudimentary conception." Hardly a term passes by, he continued, that the Court is not importuned to review convictions that apparently were influenced by inflammatory pretrial publicity. He concluded, "This Court has not yet decided that the fair administration of criminal justice must be subordinated to another safeguard of our Constitutional system—freedom of the press, properly conceived. The Court has not yet decided that, while convictions must be reversed and miscarriages of justice result because the minds of jurors or potential jurors were poisoned, the poisoner is constitutionally protected in plying his trade." Those of the media who in their liberalism have considered Vice President Agnew the most vigorous critic they have encountered in public life might consider the not inconsiderable claims of that prime favorite of the liberals, Justice Felix Frankfurter.

Justice Frankfurter's fundamental conviction never faltered, and he expressed it simply and directly in a 1950 case to which we shall have occasion later to refer: "Proceedings for the determination of guilt or innocence in open court before a jury are not in competition with any other means for establishing the charge." This is the axiom on which everything else depends, and the only possible foundation on which the issue of *Free Press v. Fair Trial* can be resolved. In the last analysis it is not the freedom of the press that is at stake nor the integrity of the court, but the right of the citizen to a fair trial, decided on the issues by the jury legally constituted to decide them, in a decision based on nothing but the evidence presented in court.

Many platitudes of this sort require repeated utterance. All too often citizens Rosencrantz and Guildenstern are caught between "the fell, incensed points of might opposites," the legal system and the press. The examples we have given heretofore have cast the press in the villain's role, the court of last appeal in the savior's. These roles can readily be reversed, and frequently they are, and then the role of the press as savior of the persecuted can be of inestimable value. The real problem comes when the courts and the press are in conflict, and the citizen is caught between them.

There is no more delicate problem than that of adjusting the respective rights of two titans of a free society, a free press and an independent court. One of the most important chapters in legal history concerns the historical process by which that adjustment has been approached, and the chapter ends when the realization is reached that the effort to preserve the rights of each must be endless as well as painstaking. The common instrumentality of adjustment from the viewpoint of the Court has been the concept of contempt of Court and the sanctions imposed on those who show it. The nineteenth century saw the lower courts striving to maintain their right to impose the kind of contempt citation that bordered on the citation for seditious libel. A series of Supreme Court decisions denied the lower courts that power. The struggle in the twentieth century has been chiefly marked by the efforts of the courts to prohibit the press from dictating court decisions, efforts which have been supported by important Supreme Court decisions. Since Court news is one of the basic staples of the press, the slow development of contempt of Court from something not far removed from the seditious libel concept to something drastically limited in meaning and application is an important aspect of our subject. Before we trace its American development, however, a word must be said about the British concept of contempt of Court, partly because it is the foundation of our own, partly because it solidified decades ago in a pattern acceptable to the British subject, and partly because it is frequently recommended as a concept worthy of American adoption.

CONTEMPT OF COURT IN BRITAIN

Few institutions in the Western world rival the British law in the panoply of office, the petrifaction of regalia, and the pomposity of procedure. That is not important. Few institutions in the Western world rival it in the impartial use of power to effect the right and protect the just. That is what really matters. Gilbert and Sullivan could parody the panoply, the petrifaction, and the pomposity. They could do so because the ridiculed surface rested on the rock of fairness and sound reason, and everyone at the Savoy knew it. One ledge of that rock is called contempt of Court.

Historians of the law have discovered contempt proceedings in England as early as the twelfth century. They had the summary, physical directness appropriate to the spirit of the age. Until it was abolished in 1641 the Star Chamber administered contempt proceedings, more perhaps by the light reflected from the gilded stars that festooned its roof and gave it its name than by the eternal lights of heaven. A century later Lord Chancellor Hardwicke incorporated criminal contempt into common law in *Riarch v. Garvan*[1] when he said, "Nothing is more incumbent upon the courts of justice, than to preserve their proceedings from being misrepresented; nor is there anything of more pernicious consequence, than to prejudice the minds of the public against persons concerned as parties, before the case is finally heard." This was the principle that twenty-seven years later Blackstone incorporated into his *Commentaries:* "A power therefore in the supreme courts of justice to suppress such contempts by an immediate attachment of the offender results from the first principles of judicial establishments and must be an inseparable attendant upon every superior tribunal."

The principle was incorporated into statute law in 1888, when mass communications had developed to the point at which the minds of the public could indeed be prejudiced against persons concerned as parties in law cases, with pernicious consequence. The Law of Libel Act provided that "a fair and accurate report in any newspaper of proceedings publicly heard before any court exercising judicial authority shall, if published contemporaneously with such proceedings, be privileged. . . ." The Libel Act recognized the legitimacy of reporting but not of prognosticating, and certainly not of influencing. In 1902 an editor and his reporter went to jail for six weeks for their failure to realize that *contemporaneously* means *at the same time as* and not *prior to*. For some time editors took their chances, especially with murder cases rich in the values treasured beyond rubies by editors, such already catalogued values as mystery and violence, the morbid and macabre. Then in 1924 came the legal episode with a title seemingly out of Dickens, the Crumbles Murder

[1] 2 Atk. 469, 471; ch. 1742

Case. The police told the witnesses not to talk, a newspaper induced them to do so, the editor was fined £1000 and told that the gates of Dartmoor would swing wide to receive him if he sinned again. Since 1924 British editors have been carefully legalistic in their approach to this particular sin.

The British law of contempt is both simple and direct. Two forms of contempt are recognized, civil and criminal. It is civil contempt to disobey the orders of a court and such contempt is legally a private wrong. It is criminal contempt to hamper the administration of justice and such contempt is subject to the penalties appropriate to a crime. An act committed in Court and ruled contemptuous is direct criminal contempt. An act committed outside Court that hampers the administration of justice is constructive criminal contempt and quite as subject to the penalties appropriate to criminal contempt as the direct kind. Britain resolves the issue in *Free Press v. Fair Trial* very effectively by the use of the contempt power. A trial in Britain is, of course, quite as truly a public proceeding as a trial in the United States, and its developments just as faithfully recorded in the English press as in the American. The people of Britain have the same taste for mystery and violence, sex and society, the morbid and macabre as their American cousins and their tastes are as adequately serviced by the British press, but they are serviced by a legal system that rests on the solid rock of fairness and sound reason. The British judge knows what contempt of Court is in Britain and he has the power to control it.

CONTEMPT OF COURT IN THE UNITED STATES: NINETEENTH CENTURY

One of the first acts of the newly created American Congress was to give the Federal courts of the new-born nation the contempt powers that courts in Britain and the colonies had exercised. The Judiciary Act of 1789 gave them "power to punish by fine or imprisonment, at ... discretion ... all contempt of authority in any cause of hearing. ..." State constitutions had already done the same for state judges.

The process of refinement started in 1831. Nowhere in the world is there land more desirable than that heartland of America known historically as the Louisiana Purchase, nor land more calculated to bring water to the mouths of speculators. By 1831 individuals with a steady eye for a good thing and an unsteady grasp on moral principles had carved out slices of Upper Louisiana for themselves. Federal Judge James H. Peck of Missouri passed adverse judgment on the propriety of their claims, and it would seem from this remote distance with good reason, but his finding aroused the ire of an attorney with a name that also has a Dickensian ring, Luke Lawless. Attorney Lawless wrote a newspaper story about what he considered the errors in Judge Peck's decision, Peck found him guilty of contempt of Court and suspended for eighteen months his license to practice law. Lawless managed to bring impeachment proceedings to Congress and to find a champion in Representative James Buchanan of Pennsylvania, a man later destined for a larger arena. Judge Peck was exonerated but Congress passed An Act Declaratory of the Law Concerning Contempts of Court. At its heart was that distinction recognized in British law between direct and constructive criminal contempt.

In a sense the issue at stake in what might be termed the Peck case was the issue at stake in the matter of seditious libel. Let us recall the definition of seditious libel: the intentional publication, without lawful excuse or justification, of written blame of any public man, or of the law, or of any institution established by law. A judge is a public man. By 1831 it was no longer seditious libel to criticize his actions since the concept of seditious libel was obsolete. Was it contempt of Court to criticize the actions of a judge and, if so, was contempt of Court merely seditious libel under another name? That was the question Attorney Lawless really asked, and Representative Buchanan asked in his name. If the concept of constructive contempt was merely the application of the concept of seditious libel to criticism of a judge, then a judge was above criticism and in one specific area the First Amendment guarantee of freedom of speech was nullified. The action taken by Congress was both wise and statesmanlike. Certainly Judge Peck had been within his legal rights in his application of the Judiciary Act of 1789 and he deserved to be exonerated. But the Judiciary Act itself needed to be reexamined in the light of the Constitution of the United States. It was, and the result was the 1831 statute named above. It provided "That the power of the several courts of the United States to issue attachments and inflict summary punishments for contempts of court, shall not be construed to extend to any cases except the misbehaviour of any person or persons in the presence of the said courts, or so near thereto as to obstruct the administration of justice. . . ." The omitted provisos bring under contempt of Court sanctions misbehavior by

court officers, and resistance by them, jurors, and witnesses to
proper court orders. The further history of contempt of Court in the
United States is the record of modifications of the 1831 statute and
interpretations of it. The first important interpretation and modifica-
tion came in the state of Arkansas, in 1855.

The editor of the Des Arc, Arkansas, *Citizen,* a man named
Morrill, entertained a deep suspicion. A man accused of murder had
been bailed under circumstances that suggested bribery to Editor
Morrill. He wrote a news story for his paper that at the very least
suggested the charge. Chief Justice Elbert H. English read between
the lines and cited Morrill for contempt. The principles on which
Justice English acted have a continuing interest and possibly a
continuing significance. He contended that only a constitutional
provision could limit the power of a court to cite for contempt and
that a statute passed by a state legislature, a coordinate and not
superior branch of government, had no power over a court. The
contempt power, he maintained, came into being with the Court
itself and as one aspect of the right to self-protection had a constitutional sanction. He pointed out that the Constitution defines the
contempt powers of Congress but not those of the courts, and he
maintained that the omission was both intentional and significant. A
legislator could defend his honor on the platform and in the press,
but for a judge to defend publicly his integrity by the tactics of
debate would be inconsistent with the dignity of the law. He
stressed the last clause of the seventh section of the Bill of Rights:
"The free communication of thoughts and opinions is one of the
invaluable rights of man; and every citizen may freely speak, write
and print on any subject—being responsible for the abuse of that
liberty." Editor Morrill was free to imply in print that a judge had
been bribed, and Justice English was free to cite him for contempt
for the abuse of liberty. There was no precedent in the Peck case,
Justice English maintained, since Judge Peck had not abused the
freedom of the press nor, by 1855, would any court find Attorney
Lawless guilty of contempt.

The conclusion Justice English reached is worthy of quotation in
full, because the entire issue of contempt of Court may be found
partly in the Peck case of 1831 and partly in the Morrill case of
1855:

Any citizen has the right to publish the proceedings and decisions of this court, and if he deem it necessary for the public good, to comment upon them freely, discuss their correctness, the fitness or unfitness of the judges for their stations, and the fidelity with which they perform the important public trusts reposed in them, but he has no right to attempt, by defamatory publications, to degrade the tribunal, destroy public confidence in it, and dispose the community to disregard and set at naught its orders, judgments, and decrees. Such publications are an abuse of the liberty of the press, and tend to sap the very foundation of good order and well-being in society, by obstructing the course of justice. If a judge is really corrupt, and unworthy of the station which he holds, the constitution has provided an ample remedy by impeachment or address, where he can meet his accuser face to face, and his conduct may undergo a full investigation. The liberty of the press is one thing, and licentious scandal another.[1]

The 1831 statute was necessary and salutary. The conduct of judges and the administration of justice in courts certainly should not be made sacrosanct and protected from criticism on the principle of seditious libel rechristened constructive contempt of Court. If there is danger that anything printed which reflects unfavorably on the conduct of a judge, whether it be true or false, may lead to punishment for contempt, then the forces of government would certainly be poised ready to stifle freedom of the press. How could anyone charge that a judge is corrupt and maintain that he should be impeached if the very act of making the charge were to open the door to contempt proceedings? On the other hand, the viewpoint of Justice English is worthy of respect. It is indeed inconsistent with the immemorial dignity of the law that a judge be forced to descend to the debating platform to defend his good name when he has been subjected to "licentious scandal." As Justice English pointed out, there are two entirely adequate means for the removal from the bench of a judge unworthy of his position, impeachment and address, the latter being removal by administrative action on the formal request of the legislature.

Freedom of the press is one of the "moral adjurations" of the Constitution. Due process is one as well; if it were not, what constitutes due process would not be a perennial point at issue in legal

[1] *State v. Morrill,* 16 Ark. 384

cases. But due process of the law applies to all aspects of court process and not merely to the rights and prerogatives of prosecution and defense. Once more we see illustrated that inescapable conflict with another right when any right of the Bill of Rights is treated as an absolute. Judges should not be above criticism; that is the doctrine of 1831. But they should be above the process of public debate; that is the Morrill doctrine of 1855. For a time the doctrine of 1831 went into eclipse and the Morrill doctrine prevailed. The result was that newspapers were cited for contempt in a number of states and then tried by the judges whom they were alleged to have treated contemptuously. Seditious libel in the guise of constructive contempt of court once more had legal standing. Once more a moral adjuration had become a jural concept, and what was valid in the judgment of Justice English, that there is a distinction between liberty of the press and licentious scandal and that the press should be held responsible for the latter with the test of truth used as the touchstone, was obscured. For the remainder of the nineteenth century the issue rested.

CONTEMPT OF COURT: 1900-1940

The issue stirred uneasily in its rest in 1907, when the Supreme Court in *Patterson v. State of Colorado* upheld the right of a state court to cite a publication for contempt if it ran material which would tend to obstruct the administration of justice while a case was pending. Justice Oliver Wendell Holmes, who wrote the Supreme Court decision, stated that pendency was the criterion. Once a case was over and done with, he made clear, there was nothing sacrosanct about the Court, the judge, the conduct of the case, or the decision. Courts in America are above neither the law nor public criticism. It was against what Justice Holmes called "premature statement, argument or intimidation" that the Court ruled.

The finding in *Patterson v. State of Colorado* struck home in journalistic circles and, indeed, in American thinking in general. It elicited in 1908 from Arthur Train one of the most trenchant attacks ever launched on the light-armed troops of the newspaper world, the yellow journals of the period, *The Prisoner at the Bar: Sidelight on the Administration of Criminal Justice.* "The judge may charge one way in accordance with the law of the land," Train stated, "while the editor charges the same jury in double-leaded paragraphs with what 'unwritten' law may best suit the owner of his conscience or his pen."[1] It was not too guarded a secret that at least a temporary part-owner of the conscience and the pen of the typical yellow journal editor was frequently an attorney currently involved in a case. There were even rumored to be very subtle divisions of yellow-journal consciences and pens which found part-ownership divided between the attorneys for both sides. Having voiced this canard, one hastens to add the definition of yellow journalism from a dictionary of unimpeachable authority: the use of cheaply sensational or un-scrupulous methods in newspapers, etc., to attract or influence the readers. Such methods were used by cheaply sensational and unscru-pulous newspapers, and not by honorable, honestly edited papers of integrity. It is the tragic fate of every occupation to be saddled with the sins of its unworthy members, and honest journalism has never been exempt from the effects of yellow journalism.

The same case also elicited in 1908 a Canon of Professional Ethics from the American Bar Association. Canon 20 gets to the heart of the matter: "Newspaper publications by a lawyer as to pending or anticipated litigation may interfere with a fair trial in the Courts and otherwise prejudice the due administration of justice. Generally they are to be condemned. If the extreme circumstances of a particular case justify a statement to the public, it is unprofessional to make it anonymously. An *ex parte* reference to the facts should not go beyond quotation from the records and papers on file in the court; but even in extreme cases it is better to avoid any *ex parte* state-ment." Even those little given to cynicism will concede that this virtual ban on one-sided statements has reached the heart of the matter far more in theory than in practice. It might even be main-tained that prosecuting attorneys in the employ of the state have been worse sinners in this regard than attorneys for the defense.

A more significant case was heard in 1917, when the City Council of Toledo, Ohio, undertook to regulate the fares and limit the franchise of the local streetcar company. The Toledo *News-Bee* let the people of Toledo know that unless the Federal judge who was to hear the case were to rule for the public and against the City Council, a public suspicion of his integrity would be indeed well grounded. The judge cited the newspaper for contempt and the case reached the Supreme Court. Behind the specific point at issue in the

[1] pp. 347–348

case was the issue supposedly decided in 1831, the soundness of the distinction between direct and constructive criminal contempt.

One recalls that the 1831 statute limited the contempt power to the control of persons misbehaving in the presence of the Court or so near to it as to obstruct the course of justice. In the *Toledo Newspaper* case the Court took a more flexible view of geography. Chief Justice Edward D. White stated in the decision,". . . however complete is the right of the press to state public things and discuss them, that right, as every right enjoyed in human society, is subject to the restraints which separate right from wrong-doing. . . . Not the influence upon the mind of the particular judge is the criterion but the reasonable tendency of the acts done to influence or bring about the baleful result is the test."[1]

The entire history of constitutional interpretation is the record of the ebb and flow of two fundamentally different philosophies, the philosophy which finds the broader constitutional principles of the Bill of Rights to be moral adjurations and the philosophy that finds them to be jural concepts. It is part of the immemorial conflict between the philosophic absolute and the pragmatic relative. The Supreme Court attempted in the *Toledo Newspaper* case to set up a "reasonable tendency" test by which published statements that concern the facts of a pending case might be distinguished from published statements that aimed at affecting its outcome. One must always bear in mind that in this, and perhaps in a majority of Supreme Court cases, there are two separate and sometimes contrasting issues. One is the specific issue at stake in the case being heard. The other is the general principle of law that informs the verdict. The Toledo paper stated that only one finding in the streetcar case was possible that would be consistent with fairness and integrity in the Court. That sort of pretrial statement simply runs counter to every instinct of fairness and propriety, and the man in the street would probably react against it, even if he was the man in the street of Toledo threatened with a higher fare and believing a higher fare unjust and unnecessary. But the difficulty with a moral adjuration is that it can be immorally interpreted and applied. It was the view of the Supreme Court that it was properly applied in Toledo and that the judge was right in citing the paper for contempt. But there are dangers in the moral adjuration concept, just as

[1] *Toledo Newspaper Company v. United States,* 247 U.S. 402

there are dangers in the jural concept. The power of constructive contempt citation is a dangerous power, capable of serious abuse and with a record of serious abuse. The reasonable-tendency test is safe in the hands of some judges, unsafe in the hands of others. The specific finding in the *Toledo Newspaper* case appeals to the sense of justice, but the reasonable-tendency principle on which it rested appeals to the sense of apprehensive caution. It is significant that there were two dissenting judges in the case, both men philosophically inclined to the moral adjuration and the pragmatic relative rather than to the jural concept and the philosophic absolute, yet both dissenting from the majority decision. They were the two justices whose legal thinking belonged not to 1917 but to the tomorrow of a distant future, Justices Brandeis and Holmes.

CONTEMPT OF COURT: SINCE 1940

Tomorrow dawned in 1941, when the Court overturned the *Toledo Newspaper* decision and returned to literal geography. The case was *Nye v. United States*[1] which concerned a guilty finding against one who was convicted of improperly coercing the administrator of an estate to dismiss a case in a Federal district court. The issue was not *Free Press v. Fair Trial*, since it concerned a litigant and not a newspaper. The Court found that the alleged offense had been committed one hundred miles from the district court in question and that geographic remoteness made improbable an obstruction to the course of justice. The lower court conviction was reversed, the principle behind the 1831 statute reaffirmed, and a case settled of oblique yet substantial importance to the press. What was more significant, the reestablishment of the geographic basis for contempt of Court nullified the reasonable-tendency test established in *Toledo Newspaper*. In nullifying the reasonable-tendency test, however, the Court created a vacuum. Common sense also has a place in the law ("The law is the embodiment of everything that's excellent," those noted commentators on the law, Gilbert and Sullivan, have assured us) and common sense says that contempt of Court can be shown in ways other than reprehensible behavior in the courtroom and the adjacent corridors. The reasonable-tendency test was based on common sense, but there are times in life when common sense is not

[1] 313 U.S. 33

enough and it is the solemn duty of the Supreme Court to make provision for that fact. The geographic test was appropriate enough, it would seem, in the *Nye* case but no one really thought it adequate to provide a general principle. The general principle came in *Bridges v. California* and it amounted in essence to the old, familiar "clear and present danger" test already met in the issue of prior restraint.

Bridges v. California came in a neatly balanced ideological package with another California case, *Times-Mirror Company v. Superior Court*.[1] The Los Angeles *Times* had run three editorials designed to instruct Judge A. A. Scott in the correct performance of his judicial duties. The last of the three was entitled "Probation for Gorillas?" The gorillas in question were two members of a labor union who had been found guilty of assaulting non-union truck drivers. "Judge A. A. Scott will make a serious mistake if he grants probation to Matthew Shannon and Kennan Holmes," the paper stated editorially. "This community needs the example of their assignment to the jute mill." Whether the community needed the example or not, the judge felt strongly that the advice, which was given a month before the date at which sentence was to be imposed, was in contempt of Court. Accordingly the Times-Mirror Company and the managing editor of the *Times* were fined $100 for each of the first two editorials and $300 for the gorilla piece. The case reached the Supreme Court under the title indicated.

Harry Bridges, a vivid personality in West coast labor ranks and a man gifted in rhetoric, also commented on the judicial situation on the coast as it affected labor. His comment came in a telegram to the Secretary of Labor and included a direful prediction that the West coast would be tied up by a shipping strike since the C.I.O. was in no mood "to allow state courts to override the majority vote of members in choosing its officers and representatives and to override the National Labor Relations Board."[2] The hand of California law also rested on him, and ultimately his fate also rested in the hands of the Supreme Court.

Once again we see illustrated what is illustrated repeatedly in the history of Supreme Court decisions. There is a difference between the specific point at issue in a case and the fundamental principle on which the decision rests, or the fundamental principle which derives

---

[1] 314 U.S. 252

[2] Quoted in Harold L. Nelson, ed., *Freedom of the Press from Hamilton to the Warren Court*, Indianapolis, 1967, p. 164.

from that decision and influences decisions to come. The simple fact was that the *Times* was an anti-labor paper, everyone knew it, and the worst the judge had to fear was the wrath of the editorial writer if his sentencing did not afford a term in the jute mill for the gorillas, to the moral edification of the community. The state had argued that judicial trials and decisions should be freed from coercion and intimidation, a thesis with which no one would quarrel. What was open to question in some minds was whether an anti-labor editorial in an anti-labor newspaper, couched though it was in admonitory tones intended for the judge presiding over the case, was coercion and intimidation in the true sense of the terms. There were those who believed that it would be a weak-kneed judge who would be coerced and intimidated by the undeviating editorial line of a newspaper. The Supreme Court reflected such thought in the verdict which reversed the decision of the state court, but the verdict was not unanimous. There were justices who believed it perilous to countenance any dictation by a newspaper to a court about an impending decision.

There was a fact of relative simplicity at the heart of the Harry Bridges case. It is not illegal to send a telegram to the Secretary of Labor. Legally a telegram of the sort Bridges sent is a form of petition, even when it contains an unpalatable prediction, and the right of petition is guaranteed by the Bill of Rights. What is more, it is not illegal to strike, not even if the strike ties up West coast shipping. There was nothing that a reasonable man would consider coercion and intimidation in what Harry Bridges did, and the verdict of the Supreme Court certainly recommends itself to the view of common sense. These two cases probably reflected an unseemly case of judicial jitters in the state of California rather than a genuine threat to judicial impartiality and decorum. Yet the Court recognized in the two cases potentialities that went far beyond the specific issues in question. What really was at stake was the validity of the Morrill doctrine of 1855, as reinforced by Justice Holmes speaking for the Court majority in *Patterson v. Colorado* (1907) and by Chief Justice White in *Toledo Newspaper Company v. United States* (1918). The fact that the Court was divided in *Times-Mirror* and *Bridges* probably reflects a division where a fundamental principle was involved more than two specific applications of it.

Justice Black, speaking for the majority, cited the applicability to the present cases of the decisions in the espionage cases which we have already considered. It is clear from his words that the majority reached its decision in *Times-Mirror* and *Bridges* on the "clear and present danger" principle. He stated,

What finally emerges from the "clear and present danger" cases is a working principle that the substantive evil must be extremely serious and the degree of imminence extremely high before utterances can be punished. Those cases do not purport to mark the furthermost constitutional boundaries of protected expression, nor do we here. They do no more than recognize a minimum compulsion of the Bill of Rights. For the First Amendment does not speak equivocally. It must be taken as a command of the broadest scope that explicit language, read in the context of a liberty-loving society, will allow.

Next Justice Black considered the extent to which a limitation on freedom of expression while a case is pending is a limitation on the freedom of the press. He pointed out the truism that interest in a case is greatest while it is pending, and the fact that cases have been known to pend for years. He found it highly improbable that to permit the sort of publication under consideration in *Times-Mirror* and *Bridges* would threaten judicial impartiality, and he held for the majority of his colleagues that to suppress criticism of the judiciary is more apt to arouse resentment and suspicion than it is to foster respect.

The real question was not answered in his decision. Were the facts of the *Times-Mirror* and the *Bridges* cases sufficiently characteristic of the sort of publication that would genuinely threaten judicial impartiality and decorum to make them an appropriate vehicle to carry the general principle that the Morrill doctrine was invalid and should be abandoned? The fact that Justices Frankfurter, Byrnes, and Roberts dissented is significant, because the basis of their dissent was not the facts of the case in question but the validity of the principle on which they were settled. Justice Frankfurter stated in his dissent, "Our whole history repels the view that it is an exercise of one of the civil liberties secured by the Bill of Rights for a leader of a large following or for a powerful metropolitan newspaper to attempt to overawe a judge in a matter immediately pending before him." California had been deprived of a means of securing for its citizens justice under law, he maintained, and what was at fault was a misapplied principle. "Free speech is not so absolute or irrational a

conception as to imply paralysis of the means for effective protection
of all the freedoms secured by the Bill of Rights. . . . In the cases
before us, the claims on behalf of freedom of speech and of the press
encounter claims on behalf of liberties no less precious." A right to a
fair trial is also a constitutional right, and a trial is not a "free trade
in ideas." "We cannot read into the Fourteenth Amendment the
freedom of speech and of the press protected by the First Amendment and at the same time read out the age-old means employed by
the states for securing the calm course of justice," he argued, and
toward the end of his dissent he voiced the viewpoint to which
everyone must subscribe who believes that the provisions of the Bill
of Rights are pragmatic relatives and not philosophic absolutes: ". . .
the Bill of Rights is not self-destructive. Freedom of expression can
hardly carry implications that nullify the guarantees of impartial
trials."

Times-Mirror and *Bridges* were unfortunate cases on which to
establish a fundamental principle. One is always in a weak position
when he tries to maintain that one side is right in terms of limited
fact and the other side right in terms of general principle. That is the
position one must maintain in these cases if he believes that the
provisions of the Bill of Rights are moral adjurations and not jural
concepts. In retrospect it is hard to see why *Bridges* ever occurred,
even at the state level. It is impossible to see how the Supreme
Court could have found in *Bridges* other than it did, and one can
recognize as strong the arguments that support its decision in *Times-
Mirror*. But it is easy to see, if one is a pragmatic relativist in such
matters, what caused three justices to dissent, one of them with due
respect to the counter-claims of Justices Black and Douglas the most
eloquent exponent of individual liberty in the history of the modern
bench, Justice Frankfurter. They saw in these two cases freedom of
speech and freedom of the press being elevated to the level of
philosophic absolutes, with the attendant danger to other rights and
freedoms. How that has worked out one can see in *Pennekamp v.
Florida* and the cases that followed.

Pennekamp v. Florida[1] arose out of two editorials and a cartoon
run in the Miami *Herald*. The newspaper viewpoint was that the
Florida courts were showing excessive leniency toward criminals and
gambling establishments through a process of non-jury proceedings.
Specifically, two recent cases had been dismissed and a third, a rape

[1] 328 U.S. 331 (1946)

case, was pending. The suggestion was that two fish had escaped the net and the third must not, and since there was not to be trial by jury the finger of accusation was leveled at one man, the judge, and not at a jury of twelve. The gentlemen of the press were indicted for contempt of Court on the grounds that they had impugned the integrity of the Court, undermined confidence in it, played free and loose with the truth, and impeded the course of justice while a case was pending. The newspaper lost in the Florida Supreme Court and won in the United States Supreme Court. The decision of the latter was based on the clear-and-present-danger principle, but the probings into implications and corollaries of that principle evidenced in the separate opinions filed by the justices give the case its chief interest and importance.

Justice Stanley Reed delivered the Court opinion. Fundamentally it is contained in the following sentence: "In the borderline instances where it is difficult to say upon which side the alleged offense falls, we think the specific freedom of public comment should weigh heavily against a tendency to influence pending cases." Freedom of discussion should be given the widest range compatible with the essential requirement of the fair and orderly administration of justice. Justice Frankfurter concurred, but expressed once more his conviction that a free press should not have precedence over an independent judiciary. The new note, however, can be detected in the opinions of Justices Wiley Rutledge and Frank Murphy. Justice Rutledge felt that no area of news is reported with less accuracy than legal news and he had some comments to add about the carelessness and haste with which reporters compound their lack of legal training. He conceded, however, that the law itself is not above reproach where clarity is concerned and that full accuracy in legal reporting is a counsel of unattainable perfection. Therefore, he held, "There must be some room for misstatement of fact, as well as for misjudgment, if the press and others are to function as critical agencies in our democracy concerning courts as for all other instruments of government." It was Justice Murphy, however, who went farthest from the defense of truth where freedom of the press in reporting legal matters is concerned. "That freedom covers something more than the right to approve and condone insofar as the judiciary and the judicial process are concerned. It also includes the right to criticize and disparage, even though the terms be vitriolic, scurrilous or erroneous."

With truth and propriety of expression removed as factors in the protection of that independent judiciary which appeared so important in the thought of Justice Frankfurter, the next corollary concerned the right of a judge to retaliate against public criticism. This was the point at issue in *Craig v. Harney.*[1] The Corpus Christi *Caller-Times* did some factually inaccurate reporting about the point at issue in a trial, with a resultant public opinion inflamed, in the view of the Court, to the point of presenting a clear and present danger to the impartial and orderly administration of justice. It proceeded to find the newspaper in contempt. The United States Supreme Court held that the tribulations of the Court arose from the nature of the case and a natural public sympathy for the defendant and not from the way the newspaper handled the story. Justice William O. Douglas wrote the Court opinion, but once more Justice Murphy went farther than the common denominator viewpoint of his colleagues, stating "Unscrupulous and vindictive criticism of the judiciary is regrettable. But judges must not retaliate by a summary suppression of such criticism for they are bound by the command of the First Amendment. Any summary suppression of unjust criticism carries with it an ominous threat of summary suppression of all criticism. It is to avoid that threat that the First Amendment, as I view it, outlaws the summary contempt methods of suppression." The logical step beyond *Craig v. Harney* came in *Wood v. Georgia,*[2] in which the right of an individual, in this case a sheriff, to criticize proceedings in a court was upheld.

TRIAL BY PUBLICITY

The record since *Bridges* makes it obvious that the press has far greater freedom now than it has ever had in its prior history to comment on pending court cases, to apply the magnifying glass to judicial proceedings, to upbraid the judiciary, and in general to pontificate about the law in all its applied as well as theoretical aspects. Justice Frankfurter may well have been right in seeing in this an ominous threat to an independent judiciary, although it is not impossible that to some extent he saw the threat through Central European rather than American eyes. The ability of the American

[1] 331 U.S. 367 (1947)
[2] 370 U.S. 375 (1962)

temperament to absorb adverse criticism, an ability not impossibly inherited as part of the Anglo-Saxon strain in our national inheritance, should not be underestimated. There is only so much influence that a revolving drum which leaves black marks on a roll of newsprint has ever been able to wield in the English-speaking world.

By and large it is the effect that greater press freedom in this area may have on the chances of a defendant to get a fair trial that should cause concern. It is nonsensical to contend that this poses the greatest threat to the poor and underprivileged when they find themselves under the heavy hand of the law. Only a very small percentage of the criminal cases that reach the courts receive any news coverage at all, and this is particularly true in the large city papers. To receive publicity, a crime story must have either an intrinsic news value of its own or features calculated to elicit reader interest. The assassination of President Kennedy and the kidnapping of the Lindbergh baby fall into the first category. The case of Dr. Sheppard, who was transformed by the press into a fit subject for Madame Tussaud, and the case of Leslie Irvin of Indiana who was metamorphosed by print into the mad dog killer exemplify the second. We have examined the steady contraction of the power of contempt citation under a series of Supreme Court decisions as it was whittled away to little more than the power to control disorder in the courtroom and adjacent precincts. Fortunately for the right of a defendant to a fair trial, there is another series of Supreme Court decisions which gives him some protection against trial by publicity. After a decade in jail Dr. Sheppard was given a new trial by Supreme Court order, and was found not guilty. In 1961 the Court found that Leslie Irvin had indeed been denied a fair trial as a result of the wide publicity given his case by press, radio, and television and therefore overturned his conviction and remanded his case for retrial. Thus at long last Dr. Samuel Sheppard received a fair trial in his own right and not in his quasi-fictional guise of Dr. Sam, and Leslie Irvin was tried as Leslie Irvin and not as the mad dog killer. But one should note that each was able to have his case carried all the way to the Supreme Court. Not all are so fortunate. Let us now consider certain of the cases in which trial by publicity was considered and condemned by the Supreme Court.

In 1950 the first crack appeared in the wall of protection erected for the media by the Supreme Court in the cases already considered, specifically *Times-Mirror, Pennekamp,* and *Craig.* The crack was made, as might be expected, by Justice Frankfurter, but it was only a crack. Two Baltimore radio stations and the Maryland Broadcasting Company had been found guilty of contempt of Court for broadcasting the record of a man arrested for a crime and a statement about his alleged confession. The Maryland Court of Appeals reversed the decision on the basis of the Supreme Court doctrine evidenced in the cases named above. The State carried the case to the United States Supreme Court, which refused to issue a writ of certiorari. Since the Court never states why it refuses to hear a case, in effect it let stand its contempt of Court doctrine and no punitive action was permitted against the broadcasting company for its pretrial publicity. But *Maryland v. Baltimore Radio Show*[1] is part of that stately set of volumes penned by the Supreme Court as a result of Justice Frankfurter's opinion about the denial of the writ. His viewpoint was precisely what it had been all along, but one point he wished to make transparently clear. It had been customary to quote in defense of full publicity about all aspects of trials at all stages in their development an aphorism by Justice Holmes: "The best test of truth is the power of the thought to get itself accepted in the competition of the market." Justice Frankfurter emphasized that to apply this aphorism to a criminal charge "would be the grossest perversion of all that Mr. Justice Holmes represents. . . ." And once more he stated his basic contention which we have already quoted: "Proceedings for the determination of guilt or innocence in open court before a jury are not in competition with any other means for establishing the charge." Juries and judges should decide criminal cases, not newspapers and television stations.

The Supreme Court refused a writ of certiorari in *Baltimore Radio Show*, but one year later it had a change of heart. Four men suspected of rape were arrested in Florida. An Orlando newspaper ran a cartoon on page one showing four electric chairs. Beneath them was the caption, "No Compromise—Supreme Penalty." The men were found guilty and on the head of the unfavorable pretrial publicity to which they were subjected, the Supreme Court upset the conviction. The endeavor to reconcile the finding in this case with the finding in *Baltimore Radio Show* is a testing exercise in semantics. In 1959 *Marshall v. United States*[2] came before the Supreme Court. Howard R. Marshall of Colorado had been indicted

[2] 360 U.S. 310 (1959)

for the illegal sale of drugs. A Denver newspaper had published articles about the defendant which dealt with his prior convictions and other subjects detrimental to him. The trial judge would not admit this material as evidence in the court trial, but it was admitted with at least adequate fanfare in Marshall's trial by publicity. The Supreme Court upset his conviction. There followed the reversal already mentioned, that of Leslie Irvin in 1961.

In between came two other reversals of substantial consequence. In 1963 the Supreme Court considered *Rideau v. Louisiana*.[1] The Louisiana television audience had been treated to a fascinating bit of life-drama by an enterprising station. Wilbert Rideau had been arrested for bank robbery and murder. Bathed in a flood light of television, as the camera and its Siamese twin the radio recorded and transmitted the scene to their fascinated myriads, Wilbert Rideau confessed his guilt to the sheriff. He was found guilty in Louisiana, the conviction upset in Washington. The case of another man, this time a man newsworthy in his own right, the financier of sorts Billie Sol Estes, reached the Supreme Court and a favorable finding because his Texas trial had been televised over his objection. There followed the most celebrated reversal of all, that of Dr. Samuel Sheppard in 1966, and the most explicit guidance the Supreme Court has ever given the lower courts about preserving the due process of justice in criminal cases from interference by the news media.

Trial by publicity is a cat of many lives, and it is capable of emerging triumphantly into life where least expected. In 1965 a civil-rights worker from Detroit named Mrs. Viola Liuzzo was shot in Alabama. Four men were arrested for her murder. The President of the United States, Lyndon B. Johnson, went on television over this case. "Mrs. Liuzzo went to Alabama to serve the struggles for justice," said President Johnson to the United States and the world. "She was murdered by enemies of justice who for decades have used the rope and the gun and the tar and the feathers to terrorize their neighbors." But he spoke in sorrow as well as in anger, as he appealed to the sinners of Alabama "to get out of the Ku Klux Klan now and return to a decent society before it is too late."[2] The mother of one of the suspects wrote to President Johnson, "I would like you

[1] 373 U.S. 723 (1963)
[2] Quoted in Donald Gillmore, *Free Press and Fair Trial*, New York, 1966, p. 62, from *The New York Times*, March 27, 1965.

to explain to me why this was done before my son was even interrogated or given any kind of a hearing or trial by jury. I feel like now my son and these other men will not have a fair trial. . . . because they were branded guilty before the nation by the President of the United States."[1] Attorney General Nicholas deB. Katzenbach stood beside his chief as the President conducted his trial by publicity. Three weeks later the Justice Department received a set of guidelines to be followed in releasing information to the media in criminal cases. There may or may not have been a connection.

There is, on the whole, a certain pattern that can be traced in the two series of cases, the one that opens with *Bridges* and the other that at least lets in a glint of daylight in *Baltimore Radio Show.* In the first series the right of the courts to use the contempt power has been steadily whittled away until nothing really remains of it except the right to preserve order in the courtroom and its adjoining precincts. In the second series the right of the defendant to be protected from the adverse effects of pretrial publicity has been steadily built up. Obviously the second is the needed corrective to the first, and the presumptive intent of the Court has been to strengthen the freedom-of-the-press clause in the Bill of Rights without infringing upon the right of a defendant to a fair trial. The basic question that must be asked is this: granted the theoretical equilibrium thus established between the right of a free press and the right to a fair trial, has a practical and effective equilibrium been established? It costs considerable money to carry a case to the Supreme Court, and it takes abundant know-how. When the action of a judge or court is criticized, it is criticized in terms of some individual or group of individuals that is to come before the Court, is appearing before it, or has appeared before it. In other words, there is no critique of a court that is not in some sense or other a critique of a defendant. If there must be room for misstatement of fact, as Justice Rutledge held, and if criticism of court action may be vitriolic, scurrilous, or erroneous as Justice Murphy maintained, then it is difficult to see what protects the defendant who does not have the means to bring his case before the Supreme Court, or at least before some higher state court, from being at least obliquely the target of comment that is vitriolic, scurrilous, and erroneous. If this danger did not exist, it would be hard to explain the action of the American bar in drawing

[1] *Ibid.*, from Richmond *Times-Dispatch*, April 5, 1965.

up codes of ethical conduct where trial by publicity is concerned, codes in which the press sometimes has shared authorship and assumed part responsibility. What the bar and the media themselves are doing about the problem is logically our next concern, but logic is accustomed to deferred recognition. Let us consider first what rights the citizen-defendant has under the letter, spirit, and tradition of the law.

RIGHTS OF THE CITIZEN

A citizen may be arrested with or without the issuance of a warrant: with the issuance of a warrant which states the reasonable grounds for his arrest and describes any place or property that may be searched or seized; without a warrant by a police officer who sees a felony committed or has reasonable grounds for believing that he is apprehending a culprit. After his arrest a confession cannot be forced from him nor can any confession he makes be introduced as evidence in his trial unless the prosecution proves that he made the confession willingly and with full knowledge that he need not make it. He has the right to counsel of his own choice and the right to insist that his counsel be present when he is cross-examined. His right to a preliminary hearing is a right provided by statute.

He has the right to be considered innocent until proven guilty, and his right to bail follows as a logical corollary of this right. He has the right to full knowledge of the accusation made against him and the right to a speedy trial based upon that accusation. The Sixth Amendment gives him the right to a trial by an impartial jury of local residents who must reach a unanimous verdict. In the course of the trial he has the right to summon and confront witnesses. He may not be tried twice for the same offense, although the specific definition of double jeopardy has varied with time and place. The tendency in the recent past has been to interpret double jeopardy with increasing rigidity.

To the extent that a set of thumbnail definitions can do justice to the legal rights of a defendant, such are the basic rights provided by the law of the United States. There are, of course, others that are not listed, like the right of *habeas corpus* and immunity to cruel and unusual punishments, and there are variations and nuances of meaning within those listed. Pervading them all is a single principle fundamental to them and indeed fundamental to the entire American concept of the human mind and heart. American law, like the British law on which it rests historically and on which it is largely modeled, is based on the thesis that man is good by nature and that the burden of proof that a particular man is not virtuous in respect to a particular action rests upon society which makes the charge. In the ultimate analysis it is that principle which separates the concept of democracy from the concept of benevolent dictatorship, which makes man the protected creature of his society, and the concept of regimented dictatorship, which makes him its pawn. The principle of the native goodness of man cannot be separated, in the democratic concept, from its ideological twin, the principle that man is mentally competent to be master of his own destiny. All the American law and its major prophets abide by these two principles, that the citizen is mentally and morally responsible for his acts and that they are virtuous acts unless proven otherwise. It is the solemn obligation of every other American citizen, and this includes policemen, judges, jurors, editors of newspapers, and managers of radio and television stations, to abide by the same two principles when they pass private or public judgment on the actions of their fellows. If the one absolute right is the right to live a life of virtue, the right most closely related to it is the right to one's good name until that right has been forfeited. The right to a fair trial is a development from that right, and the right of others to the truth must be exercised with moral as well as legal observance of the two principles which derive from the right to lead the life of virtue. There would be no such case as *Free Press v. Fair Trial* if this injunction were universally observed. It is not, and that is why we have codes of behavior drawn up, now by the bar, now by the press, now by both and the other media jointly. We may now return from this detour through the paths of philosophy to the logical next concern: what the bar and the media are doing about the problem. We may start with the bar.

CODES OF BEHAVIOR: THE BAR

We have already seen a certain seesaw quality to the American concept of contempt of Court. At first the power of a judge to rule on contempt of Court was broad indeed, excessively broad in the light of the tender sensitivity of some judges to criticism. Then, out of the Peck case of 1831, came the legislation which limited the power of a judge to find persons in contempt to those who had expressed their contempt by intolerable conduct in the courtroom or its immediate environs. This concept lasted until the Morrill case of 1855 established a widely accepted principle extending the exercise of the contempt power to the punishment of editors guilty of publishing "licentious scandal." This concept was reaffirmed by the Supreme Court in 1907 when Justice Holmes wrote the Court decision in *Patterson v. State of Colorado,* upholding the right of a state court to cite a publication for contempt if it ran material detrimental to the course of justice during the pendency of a case.

This finding struck home, because it was a very loosely guarded secret that the common source of such material was the slanted disclosures of prosecuting and defense attorneys. Within a year the American Bar Association published its Canon of Professional Ethics. Much of it is not pertinent to our subject, but Canon 20 is. It condemns one-sided statements issued to the press by attorneys during the pendency of a case with an eye to influencing its outcome. No one has ever questioned the piety of purpose that inspired Canon 20, nor has anyone ever found evidence of its influencing to a measurable degree the conduct of the profession. On the whole Canon 35, which was added in 1937, has worked better, assisted as it has been by judges from the Supreme Court in the cases of Wilbert Rideau and Billie Sol Estes, and no doubt by its inescapably explicit nature. "The taking of photographs in the courtroom, during sessions of the Court or recesses between sessions, and the broadcasting of court proceedings, degrade the Court and create misconceptions with respect thereto in the mind of the public and should not be permitted." Hence comes the dignified and non-degrading pencil sketches of principals in law cases which enliven newspaper accounts of court trials and provide variety to the pictorial images on the television screen.

In 1953 the New York County Lawyers Association accepted a code of ethical behavior prepared for it by its committee on fair trial and free press. After affirming that both ideals should coexist with neither expanding at the expense of the other and agreeing that "in recent years the cause of justice has suffered by reason of newspaper and other publicity during or immediately preceding trials, as well as subsequently thereto during the pendency of appeals," the Association proceeded to its avowed principles. The public is entitled to factual, unslanted statements of events in the courtroom; it should be protected from revelations injurious to public morality; attorneys should avoid testing their cases in advance in the press, criticizing court officers, and evading the professional imperative contained in Canon 20; the press should not seek out in advance the testimony to be given by witnesses nor publish articles about a case prepared by witnesses until the final disposition of the case has taken place; the press should avoid the expression of opinions about the credibility of witnesses, the use of sensational headlines not strictly based on fact, and the publication of testimony ruled out by the judge. A defendant's record should not be published until the case is finished, a reputed confession should not be published until admitted as evidence in the trial, and no effort should be made to influence the terms of a sentence to be imposed by a judge.

The New York code is the prototype of them all. Except to lovers of monotony, there is a tedious quality to the reading of the various ethical codes adopted in the several states by the bar, the press, or the two in conjunction. Three such codes may serve as examples. In 1964 the Philadelphia Bar Association adopted a policy regarding the release and publication of information in connection with criminal proceedings. It is a lengthy document, entirely consistent in spirit with the earlier code of the New York County Association but very much more detailed in the way it spells out the specific actions deemed permissible for bar and press. It was greeted with vigorous editorial hostility by newspapers throughout the country, a hostility directed more at the way the principles would be implemented than at the principles themselves. Virtue has always aroused more umbrage in its practice than in its theory, but it may be significant that in 1966, the year in which the Supreme Court ordered a new trial or freedom for Dr. Samuel Sheppard, the Philadelphia Statement of Policy was adopted by the Cleveland Bar Association, the Cleveland *Plain Dealer,* and the Cleveland chapter of the national journalism society Sigma Delta Chi.

It may be cynical to point out the coincidence, just as it may have been cynical to point out the coincidence between the trial by publicity which President Johnson conducted on television of the members of the organization he deemed guilty of killing Mrs. Liuzzo and the announcement three weeks later of a Statement of Policy Concerning the Release of Information by Personnel of the United States Department of Justice Relating to Criminal Proceedings. The statement itself follows the predictable lines. In a sense all such codes are merely exhortations addressed to the bar by itself to observe in practice the rights guaranteed to defendants by American law.

CODES OF BEHAVIOR: THE PRESS

The first important formulation of a code of newspaper ethics took place in 1923 and was the work of the American Society of Newspaper Editors. Canons 6 and 7 of its Canons of Journalism, entitled Fair Play and Decency, are pertinent to our subject. Canon 6 provided that "A newspaper should not publish unofficial charges affecting reputation or moral character, without opportunity given to the accused to be heard; right practice demands the giving of such opportunity in all cases of serious accusation outside judicial proceedings." Under the head of *Decency* the editors averred,

A newspaper cannot escape conviction of insincerity if, while professing high moral purpose, it supplies incentives to base conduct, such as are to be found in details of crime and vice, publication of which is not demonstrably for the general good. Lacking authority to enforce its canons, the journalism here represented can but express the hope that deliberate panderings to vicious instincts will encounter effective public disapproval or yield to the influence of a preponderant professional condemnation.

Conditions, unfortunately, were not ripe for virtue. Within a year Leopold and Loeb were tried and found guilty of murdering Bobby Franks, eliciting what the Chicago *Tribune,* one of the worst offenders, afterwards contritely called "a three months moral pestilence imposed upon our people."

Another code of journalistic righteousness was penned in the melancholy calm of repentant retrospect after the trial of Bruno Hauptmann for the kidnapping and death of the Lindbergh baby, a journalistic saturnalia that rivalled in morbid luxuriance the Hall-Mills and Sam Sheppard cases. The American Newspaper Publishers Association and the American Society of Newspaper Editors joined the American Bar Association in 1936 in denouncing the trial of Hauptmann as "the most spectacular and depressing example of improper publicity and professional misconduct ever presented to the people of the United States in a criminal trial" and calling for "standards of publicity of judicial proceedings and methods of obtaining an observance of them, acceptable to the three interests represented." As might be foreseen, the committee of eighteen came out vigorously in favor of the rights which the law is supposed to guarantee to defendants anyway and therefore in favor of the principles of ethical behavior inseparable from documents of this sort. As a nod to technology, which had advanced since Hall-Mills, it called wholly indefensible the surreptitious procurement of sound records, and as a recognition that the public-opinion poll was now a fact of life it ordained that "no popular referendum ought to be taken during the pendency of the trial." A rather strange prohibition, the reason for which diligent search has not unearthed, was the forbidding of officers of the law to take part in "vaudeville performances" during the progress of a trial. Except for these grace notes, the old, familiar melody remained unchanged.

Its notes re-echo in the codes adopted by bar and press in various states in the years that followed. The Oregon Bar, press, and broadcasters adopted a code of admirable brevity and total freedom from novelty in 1962. In 1963 a Massachusetts Bar-Press Committee adopted a more detailed and specific code which seems, somehow, to have escaped the editorial brickbats thrown at the Philadelphia code of unhappy memory. In 1965 the Kentucky Press Association adopted a long and leisurely code which spelled out with the cultured loquacity that goes with blue grass what all had been saying all along. The unanimity with which virtue is applauded in these documents is reassuring, the support given to principles long since spelled into law is heartening. What is totally lacking is any evidence of an intention to provide implementation of any sort or scope to the objectives tersely or verbosely spelled out. This gives a certain interest to a Minnesota development of the winter of 1972.

In January the creation of an eighteen member Minnesota Press Council was announced, nine of the members professional journalists and nine representatives of the public. The chairman, C. Donald Peterson, is an associate justice of the Minnesota Supreme Court. The Council is the creation of the Minnesota Newspaper Association and its avowed purpose is to create a forum to which a person who considers himself injured in print may appeal without facing the cost and delay of a libel suit. It has no power to enforce its findings, but by and large the Minnesota papers have agreed to publish reports of Council proceedings and recommendations about corrections and retractions. It is ironical that the first case the Council heard was directed against the editor of a labor newspaper, a man actively instrumental in creating the Council. It concerned the charge that a Minnesota legislator had listened to the effective blandishments of two lobbyists one night in a St. Paul restaurant, one of whom the legislator maintained he had not addressed and the other he stated had not even been present. The Council vindicated the legislator, publicized its findings, urged the labor newspaper to report them. It is much too early to determine how effective the Minnesota Press Council will be, but at long last the pious expression of principles is linked to a form of implementation. The omen, at least, is favorable. The best way to stay out of the hands of the police always has been to police one's own conduct.

FREE PRESS

The case, then, is still unsolved, as all cases tend to be that have two laudable and diametrically opposite objectives. The press must indeed be free, the trial must indeed be fair. But this is a case in which the two principals are overshadowed by a third. The public curiosity must indeed be satisfied. Therein lies the really abrasive rub.

The statement is often made that only a small percentage of crime stories ever appear in print. This is indeed true. The problem we are considering has nothing to do with the ordinary thug. His rights are very properly protected by the courts, over-protected in the view of many police officers and other critics of the Warren Court, and they are immune to injury by the press because his deeds have not aroused the public curiosity. It is the relatively small percentage of cases which legitimately arouse the public interest or by manipulation whet the public curiosity that cause the trouble. There would have been no problem of press coverage where the shooting of Patrolman Tippit was concerned if it were not an episode in the assassination of President Kennedy.

A valid distinction exists between the cases that arouse public interest and the cases that whet public curiosity. To say that the assassination of a President arouses public interest is, of course, a ludicrous example of under-writing, but in this matter a common denominator term is necessary. It does not take Armageddon to arouse public interest. Public interest may be aroused legitimately and naturally by any number of criminal matters less cataclysmic in nature; the revelation of dishonesty in high places, shady dealing in corporate enterprise, inadequate protection of the public safety are examples. All such matters by their nature should lead to court trials, and it is part of one's responsibility as a citizen to be interested in them.

Here is the field of widest scope for the exercise of freedom of the press in the public interest, and in it the record of American journalism is full of splendid examples of public service. It may seriously be questioned if there is a better example, and even inspiration, that the press can offer than the persistence with which the St. Louis *Post-Dispatch* aided Senator Thomas Walsh of Montana in the investigation of oil leases during the Harding administration, the money it spent in the process, the way it pushed on despite ridicule and overt hostility, and the way it brought a house of corruption tumbling down about the heads of the men who betrayed the nation that honored them, the President who trusted them, and the consciences that God gave them. What the *Post-Dispatch* did in the Teapot Dome case, other papers have done in cases so numerous that it would be as invidious to single out examples as it is unnecessary. Many of these cases have been so local in nature as to arouse no interest outside the immediate locality, and yet the service done the public interest has been no less valuable in nature than the service done in cases that interest the nation and the world. It may have been the bribery of city officials, the unholy alliance between crime and law enforcement, the shabby and shoddy bit of construction that later may cost lives. Repeatedly newspaper sleuths have run down and exposed such matters, to the great and lasting public good.

The distinction must always be borne in mind between an investigation and a trial. Repeatedly the investigation has been instigated and carried on by a newspaper before the law enforcement process was initiated, and sometimes initiated as a result of press prodding. This is a part of the field wide open to the press, and in the public interest must be kept permanently and totally open. Nor, indeed, is there reason for limiting activity in the field once the pretrial procedure and the trial processes get underway. What is to be limited is the improper publishing of information and even more of speculation during the pretrial and trial periods. The theoretical basis for limitation is spelled out in the ethical codes adopted by bar and press in state after state for the past twenty years. A thumbnail spelling is possible: stick to the facts; avoid prejudicial press releases;

do not publish forthcoming testimony in advance nor evidence ruled out of Court unless identified as such; do not publish a defendant's prior record nor confession unless admitted into the court record; do not try to influence either the jury finding or the judicial sentence. Once the case is over and any appeals settled, then the total record may be printed and the total record may well contain information that never came out in Court or did come out and was barred by the rules of evidence. The press that acts in this fashion is both free and responsible. Responsibility is the obverse imprint on the coin of freedom.

Then there is the other kind of case, the kind that whets the public curiosity, the Professor Webster, Lizzie Borden, Hall-Mills, Leopold-Loeb, Sam Sheppard, Finch-Tregoff sort of case. Here we deal with the material of fact but the technique of fiction. Such cases are natural circulation builders, and the Fourth Estate has a sixth sense for such. In 1946 Chicago produced a violence-morbidity classic, the case of a youth named William Heirens. His competition for prominence during his trial was the atomic bomb tests at Bikini, the immediate postwar problems of the Office of Price Administration, and the matter of getting Britain back of its fiscal feet, all matters of importance and worthy of public interest. A study of eighty-five issues of Chicago newspapers revealed that the Office of Price Administration got eleven top headline billings, the bomb tests four, the loan to Great Britain two, and William Heirens sixty-two.

There is no reason for thinking of cases that when adequately ballooned whet the public curiosity as if they were cases that arouse a natural and justified public interest. It is, of course, conceivable that there could be shady dealing in the handling of such cases by law enforcement or judicial officers. The revelation of such would then be a public service by the press. However there is no particular reason for the public conscience to twitch in this matter. Sex, glamor, violence, society, and morbidity are their own excuse for being. They do not need the public interest to justify their treatment in a way calculated to increase newspaper circulation and elevate television audience ratings. The corollary is that sentiments about the freedom of the press, the guarantees of the Bill of Rights, the immemorial tradition of freedom in the English-speaking world, and the absolute priority of truth, however eloquent in expression and ennobling in nature, are not strictly applicable. Hall-Mills and Leopold-Loeb did not need the the Constitution of the United States to become household words. Sex and morbidity were quite adequate.

The conclusion, however, is in no way different from the conclusion reached about cases that legitimately arouse the public interest. The public is indeed curious about such matters, morbidly curious if one wishes, and in a free society with a free press that sort of curiosity will be satisfied. The press and the other media will have no higher standards than the society that supports them, and there is no way to make life better other than to make men and women better. In such cases just as truly as in the case of a great national tragedy like the assassination of a President or a great national scandal like Teapot Dome, there is a distinction between an investigation and a trial. The same rules that govern the reporting of trials that concern matters of legitimate interest govern the reporting of trials that concern matters of artificially aroused curiosity. The difference is that they are, if anything, harder to enforce in the second sort of trial than in the first. The assassination of President Kennedy and the pillaging of Teapot Dome did not need the techniques of fiction to make them matters of massive importance and grave interest. The charges leveled at Dr. Sheppard and Dr. Finch did, and the techniques of fiction persisted in the coverage of their cases. It would have been a matter of all but insuperable difficulty to give Lee Harvey Oswald a fair trial, but he was an American and entitled by American law to one. It was a matter of artificially contrived difficulty to give a fair trial to persons in the position of Lizzie Borden and Sam Sheppard. The austere fact remains unchanged. Professor Webster, Miss Borden, Reverend Mr. Hall, Mrs. Mills, Harry K. Thaw, Leo Frank, Nathan F. Leopold, Jr., Richard A. Loeb, Bruno Richard Hauptmann, Dr. Samuel Sheppard, Dr. Bernard Finch, Miss Tregoff, and all other men and women tried in American courts under American law but also under the manipulated klieglight of publicity had the rights of citizens. Again and again those rights have been cynically flouted in the name of newspaper circulation and television ratings. It is a prostitution of a noble ideal to attempt the justification of that fact in the name of a free press, the Bill of Rights, and the sanctity of truth. What can be done about it without injustice and injury to a free press and the sanctity of truth, and with observance of the moral adjurations of the Bill of Rights, is our remaining concern.

FAIR TRIAL

The first thing that can be done about it is so transparently obvious that it almost appears derisive to point it out. The press can follow the rules of conduct repeatedly codified by the press associations. This appears quixotic. No one has ever contrived a way in this sinful world of making men and corporations follow counsels of perfection if they are devoid of sanctions. Sanctions may be self-imposed or they may be imposed from outside. The former are always the more desirable, provided they are sincere and not a cynical mask for corruption within. The true professions like medicine and law do police themselves, not always guided perhaps by the clear, unwavering light of perfect justice but guided at least by that uncertain light which is all we sub-celestial creatures are vouchsafed. The press has guidelines galore but until the recent creation of the Minnesota Press Council and its adjudicating forum there was no set of guidelines equipped with a process of sanction. As we said before, it is much too early to know how things will work out in Minnesota, but at least one state press has linked principles to a form of implementation. At least in theory the Minnesota way of self-discipline is the best way.

Then there is the British way, reliance on the power to punish for contempt of Court. Britain frowns in practice upon about the same press actions that are denounced in theory in the United States. A newspaper and its officials may be held in contempt of Court and punished for printing evidence not admissible in Court, for publicizing the prior record or the purported confession of a prospective or present defendant, and for editorializing about a case while it is pending. In Britain courts can and do enforce a code of conduct by the press entirely acceptable in theory to the American press, if the codes of conduct adopted by American press associations represent their true convictions. There has always been a substantial body of opinion in the United States which has held that we should adopt the British system. We might put it into terms consistent with the American history of contempt of Court and say that we should return to the Morrill principle of 1855.

In the writer's opinion this would be a grave mistake. The differences between the British and American tradition, temperament, patterns of living, legal and political procedures, even the physical size of the two nations are too great to pin much faith on the thought that what works well in Britain would work well in the United States. We have, of course, the same end in view which the British very successfully reach by the power of contempt of Court. The question concerns the practicality here of the means that work so well there.

Great Britain is a small, relatively unified country, with an ancient tradition of respect approaching awe for the law and its workings. Its bar is very limited in number, and those who plead in Court even more limited. Furthermore, in Britain the defense attorney in today's case may be the prosecutor in tomorrow's. There is a great gulf between politics and the law in Britain, and an immunity in the legal process from political pressure that approaches total isolation. If there is an ancient tradition of respect for the law, there is a tradition equally ancient of justice within the law. The record of the British in administering justice to peoples whom the Lord in His inscrutable wisdom chose not to make British is not immaculate, but the record is amazingly free from stain where the legal treatment of the British by the British is concerned. The supreme justification of the British system is the pragmatic one. It works. One gets a fair trial there.

There is no convincing evidence that it would work nearly so well in the United States. When the 1831 doctrine prevailed which limited the contempt power to the preservation of order in the courtroom, the field was left wide open for yellow journalism and a field day followed. When the Morrill doctrine of 1855 prevailed, the field day at least entered a twilight but the dangers present in the concept of contempt of Court soon showed themselves. Newspapermen were cited for contempt and tried by the judges whom they had treated contemptuously. The contempt of Court power is one of the genuine and grave threats that exist to freedom of the press. What is even graver, it is one of the genuine and grave threats to the basic welfare of the citizen for whom both press and courts exist.

It is well to recall, if one lives in a state in which judges are appointed, that in most American states judges are elected. In most states a judge is a cog in a political machine and the alliance between the Court and politics, which is as close to totally absent in Britain as is possible in an imperfect world, is a very real and close one. Grant a close tie between the courthouse and the state house or city hall, grant a judge elected by the help of a corrupt state or city administration, grant a crusading newspaper which reveals the corruption and the tie, and there will be neither a fair trial nor a free press. This is the extreme case. The typical one may well be worse. If truth loves the light, falsehood loves the darkness. A dishonest judge really skilled in dishonesty would never stir the dogs of the press, but the press would know that the courthouse has dogs too. The great danger in a contempt of Court power analogous to the British but operating in the American political system is that the citizen would be caught between two conflicting forces—law and press. What if it is the citizen and not the press who first raises the issue of corruption? The man in the street can be held in contempt just as readily as the man in the editor's office, if the contempt power is broad enough.

Another way of handling the problem that has frequently been suggested is to limit by law the nature and extent of the information about a suspect or defendant that can be released by law enforcement officials to the press. An example of the sort of legislation that has been proposed to this end was Senate Bill 290, filed in 1965 by Senator Wayne Morse of Oregon. This piece of legislation would have made it illegal for a Federal employee, a defendant, or a defense attorney to "furnish or make available for publication information not already properly filed with the Court which might affect the outcome of any pending criminal litigation, except evidence that has already been admitted at the trial." S 290 concerned only Federal courts, but similar legislation curbing the power of state and local law-enforcement officials has been repeatedly proposed. Sometimes the sanction which the proposed legislation would apply to the public official has been extended to the press that published the unpermitted news release or to the newspaper that published improperly the prior record or reported confession of a suspect or defendant. In a manner of speaking, all such proposed legislation would enact into law the sort of sanction that is exercised in Britain by the contempt of Court power, that has been frequently proposed and, by the Morrill doctrine of 1855, actually exercised in the United States.

The basic arguments against extensive contempt of Court power after the British model are less applicable to the approach by statute, although they do have some validity. A distinction must be drawn between the freedom of the press to investigate and the freedom of the press to publish. Another distinction must be drawn between the freedom of the press to publish now and the freedom of the press to publish later. Anything like a blanket prohibition on the freedom of the press to publish during the pretrial and the trial period would certainly have a dampening effect on the enthusiasm of the press to investigate. In the last analysis news is a commodity the press sells, and no store stocks goods that cannot be sold. A blanket prohibition would imply the same sort of total trust in the integrity of the legal system that full power of contempt of Court implies. Reasonable and proper pretrial and trial publicity helps to preserve the integrity of the legal system and may be helpful in its effective operation. Facts may be brought to light, witnesses discovered, aspects of a case unearthed that otherwise might remain hidden to the detriment of justice and quite possibly to the injury of an innocent citizen.

It is never difficult to speak in favor of what is reasonable and proper. The difficult thing is to define it and then to say how it should prevail. There are certain things the press can and should do on its own initiative to improve the reasonable and proper coverage of crime stories and criminal cases. The first is to train crime reporters and reporters conversant with the principles and operation of the law. We hear of the profession of journalism. Journalism is not a profession nor has it taken any really significant steps to make itself such. The true professions like theology, medicine, and law require intensive and protracted periods of professional training. At least a newspaper might give a neophyte in the field of crime and court reporting some apprenticeship training under a reporter experienced in the field. Crime and the law are multi-billion-dollar businesses. They deserve, however ironical the word may sound, to get the sort of informed reporting big business gets on the financial page.

We have drawn a distinction between freedom of the press to publish now and freedom of the press to publish later. One of the cornerstones of newspaper work is the release date. Organizations of every sort and size turn in stories to newspaper offices with release dates typed at the top. There is a natural and proper system of release dates implicit in every court trial. As a rule it ties in with the time that evidence is admitted by the Court. Observance of this sort of release date is consistent with true professional standards. If the press observes with pious rectitude the release date set by General Motors for information about next year's models, and indeed it does, it should observe with the same rectitude the release dates implicit in the trial of a citizen for a crime. The press is entirely free to criticize the conduct of that trial as it is conducted, just as it is entirely free to criticize the offerings of General Motors, now that Ralph Nader has revealed the previously unsuspected truth that such press criticism is possible. It should not as a matter of professional integrity criticize the conduct of a trial before it takes place, appraise the evidence before it is submitted and accepted, reach the verdict before the jury does, and sentence the convicted before the Court passes sentence. The citizen on trial has just as much right to the honoring of release dates as any corporation that manufactures automobiles or any fraternal lodge that runs a dance.

One may be reassuringly certain that the press will not publish the charge by *Consumer Reports* that a particular vacuum cleaner is null and void in operation without getting the case for the defense from the vacuum cleaner manufacturer. When a civil war for control rages between two corporate owners of massive blocks of stock in a corporation, the financial page carries with meticulous care balanced statements by the generals of the opposing sides buttressing the eternal justice of their respective cases. There is no reason that the same cannot be done in criminal cases and curiosity-rich civil cases and the proof that it can be done is the fact that the good newspapers do it. If the prosecution issues a statement, the balancing statement by the defense should be elicited and published. Each pro should have its con, each positive its negative. Most important of all, perhaps, should be the ruthless editing out of courtroom stories editorializing comment and even the sort of adjective or adverb that carries an editorial connotation. These are some of the things the press can do. Then there are things the Courts can do, short of exercising contempt of Court power.

There are two obvious things the Courts can do, grant a postponement of a trial and give a trial a change of venue. The first device is based on the pragmatic consideration that man has a short memory and waves of publicity soon subside. Furthermore, when the whetted curiosity of the public has lost its edge, it is hard to whet it again. The suspect in whose case an impartial jury would be hard to assemble one year may be tried before a serenely impartial jury in the same courtroom a year later. Forgetfulness is one of the automatic human virtues. A change of venue frequently can produce the same result without the passage of time. A suspect who cannot hope for a fair trial in one county because the winds of publicity have whipped up a local storm about his head may find a courtroom of halcyon calm in a county in another part of the state. These are practical devices that often work in cases where natural interest is limited in geographic extent or where artificially stimulated curiosity has relatively little on which to feed. They cannot be expected to work in cases of great moment. After the Dallas debacle Lee Harvey Oswald would have needed a change of venue to the dark side of the moon.

Yet there is something about a postponement or a change of venue that goes against the grain. They are practical and realistic devices, but they are based on the premise that the law must bow to the superior force of publicity. They are grounded on the thesis that intelligent and responsible men and women cannot realistically be expected to retain their intellectual detachment and fairness in the face of a barrage of publicity leveled by the communications media. This may indeed be true, but the postponement of a trial and the granting of a change of venue are confessions that the law as an institution has lesser strength than the press as an institution and therefore a prudent defendant may be wise to give up his rights to a speedy trial or a trial by a local jury, or possibly to both. This should not be. If *Free Press v. Fair Trial* is to be a battle, then Fair Trial will never win by retreating. The law must launch a counter-offensive of its own.

A counter-offensive is possible. One device available to the Court is the power to declare a mistrial. There is no reason that the improper release of prejudicial statements by either prosecution or defense clearly designed to affect the outcome of the trial should not be grounds for declaring a mistrial. There is no reason that bar associations should not be empowered to investigate the grounds for such mistrials and to take such disciplinary action as lies within their frequently quite adequate powers. Police commissioners have very adequate powers to investigate and discipline members of the force, if the improper statements are issued by the police. There is no unit in the press powerful enough to remain permanently indifferent to the reaction of the citizen to its deeds, and the very fact that a mistrial has been declared as a result of an abuse of press freedom would carry its own implicit rebuke to the press. A strong judge can run a good, honest trial if he makes up his mind to do so.

Furthermore, he will have the United States Supreme Court to back him up. In case after case the Court has reversed a lower court judgment when it was clear that abuse of the privileges of the media had denied a defendant a fair trial. Justice Frankfurter, as we have seen, pointed the way in his minority opinion in the *Baltimore Radio Show* case of 1950, when the Court refused a writ of certiorari in a case in which a local radio company had broadcast the prior record and alleged confession of a man arrested for murder. The Frankfurter dissent, lonely though it was, was rich in significance as later decisions showed. The Court had destroyed the 1855 Morrill doctrine of contempt in the *Bridges, Pennekamp,* and *Craig* cases but had put nothing in its place. Justice Frankfurter saw before the rest how perilous this was to the constitutional guarantee of a fair trial and the necessity for putting a counter-balance on the scale now that the contempt power had been drastically limited. Within a year the Court had a change of heart. An Orlando, Florida, paper expedited the conviction of four men for rape by running the cartoon already mentioned. The Court reversed the conviction on the grounds that improper pretrial publicity had destroyed their right to a fair trial. On the same grounds it reversed lower court convictions in *Marshall* (1959), *Irvin* (1961), *Rideau* (1963), and *Sheppard* (1966). The judge who declares a mistrial on the grounds of prejudicial publicity and the appeals court that reverses a lower court verdict on the same grounds and orders a new trial have, to buttress their position, case after case in which the Supreme Court has shown a deep awareness that the citizen may be caught between the jaws of a potent vise, if it is his ill luck to be the central figure in a case that arouses natural interest or what is worse, in a case in which curiosity is artificially stimulated. The case may bear his name, but he is the hapless third party in *Free Press v. Fair Trial.* When new trials were ordered for Marshall, Irvin, Rideau, and Sheppard, the Supreme Court showed that the law has other strategies available besides the retreat technique of the postponed trial or the changed venue.

There is a device open to the citizen himself, in his capacity as a citizen. In most American states judges are elected. In some they are appointed. Neither system is perfect and generalizations are by their nature suspect, but the person who argues that the states with appointed judges have better courts than the states with elected judges has the stronger side in the debate. The elected judge is a concept that has come down from the rather crude and leveling democracy of Andrew Jackson. The concept is one that appeals to the person who prefers the ideological absolute to the pragmatic relative. The United States is a democracy. In a democracy all public officials are elected. A judge is a public official. Therefore a judge should be elected.

The truth is that a judge is a public official with a difference. The selectman, city councilman, mayor, legislator, governor, or senator is not supposed to be aloof, disinterested, austerely removed from his constituents. He is elected to serve their interests, and the fact that he should do so fairly and impartially does not mean that he is to be emotionally detached from them and the interests to which he is to be dedicated. But a judge should be not only fair and impartial, but he should be aloof, disinterested, austerely removed from any intellectual or emotional commitment to the parties that come before him. Most important of all, he must be totally independent from any pressure direct or indirect that they can exert. How can he be when he must present himself to them periodically for re-election? He has a much better chance of preserving the ideal of justice when he is appointed and secure in his appointment unless he forfeits it by misconduct than he is if his security extends only to the next election.

On the other hand, there is the inertia of tradition, and tradition in most states has it that judges be elected. The American Bar Association has wrestled with what is always a difficult problem in an area where emotions can run high, the problem of reconciling respect for tradition with the need for progress. The Association has suggested that a judicial committee representative of the profession and the public assemble a slate of judges from which the governor may choose and appoint. After a judge has been on the bench for an adequate period the votors would decide whether or not he should remain there. If they voted him out of his position, it would be filled by another appointment by the governor. The basic objection to the elected judgeship remains, that a judge must please the electorate to stay on the bench, but at least the objection has been modified. Potential judges would be screened by a committee working in an atmosphere of deliberation and composure, the voting process would be removed from party politics, and in practice it is likely that a judge would be considered "innocent" and hold his job unless he had been guilty of arousing the public ire. As a compromise with tradition, it might well be worthy of a trial. It might contribute to the most important single component in the right to a fair trial for the citizen, an impartial and a strong judge.

Thus there are steps the legal profession can take and steps that the press can take to end *Free Press v. Fair Trial*, that perennial case which never should have reached the docket. The citizen, too, is not without resources. In addition to the elective process, simplistic or refined as suggested above, the citizen has a potent legal weapon and a legally protected right, the right to sue for libel. This is one aspect of the relationship between the citizen and the press which extends far beyond the limited relationship which exists when the citizen is in the coils of the law. The aspect is so important that it merits a chapter by itself in any study of the citizen-press relationship.

Part III

LIBEL

The entire concept of libel, no matter how many its ramifications and how subtle its legal nuances, rests upon a concept of stark simplicity. No one ever put it better than Iago, about the least deserving of this honor of all Shakespeare's creations. "Good name in man and woman, dear my lord, Is the immediate jewel of their souls . . . he that filches from me my good name Robs me of that which not enriches him And makes me poor indeed." One other unpoetic but vital phrase must be added to make the definition valid: he must do it in print.

A libel is a published statement about an identified or easily identifiable person which makes the reader think worse of him. To make it libel the triad must be complete: publication, identification, defamation. The concept of libel is rooted in that already mentioned philosophic concept on which the entire body of American law and English law before it is based. It is the basic assumption of the law that a citizen is a person of moral integrity and mental competence. That is what we really mean when we say that a person accused of a crime is considered innocent until proven guilty. In the criminal process the citizen himself fouls the immediate jewel of his soul by the criminal act. The law then must prove that he did it.

There is nothing fixed and final about the concept of libel and its legal consequences. It is slander for a person to make an oral statement calculated to defame another. It is libel to put the statement into print. Historically the law has been so lenient toward slander as virtually to ignore its existence. But what if the slander is voiced on a coast-to-coast broadcast? Today it is possible, just as it was in the thirteenth century, for the concepts of slander and libel to merge, and conceivably the slanderous statement may be the more libelous form of the two. The truth is that far from being a fixed, unchanging concept, the concept of libel has undergone a series of changes of prime significance to the citizen in his relationship to the press, and now the concept of slander is undergoing a rapid transformation equally significant to the citizen in his relationship to the media that use the spoken word. The former series of changes has a long history, to which we must now address ourselves. The latter transformation is a new phenomenon, one almost without history but one certainly ripe for speculation.

INFAMOUS LITTLE BOOKS

We have already seen that the very concept of freedom of the press arose as the obverse of the concept of libel. In the late eighteenth century there were four kinds of libel recognized, seditious, defamatory, blasphemous, and obscene. A piece of writing free from all four might lawfully be published. We have considered under the head of Prior Restraint the implications of seditious libel and the development of the concept. Now our concern is defamatory libel, the libel injurious to the good name of a private citizen as distinct from a public official. Its history begins in ancient Rome.

Roman law dealt severely with statements made in public that defamed the good name of Roman citizens, the sort of statement that was "an insult to good manners" (*convicium contra bonos mores*). The essence of the offense was its public nature, the insult being offered not merely to an individual but also to proper conduct. Hence it did not matter whether the substance of the insult was true or false. Roman law also dealt with defamatory statements that were made in private. Such statements insulted, not proper conduct but an individual. Consequently in them the truth was a defense, even if their substance was false but erroneously believed to be true.

At first there seems to have been no distinction drawn by the Romans between slander and libel. The offended party sued in what we would call a civil action for a monetary penalty, basing his suit on the public nature of the offense in the first instance and the alleged falsity of the charge in the second. The basis for the legal distinction between public and private utterance of a defamatory nature was to make possible the often necessary disclosure of flaws in the character of Roman citizens without subjecting them to unnecessary public contumely.

It is a commonplace of classical studies that the Romans were original in only one literary form, satire. Not only were they original in it; they have never been surpassed, not even by the French. They created Horatian satire, witty, urbane, cultivated, and devastating; they created Juvenalian satire, bitter, vindictive, unrelenting, and devastating. "Infamous little books" (*libelli famosi*) of satire circulated about the ancient city, and under the Empire they came to be feared and dreaded, and therefore hunted down and their authors punished with extreme severity. A Roman emperor was a god, and a satire on a god is seditious, blasphemous, and obscene, as well as defamatory. The four concepts blended into one when an infamous little book made an emperor its target, and when it did, the truth or falsity of the satire was totally irrelevant. Thus the four concepts of libel that persisted into the time of the American Revolution had their genesis in ancient Rome, and one can see how the link between libel and sedition, the link that joins libel to blasphemy and obscenity, as well as the link between libel and defamation were established. One can also see why truth so frequently was no defense in libel. Then one may also see the origin of the English word *libel,* a derivative of the Latin diminutive *libellus,* the little book that became so infamous and hated.

By and large the "infamous little book" concept was taken over by the English from Roman law, with a bland disregard for the limitations with which the later Romans hedged the concept. Not unnaturally, the earliest English concept of libel did not distinguish it from slander. There were civil actions for libel as early as the reign of Edward I (1272-1307) but the crime of spreading false reports about the magistrates (*scandalum magnatum*), an expansion of the "infamous little book" concept quite unwarranted by Roman law and practice, and the punishing of it by statute law as a breach of the peace seems first to have appeared in Star Chamber proceedings under James I (1603-1625). By then the concept of seditious libel was full-blown but its further history, to which we paid some limited attention in Part I, no longer is our concern. Both concepts, defamatory libel and seditious libel, were taken over bodily from Roman law, but their history in the English-speaking world is the history of two separate and very different concepts having very little in common except a point of origin.

LIBEL IN THE NINETEENTH CENTURY

The concept of defamatory libel, which we may for the sake of convenience hereafter term merely libel, remained fairly fixed through the nineteenth century in both Britain and America, and as a concept just about the same in both countries. A distinction was observed between oral slander and printed libel, with the latter deemed far the more serious offense. One may be spontaneously and unthinkingly slanderous in the heat of sudden anger, but it takes time, thought, and deliberate intent to be defamatory in print. Furthermore, print is permanent and public, and no form of slander that the nineteenth century knew could be broadcast after the manner of printed libel. Hence the actionable grounds of slander were rigidly limited: the allegation that a person had been guilty of a prison offense, that he had a serious contagious disease, or that he was gravely incompetent in his profession were the major grounds for action, and in the case of the last legal action would be entertained only with evidence that the slander had gravely injured him in his profession. For that matter, the offended could collect in the first two instances only if he had not been threatened by Old Bailey or the pest house. Truth was fundamental, and there could be no recovery of damages unless it could be proved that damages, and pecuniary damages at that, had actually occurred.

There was no comparable limitation to special grounds where actions for libel were concerned. Any defamatory statement that made its butt an object of ridicule, obloquy, or hatred was libel, and everyone involved in the production of the libel—author, printer, and publisher alike—was at least potentially liable to an action. A libel did not have to be direct and explicit. Libel by innuendo ("John Smith was sober again today") was actionable, and the jury might test the subtlety and effectiveness of the innuendo in reaching its verdict. But there was a legal staff of oak on which a defendant could always lean: he could always justify his libelous statement by the defense of truth.

The ordinary supposition behind libel law was that a libel was intentional in nature and malicious in purpose. Hence the proof of truth rested on the defendant. But there are circumstances in which the exact opposite is true. If the average citizen said, "John Smith is a thief," the ordinary supposition was that the libel had behind it a malicious purpose. If the king's attorney, or the district attorney, or the chairman of the grand jury stated, "John Smith is a thief," the statement might be true or false and the legal supposition was that it was false until proven true by a courtroom trial, but it was not considered malicious. The proof of truth in such an instance rested on the plaintiff. It is out of this distinction based on the presumptive motivation on the one hand of the private individual and on the other of the public official that the concept of privileged utterance arose. The private libeler presumably is grinding his axe, the public libeler is not. Hence arose the privileged nature of statements made in judicial and legislative proceedings. By extension there came into being the relatively privileged nature of statements by those whose professions require them to pass judgments, frequently disparaging, on the achievements of their fellows. Especially outside the court-room and the legislative hall, the distinction between criticism and libel is easier to recognize in practice than to define in words. "Last night John Smith gave the worst performance of *Hamlet* in the history of the English speaking stage" is criticism, good, bad, true, or false as the case might be. "Last night John Smith gave the worst performance of *Hamlet* in the history of the English speaking stage because he was drunk" is libel. A further extension of the concept of privileged utterance protected defamatory statements about the character of prospective employees, the integrity of prospective borrowers, the competence of prospective students, and the like. In all such cases the plaintiff, whether employee, borrower, or student, would have to prove malice to make the defamation actionable.

The concept of criminal libel, historically a subdivision of sedi-tious libel, tended to wither away during the nineteenth century. In practice it was limited to seditious libels calculated to disturb the peace. "To arms! The sheriff of Nottingham and his accomplices are about to drive us from our homes and burn our crops" was the sort of hypothetical libel that might find a defendant facing the charge of criminal libel. The truth or falsity of such a libel was not the point at issue, since the charge of criminal libel would be based upon its threat to the peace and order of the realm. In practice there were very few occasions on which the issue of criminal libel was raised, and except for a new and still largely unsolved problem of libel law, the problem of group libel, one might say that the issue is dead today. Its implications have been fused with the implications of the laws against sedition and the practice of prior restraint, and there are other statutes entirely adequate to control threats to the peace. Even in the nineteenth century, however, there was little life left in the concept of criminal libel.

On the whole the nineteenth-century law of libel substantiated the benign judgment of Gilbert and and Sullivan that the law is the embodiment of everything that's excellent, rather than the libelous statement attributed to Mr. Bumble that the law is an ass. It was the end product of over two thousand years of jurisprudence, and into it had gone the wit, wisdom, and ripe experience of generation after generation of jurists and legislators. It was very important that the concept of libel be separated from the concept of sedition, and it was also of supreme importance to determine what sedition itself was. It was practical and useful to separate the concept of libel from the concepts of blasphemy and obscenity, and this was done very early in the century. The distinction between slander and libel was a valid one, and yet it is a distinction that illustrates how true it is that the law can never stay fixed and that there can be no satisfactory system of jurisprudence that does not have a good measure of pragmatism in its operation. When the distinction was drawn, no one dreamed of a day when the spoken word could literally be heard around the world and down from the moon. The concept of libel held in Britain was the concept held in the United States, and in the last analysis it was the concept held in ancient Rome. This concept is the natural starting point for a consideration of the development of libel law in the twentieth century. It is still the fundamental concept, but enough has happened to libel law in the modern age for one not to rely entirely on the concepts held in Victorian Britain, or for that matter Victorian America.

Libel and the Public Man

It is an observable fact in the history of the law that the law is quite capable of a complete somersault. Sir Edward Coke (1552–1634), lord chief justice of England, once defined libel as "written blame, true or false, of any man, public or private; the blame of a public man being a more serious matter than the blame of a private man." It is the second half of that definition which has come about a complete turn in somewhat more than 300 years, with most of the turn taking place in the twentieth century. Our first concern in the twentieth-century development of the libel concept involves the libel of the "public man," and the extension of that concept to those whose publicity arises from areas other than the political.

The absolute privilege of the press to report on administrative, legislative, and judicial proceedings was the intended result of the First Amendment to the Constitution, and it is a privilege made explicit by statute law in the various states. Terminology differs from state to state, but the law of Oklahoma is typical: "A privileged publication or communication is one made ... by a fair and true report of any legislative or judicial or other proceeding authorized by law, or anything said in the course therof, and any and all expressions of opinion in regard thereto, and criticism thereon, and any and all criticisms upon the official acts of any and all public officers, except where the matter stated of and concerning the official act done, or the officer, falsely imputes crime to the officer so criticized." In general, statute law in the various states gave absolute privilege to reporting and editorializing about matters of governmental concern, short of malicious falsehood. The latter phrase, however, indicates a distinction between the literal act of reporting what transpired and the addition of extraneous matter or editorial comment. Once the newspaperman moved beyond the bounds of exact reporting, his absolute privilege was modified into a conditional privilege subject to the limitations of truth and honesty of purpose. Furthermore this conditional privilege was itself limited. In no way did it extend to editorializing about the lives of public servants. Arizona law put it succinctly: "Libelous remarks or comments connected with such privileged matter receive no privilege by reason of their being so connected."

At this point came the division of opinion about the libel of "the public man." To what extent must the discussion of the acts of a public official be based upon the truth? Or, to put what is for practical purposes the same question the other way around, to what extent does libel law protect the public official? At the mid-point of the twentieth century most states held that the privilege of fair comment and criticism of the acts of public officials was to be limited by the truth, and that defamatory statements about public officials, if false, were just as actionable as such statements would be if made about private citizens. As one Federal Circuit Court of Appeals stated, "The mere fact that a man is a public officer or is a candidate for public office does not constitute a warrant, either to the ordinary citizen or to a newspaper, to spread false charges against him of criminal acts or disgraceful conduct."[1]

This view, cogent though it seems to the layman and rooted though it undoubtedly is in justice, is not the only view that can be held, nor is it the view that has prevailed. There is many a truth that is known but cannot be proved, there is many a statement made that is false yet made with honest intent. Can the press do its full duty in informing the public about the actions of public officials and the qualifications of aspirants to officialdom if it cannot print in good faith and without malice statements that it cannot prove and statements that may in fact be false? A minority of states at mid-century

---

[1] *Nevada State Journal Publishing Co. v. Henderson,* 294 F. 60.

held to this concept by statute law. The principle was put with a succinctness to rival Arizona brevity in the adjacent state of California: "Doctrine of privileged communications rests essentially upon public policy. Under proper circumstances the interest and necessities of society become paramount to the welfare or reputation of a private individual, and the occasion and circumstances may for the public good absolve one from punishment for such communications even though they be false."[1]

The case which was to be the direct harbinger of the late twentieth-century doctrine was heard early in the century, as early as 1908, in Kansas. In *Coleman v. MacLennan*[2] the plaintiff sued the Topeka *State-Journal* for what he alleged was a libel against him in his official handling of a transaction that involved school funds. The Kansas Court stated, ". . . it must be borne in mind that the correct rule, whatever it is, must govern in cases other than those involving candidates for office. It must apply to all officers and agents of government—municipal, state, and national; to the management of all public institutions—educational, charitable, and penal; to the conduct of all corporate enterprises affected with a public interest— transportation, banking, insurance, and to innumerable other subjects involving the public welfare." This was an expansion, as expansive in the view of many students of the law as the Kansas prairies themselves, of the entirely limited and licit principle on which *Coleman v. MacLennan* was decided: "Under a form of government like our own there must be freedom to canvass, in good faith, the worth of character and qualifications of candidates for office, whether elective or appointive, and that by becoming a candidate, a man tenders, as an issue to be tried out publicly before the people or the appointing power, his honesty, integrity, and fitness for the office to be filled."

Echoes of *Coleman* did not reverberate in Washington until 1964, but something like an echo of this old Kansas case was heard in Connecticut in 1955. A politician on the hustings electrified workers of Meriden by telling them in a radio speech that their company was about to go out of business and they were about to go out on the street because the Republican administration in power was indifferent to the welfare of business and workers alike. The statement was

[1] *Jones v. Express Publishing Co.*, 87 Cal. App. 2460
[2] 78 Kans. 711

calculated by its nature to injure the business firm and had the further disadvantage of being false. The firm brought suit against the source of the libel, maintaining that although there was a campaign on and the speech was made by a candidate for public office, its fiscal soundness was not a matter about which false statements could be made under the immunity accorded statements that concerned the public interest. The Connecticut Court ruled that prospective unemployment is a matter of public interest and hence that the company position on the issue was not legally sound. The inference, that any enterprise large enough is automatically vested with a public interest and so by the Kansas-Connecticut doctrine is denied the protection against libel accorded economic lesser fry, seems inescapable. So far it has escaped explicit acceptance by the Supreme Court of the United States, but the Kansas case was the foundation of what has come to be called the New York Times Rule and the Rule has been extended to non-political luminaries. By it a new curse has been added to greatness.

THE NEW YORK TIMES RULE

L. B. Sullivan, Commissioner of Public Affairs for Montgomery, Alabama, was an exceedingly angry man. *The New York Times* had carried an advertisement which described alleged violence done in his domain to demonstrators opposed to racial discrimination. The advertisement contained certain statements which Commissioner Sullivan held were false, and which he further maintained could be demonstrated to be false on the basis of news stories carried in the same *New York Times.* He sued for libel and was awarded $500,000 by the Alabama trial jury, an award which was sustained by the Alabama Supreme Court. The case was appealed to the United States Supreme Court and the verdict reversed. Justice William J. Brennan wrote the Supreme Court decision.[1]

Justice Brennan pointed out that by Alabama law a publication is libelous if it "tends to injure a person . . . in his reputation" or "bring him into public contempt." The only defense Alabama law provided for such a libel was the truth, and the fact of fair comment had to be predicated on the fact of truth. A showing of actual malice was necessary for an award of punitive damages. Justice Brennan contin-

[1] *New York Times v. Sullivan*, 376 U.S. 254 (1964).

ued in his outline of the Alabama law, "Good motives and belief in truth do not negate an inference of malice, but are relevant only in mitigation of punitive damages if the jury chooses to accord them weight . . ." He then defined the actual question as the Supreme Court saw it: "The question before us is whether this rule of liability, as applied to an action brought by a public official against critics of his official conduct, abridges the freedom of speech and of the press that is guaranteed by the First and Fourteenth Amendments. . . ."

That freedom of expression about public issues is a constitutional guarantee, he continued, has been established by numerous court decisions. The question, then, is whether "by the falsity of some of its factual statements and by its alleged defamation of respondent" the advertisement forfeited that guarantee. Justice Brennan then cited a number of findings that indicated that neither falsity nor defamation forfeited the constitutional safeguard that protects one who comments on the public acts of a public official. Only if the official could prove that a published falsehood was inspired by reckless malice could he collect for a libel on his public conduct, was the decision of the Court. "The constitutional guarantees require, we think, a federal rule that prohibits a public official from recovering damages unless he proves that the statement was made with actual malice—that is, with knowledge that it was false or with reckless disregard of whether it was false or not." Justice Brennan then cited the Kansas case of *Coleman v. MacLennan* in support of this viewpoint, and indicated an analogy between it and the Court finding in *Barr v. Matteo*[1] in which the Court held that a public official was protected absolutely from libel suits for statements about private citizens made within the "outer perimeter" of his duties. "It would give public servants an unjustified preference over the public they serve, if critics of official conduct did not have a fair equivalent of the immunity granted to the officials themselves." Toward the end of the decision Justice Brennan voiced what may well have been the rationale underlying the whole. "This proposition has disquieting implications for criticism of governmental conduct. For good reason, 'no court of last resort in this country has ever held, or even suggested, that prosecution for libel on government have any place in

[1] 360 U.S. 564

the American system of jurisprudence'. . . . [1] The present proposition would sidestep this obstacle by transmuting criticism of government, however impersonal it may seem on its face, into personal criticism, and hence potential libel, of the officials of whom the government is composed." The decision of the Supreme Court was unanimous, and the only suggestion of dissent came in the concurring opinions of Justices Black, Douglas, and Goldberg who felt that the Court had not gone far enough. Their view is crystal clear in Justice Goldberg's words: "In my view, the First and Fourteenth Amendments to the Constitution afford to the citizen and to the press an absolute, unconditional privilege to criticize official conduct despite the harm which may flow from excesses and abuses."

Thus ended a concept ancient as ancient Rome. The concept of seditious libel had evolved in Roman law when infamous little books attacked the emperor. It was expanded in British law to protect all magistrates from adverse criticism. The repudiation of the concept was a motivating factor behind the passage of the First Amendment, and was confirmed by the fate of the Alien and Sedition Acts. With the establishment of the New York Times Rule, the final sod was thrown on the grave of seditious libel. Even then, Justices Black, Douglas, and Goldberg had a dread that the sad relic might somehow stir in its grave. Malice remained grounds for a libel action, and *malice* was defined as "knowledge that it (i.e., the libelous statement) was false or with a reckless disregard of whether it was false or not." Jurors have been known to prefer politicians to publishers, and a jury might well take a jaundiced view of what is claimed to be a non-malicious falsehood and might be more austere in its definition of reckless disregard than an editorial writer.

In the opinion of the writer, this is precisely the way it should be. One returns as always to the distinction Judge Learned Hand drew between the broader provisions of the Constitution viewed as moral adjurations and viewed as jural concepts. Once any provision of the Bill of Rights is viewed as an absolute, even freedom to criticize public officials as "an absolute, unconditional privilege" in Justice Goldberg's phrase, sooner or later that absolute right will meet another right head-on. It is certainly true that the press must be free to criticize the conduct of public affairs. It is certainly true that this means a freedom to criticize the conduct of individuals in the public

[1] *City of Chicago v. Tribune Co.*, 307 Ill. 595, 601.

service. On the other hand the person in the public service has precisely the same right to his good name as any other citizen. The distinction between criticism of a person's public acts and criticism of his private morals is extremely difficult to observe in practice, as even the most casual study of campaign utterances will reveal. A jury certainly should be free to decide whether or not a publication critical of an official's public conduct is properly limited to an objective criticism of that and that alone, or whether one is intended to infer from it the real butt of criticism, the manners and morals of the man attacked. A jury certainly should be free to determine what appears to twelve average citizens malicious and what does not.

The problem of truth or falsity is a most difficult one. It is much easier to prove that a statement is false than it is to prove that it is knowingly false. It may be easier to prove that it was made with a disregard of its falsity, since proof may be available that its truth was inadequately investigated before the statement was made. (One recalls Commissioner Sullivan's contention that the advertising staff of *The New York Times* could have spotted falsities in the advertisement "Heed Their Rising Voices" by reading the news columns of their own paper). Here, it would seem, is the crux of the whole matter, the basis for the vital distinction between the moral adjuration and the jural concept. Certainly the press must be free to criticize the conduct of public affairs. That does not mean it must be free to voice the criticism before it investigates its truth or its falsity. The Constitution guarantees freedom of the press. It does not guarantee instantaneous publication by the press. One can easily conceive of the jury which would consider the rush into print that falsely defames a citizen who happens also to be a public official "a reckless disregard of whether it was false or not."

A good example of the peril present in the doctrinaire New York Times Rule was provided in the summer of 1972 when the fate of Senator Thomas Eagleton of Missouri as vice-presidential candidate of the Democratic Party was sealed partly by the carefully investigated and properly authenticated disclosure that he had a record of repeated treatment for mental problems and partly by the inadequately investigated and entirely unauthenticated charge that he had a record as a reckless, drunken driver. There is reason to believe that the inadequately investigated and later retracted charge played its part in his downfall as apparently corroborative of the carefully documented disclosure. The disclosure was made by the reporters of the Knight papers in the best tradition of responsible journalism. The charge was followed by a total withdrawal and apology by the commentator who made it. There is certainly a difference between the two, but under the New York Times Rule the standings of the substantiated disclosure and the repudiated charge are precisely the same. Truth and falsehood should never stand side by side on the same pedestal.

The full implications of the New York Times Rule have not as yet developed. Probably the most important single implication is what courts less libertarian than the Warren Court for which Justice Brennan spoke will consider a reckless disregard of whether a statement is true or not. This is a nation with a governmental structure dependent on the concept of checks and balances. That concept permeates American life, and is the concept which has enabled a naturally spirited and effervescent people to sustain internal dissensions that would tear apart the fabric of other societies. Underneath the philosophy of checks and balances is a vital, unphilosophic, typically American belief in fair play. There is something fundamental in the American psyche that rebels when play is not fair, and every now and then some massive power in American life becomes aware that it has offended that spirit of fair play and aroused the antagonism of something stronger even than itself. On the whole the news media are safer in operating even under the very questionable New York Times Rule with its recognition that there is such a thing as malice and such a thing as reckless disregard for the truth than under the thinking of Justices Black, Douglas, and possibly Goldberg who have elevated press freedom into an absolute. Yet it will be a sad day for the American press if reliance on the New York Times Rule brings it into a direct confrontation with the American spirit of fair play. The newspaper can print and publish; the individual, whether he is a private citizen or a public official, can print and publish only through the medium of his antagonist, the newspaper itself. The citizen is thoroughly aware that the newspaper is both defendant and judge. Most important of all, the citizen is thoroughly aware that the newspaper is also a censor. There is no power the press has quite so potent as the power to leave things out. At least the citizen should have a jury to which he can appeal.

One should note that the safeguard of honest and honorable conduct is quite as open to the gentlemen of the news media as it is to the American citizen in general. If editorial comment is based, to the degree possible, on facts that can be proven true, if criticism of official conduct is limited to what seems warranted by the facts as understood, if reasonable effort is made to verify the bases on which criticism rests, and if the editorial staff bears forever in mind that it cannot compete in speed with radio and television, and so it should make up in accuracy of statement and solidity of judgment its failure to share with its competitors the speed of light, then it is unlikely that it will fall into the toils of a censorious and even a vindictive jury. On the whole all America, the press included, is better off if the politicians have a healthy respect for the power of the press and the press has a healthy respect for the power of the jury. The only way that the scales can be balanced, in the newly created case of *Free Press v. Public Official,* is for the courts to hold the press to a reasonable standard of care in determining the truth of what it prints and for the courts themselves to be guided by a reasonable interpretation of the phase "reckless disregard." In that way fair play will be insured and the operational basis of a land of checks and balances maintained.

The New York Times Rule Applied

Eight months after promulgating the New York Times Rule the Supreme Court had occasion to apply it in a case involving that legal rarity, criminal libel. District Attorney Garrison of Orleans Parish, Louisiana, was appalled at the freedom with which he saw vice flourishing in the carefree, fun city of the South, New Orleans. He traced the fault back to the urbane and sophisticated inertia of the municipal judges of the city, and not impossibly when he charged that they were unwilling to make available to his office funds that existed for the purpose of suppressing vice, he suggested something more venal than urbanity and sophistication. In any event, he was indicted and found guilty of criminal libel. He carried his case to the Supreme Court and the Louisiana verdict was reversed.

The Court faced in *Garrison v. Louisiana*[1] a perennial problem of the law and an unusual twist. The first is the problem of the double issue, one aspect extraneous in nature to the other but in the specific case inextricably interwoven with it. Whatever crime the crusading Attorney General may have been guilty of, it was certainly not the

[1] 379 U.S. 64

crime of causing a breach of the peace. It was specifically to meet this crime that the concept of criminal libel has existed through the centuries. Was he guilty, however, of something in voicing his dark suspicions about the dedicated alertness of the local bench? The Supreme Court decided that he was not, since by the New York Times Rule the states were limited in their power to apply criminal sanctions for criticism of the official conduct of men in public office.

The unusual twist to the case arose from the fact that one public official was criticizing the official actions of a group of other public officials. Furthermore, they were at the best middle echelon public officials. The *Garrison* case naturally gave rise to the question, what is meant by a public official? How far down on the occupational scale may a public official be and still be subject to the slings and arrows under the Rule? Evidently it applied to appointed as well as elected officials. Did it apply, as the Kansas Court said in its anticipation of the Rule, to all officers and agents of government, to all who administer public institutions of all sorts and dimensions, and to all who manage industry sufficiently important to make its management a matter of concern to the public? The Court was aware that this problem existed. In his decision on Commissioner Sullivan's case Justice Brennan had stated, "We have no occasion here to determine how far down into the lower ranks of government employees the 'public official' designation would extend for purposes of this rule, or otherwise to specify categories of persons who would or would not be included." The *Garrison* case made it clear that at least it extended down to municipal judges.

At the risk of an invidious distinction among the echelons of the public employ, one may say that the 1966 case of *Rosenblatt v. Baer*[1] carried it down a notch or two lower. The Laconia, New Hampshire, *Evening Citizen* made allegations about the misdirection of public funds which the supervisor of a recreation area thought directed at him. A New Hampshire jury thought so too, and in the resulting libel suit awarded the supervisor $31,500 damages. The Supreme Court overturned the decision, ruling "Where a position in government has such apparent importance that the public has an independent interest in the qualifications and performance of the person who holds it, beyond the general public interest in the qualifications and performance of all government employees . . . the New York Times . . .

---

[1] 383 U.S. 75

standards apply." It cemented this viewpoint more solidly in *Henry v. Collins*[1] in which it applied the Rule to chiefs of police and county prosecutors.

If the local chief of police is a public figure sufficiently important for the public to have an independent interest in his qualifications and performance, what about the president of a massive industrial organization, the television commentator who commands a national audience, or for that matter a public figure whose official capacity belongs to the past, such as a former President of the United States? Are they covered by the Rule? What about a churchman of great dignity and prominence, or the professor at a university of national prestige with a flair for transmuting institutional prestige into personal prestige? Or what about some folk hero of the American people, a great professional athlete for example, an actor or better still an actress who walks the land like a goddess, or the sort of genius for the contemporary who can ride to the skies some such cause as ecology or women's lib? One might call this herring red and say that the Rule was clearly designed to give the privilege only to the criticism of officials in the public employ in the performance of their official duties. The herring is not red. The principle enunciated in a Kansas court in 1908, that criticism of anyone important enough is privileged whether he is in the public employ or not, has come to life again in the years since the Rule was promulgated.

It came to life in Alaska in 1966 and by one of the twists that can give life its ironic delights the victim of the rule was a newspaperman. The Fairbanks *Daily News-Miner* called the late Drew Pearson "the garbage man of the fourth estate." Mr. Pearson, a recognized authority on epithets, took umbrage at this one and sued for libel. The important point is not his failure to collect but the grounds on which he was denied collection. The Alaska Superior Court ruled that "Drew Pearson, a public figure and internationally known newspaper and radio columnist of no mean proportions, should occupy the same standing in the law of libel as Senator Gruening whose cause he was publicly supporting. . . ." This was obviously an extension of the New York Times Rule and, in principle at least, an application of the Kansas doctrine which extended privileged criticism "to the conduct of all corporate enterprises affected with a public interest." Newspaper columns and radio programs are such.

[1] 380 U.S. 356

In two cases heard in 1967 the United States Supreme Court extended the Rule to include the Kansas doctine. The first involved the actions of General Edwin A. Walker (U.S. Army, ret.) during a disturbance at the University of Mississippi. An attempt was being made to enroll a black student and the attempt was meeting with resistance. The Associated Press reporter on the scene filed a dispatch in which he stated that General Walker commanded the crowd, led the charge against the Federal marshals, encouraged the rioters to use violence, and gave them professional advice on how to combat the effects of tear gas. The general sued for libel, the case reached the Supreme Court, and the general lost the half million dollars awarded him by a Texas court. The Supreme Court decision was unanimous.

The second case involved the actions of Wallace Butts, athletic director of the University of Georgia. A crossed telephone line permitted a listener to overhear a conversation between Butts and Alabama football coach Paul Bryant. The conversation was quite technical in nature, evidently concerned the playing patterns of the Georgia team, and was interpreted as a conspiracy by the two sports figures to fix the forthcoming football game between the two state universities. It goes without saying that epochs are made every time Georgia plays Alabama, and that anyone closely related to athletic titans of their dimensions is automatically a public figure. The listener thought so, and so did the Curtis Publishing Company to whom he told his lurid tale. It duly appeared in the *Saturday Evening Post*. Butts sued for libel and was awarded $460,000. The case ultimately reached Washington and the verdict was upheld by a five to four decision of the Supreme Court.

The Butts case has a legal importance that transcends even the importance of a football game between Georgia and Alabama. Four opinions were filed by the Supreme Court justices. On one point the nine justices were in agreement: constitutional safeguards against libel suits extend beyond public officials to public figures. At this point agreement ended. Chief Justice Warren and Justices Brennan, White, Black, and Douglas held that the New York Times Rule should apply exactly to public figures. Justice Harlan wrote an opinion in which Justices Clark, Stewart, and Fortas concurred which would allow damages "on a showing of highly unreasonable conduct constituting an extreme departure from the standards of investigation and reporting ordinarily adhered to by responsible

publishers." They found the Curtis Publishing Company guilty of
such highly unreasonable conduct in publishing an accusation based
on an accidentally overheard telephone conversation without view-
ing the notes taken of the conversation, without interviewing another man present when the conversation was overheard, without
checking films of the game to see if suspicious deviations from
anticipated play occurred, and by assigning the writing of the story
to a man who was not a football expert.

The case was one of unimaginable tightness for Wallace Butts.
Two justices, Black and Douglas, reiterated their often expressed
view that all libel suits violate freedom of the press guarantees and
hence that all defamation suits are without constitutional basis.
Justices Brennan and White adhered strictly to the New York Times
Rule. It was only the fact that Chief Justice Warren agreed with the
conclusions of Justice Harlan and his three associates without accepting their process of reasoning that saved the reputation of
Wallace Butts. He agreed that "slipshod and sketchy investigatory
techniques employed to check the veracity of the source and the
inferences to be drawn" did comprise unreasonable conduct on the
part of the publisher. His conclusion is one that appeals in so simple
and direct a fashion to the average person as to gloss over its
implications where the thinking of some justices is concerned:
"Freedom of the press under the First Amendment does not include
absolute license to destroy lives or careers." But it does, if one
believes that all libel suits are unconstitutional.

It seems impossible to escape the conviction voiced by Justice
Black, a believer in the unconstitutional nature of all libel suits, that
the Supreme Court listened to the Walker and Butts cases not as a
Court but as a jury, and based its verdicts on the facts. But the
Supreme Court does not exist to be a jury of the last resort. Its
responsibility is the interpretation and application of the law, not the
determination of the facts. And yet, if it chooses to hear cases under
the New York Times Rule with its proviso for libel suits that are
tenable only if malice is shown or a reckless disregard for truth, it is
difficult to see what else the Supreme Court can be except a jury of
the last resort. When all is said and done, the Supreme Court really
ruled in *Walker* that the Associated Press had not acted with a
reckless disregard of truth and that in *Butts* the Curtis Publishing
Company had. But this is a decision based on facts.

In extending the Rule in *Walker* and *Butts* to those who play prominent roles in what, by the broadest extension of the term, may be called public affairs the Supreme Court gave rise to two thought-provoking questions. Is it the intent of the Constitution that persons prominent for reasons other than public service should have only the most meager protection against libel of their conduct and morals? If such is not the intent of the Constitution, does not the New York Times Rule deny to the prominent the due process of the law? It twists the nature of the occupation out of all semblance to the normal meaning of the term to make the athletic director of a state university a public official, and it is utterly impossible to differentiate between a criticism of such a person's official conduct and a libel on his morals when the charge is that he conspired to fix a football game. It simply outrages the American sense of fair play to say that a man in the position of Mr. Butts should be denied all but the barest protection of the law when his morals are libeled, merely because his position is one in the public eye.

In these two cases the justices were in unanimous agreement that the Rule should apply to all persons sufficiently bathed by the public limelight. Five justices held that the Rule should apply in exactly the same way to public officials in the strict sense and to public personages. Four justices would allow damages to the latter "on a showing of highly unreasonable conduct constituting an extreme departure from the standards of investigation and reporting ordinarily adhered to by responsible publishers," evidently a modest toning down of the "reckless disregard of whether it was false or not" phraseology of the Rule. Chief Justice Warren held that the distinction between public officials and public figures and "adoption of separate standards of proof for each has no basis in law, logic, or First Amendment policy." Justice Black went his usual absolutist way: "I think it is time for this Court to abandon *New York Times v. Sullivan* and adopt the rule to the effect that the First Amendment was intended to leave the press free from the harassment of libel judgments."

There is some merit at this point in stating precisely what the First Amendment says about the press. The statement is simple and direct: "Congress shall make no law . . . abridging the freedom of speech, or of the press. . . ." The omitted words concern the prohibition of an establishment of religion and the guarantee of the rights of assembly and petition. In recognizing malice as grounds for legal action when a public official or public personage is libeled, the Supreme Court certainly did nothing to abridge press freedom. No one's freedom is abridged when he acts with the knowledge that he must face the consequences of his action, unless one wants to pervert the meaning of freedom into uncontrolled license to do wrong. But to maintain that "... the First Amendment was intended to leave the press free from the harassment of libel judgments" is in effect to maintain that the Founding Fathers intended to put journalism, the only occupation that has a constitutional guarantee of its freedom, entirely above the law. There is nothing in American history, any more than there is in logic and justice, on which to base that reading of the nation's ancestral mind. There is also the Fourteenth Amendment to consider: "No state shall make or enforce any law which shall abridge the privileges or immunities of citizens of the United States; nor shall any state deprive any person of life, liberty or property without due process of law; nor deny to any person within its jurisdiction the equal protection of the laws." It would certainly be denying the equal protection of the laws to hold that the average citizen could be sued for libel but the town newspaper could not, or that the average citizen could collect when libeled but the public official or the celebrated personality could not. The Constitution cannot be unconstitutional.

The point is essentially a simple one. A national magazine of massive circulation runs a feature article the gist of which is that the athletic director of a state university conspired with the coach of an athletic rival to fix a football game. Every court up to the Supreme Court found that Mr. Butts had been libeled by that story. Precisely what redress could Mr. Butts have had if the press had an absolute protection against libel suits? The newspapers of Georgia and Alabama might well carry his denial of the charge, and for that matter so might the national press associations, but a denial is not a vindication. The only way that a vindication can be obtained is by a fair, honest, open trial in a public courtroom, in which an impartial jury hears the case and decides its merits.

There is never much difficulty in obtaining information about the ways in which the law denies equal treatment to the poor and underprivileged. Political careers are made out of that theme. The most important single development the twentieth century has seen in libel law has nothing whatever to do with the poor and underprivileged, and everything to do with the wealthy and privileged, or at least those privileged enough to hold some political office from chief of police up to President of the United States. Whatever other outrages the poor and underprivileged may suffer, they are seldom if ever libeled as individuals in the public press. It is the public official and the public personage who must face that risk.

It must always be borne in mind that the press includes every unit that carries what purports to be news. It includes the small town weekly, the paper published in the county seat, the paper that serves a suburban area, the "throw away paper" that seasons the advertisements with local news and is distributed without charge, and the small city paper as well as the metropolitan daily. It includes magazines of every sort and size of circulation, and they sound every note on the gamut from the most austerely learned to the most basely scurrilous. Can it be seriously argued that the small-town newspaper should be free to print whatever it chooses about the public conduct of the local selectman and he be denied any right to legal vindication? There are frogs of all sorts and sizes, and there are ponds of all sorts and sizes, and one may be a public personage in terms of Grover's Corners quite as truly as in terms of New York City. One might add that there can be blackmail in Grover's Corners also, and blackmail flourishes most luxuriantly where blackmail cannot be effectively checked.

The important thing is not to get a verdict in *Free Press v. American Citizen*. The important thing is not to let grounds for the case exist. Once the American public becomes convinced that any institution has been placed above the law, or has clambered to a position above it, that gyroscopic quality in the American spirit that we call fair play begins to work. Things will be leveled off. The New Times Rule is strong medicine and dangerous. All one has to do is picture the frame of mind of one in the position of Mr. Butts, of a man accused from coast to coast by a national publication of the sort of despicable act of which no court ever found him guilty, who would be denied access to a court and therefore, however free he might be to voice his denial of the charge and however widespread his denial might be broadcast would be denied the only true vindication open to an American citizen, vindication in an open trial. Other American citizens would have no difficulty picturing his frame of mind, and conjuring up the same frame of mind themselves. No moral adjuration should be taken more to heart by all units of the news media than the adjuration not to lean too heavily on the New York Times Rule. There are other rights besides the rights of a free press, and one of the most precious is the right of the citizen to his good name. Coupled with it is his right to the equal protection of the laws and access to their due process.

Once more we see illustrated the fundamental thought: if any right of the Bill of Rights is treated as a legal absolute, sooner or later it comes into direct collision with another right. The twentieth-century destruction of the seditious-libel concept is now completed, but from the ashes of that concept has arisen a counter-concept equally dangerous, the concept that the press can libel with legal immunity anyone prominent enough or anyone with standing in the public employ. Politicians are also American citizens, and so are public personages such as business executives, athletic idols, actors and actresses, and those human meteors who flash across the national sky for a variety of transient reasons too numerous and varied to reckon. The wisest course is to protect their rights also, and the course is wisest for the press as well as for the nation at large. Only when the rights of the prominent and powerful are observed are the rights of the poor and underprivileged safe. The unusual form of the statement is just as true as its customary reverse: only when the rights of the poor and underprivileged are observed are the rights of the prominent and powerful safe. The rights of different groups face different dangers, but none are really safe unless all are safe. This brings us naturally to the other important twentieth-century development of libel law, the concept of group libel.

Group Libel

There is no aspect of libel law that poses more problems calculated to make Solomon gray than group libel. There is no difficulty in framing the questions. What is a group? How large can a group be and still be capable of suffering actionable libel? Must every member of a group suffer before the group is libeled? Must the group suffer a financial loss before it can recover for libel? If the loss is other than financial, how is it to be measured? The problem is to find solutions, and no small part of the problem is that no solution will stay found very long.

Let us start with the last aspect first. At the moment of writing black Americans feel an acute sensitivity to libel and one should expect to find a positive and sympathetic reaction to that sensitivity on the part of courts and juries. Yet during most of the history of this country there was no group that could be libeled with greater safety, and indeed was libeled with greater frequency and immunity, than black America. There has always been a strong Jewish sensitivity to libel, a sensitivity that grows more acute and then abates as anti-Semitism rises and falls as a public aberration. Anti-Catholicism has had much the same history. It should go without saying that there is never reason for libeling a racial or religious group but group libel does exist. It is the group that is libeled and the concept of what constitutes group libel that keeps changing.

It is currently the fashion to think of groups in terms of race or religion. It was not always the fashion, and indeed the group that has been most frequently the plaintiff or defendant in a group libel action has been the corporation. Corporations have business reputations that can sustain injury from libel and a loss in reputation is directly translated into a loss in pocketbook. A corporation, to be sure, does not have a character in the personal sense but it does have a property right implicit in its credit rating. While the matter is deeply conccaled in the maze of corporate law, a maze from which we are blessedly delivered by our subject, the general tendency of the courts would appear to be to admit libel suits by corporations based on the contention that financial loss has resulted from libel but not to accept them if their officers have been libeled as individuals. Historically the officers have had the right to sue for libel as individuals. Whether they still retain that right if the corporations are large enough depends on the still unplumbed implications of the New York Times Rule.

There is another unsolved problem implicit in the Rule where group libel is concerned. What about the non-profit institution, perhaps the charitable institution, the institution of learning, the religious congregation viewed not as a religion but as a congregation, that is libeled? Being non-profit, it suffers no diminution of profit. Being a group, it has no personal reputation. The long established principle is clear enough, as established in a New York and later a Massachusetts case. The New York *Evening Graphic* once made a most unexpected and quite deplorable turning of the tables by accusing the New York Society for Suppression of Vice of highly irregular and even criminal acts. The newspaper defense might well give pause to those who believe that the press should have absolute freedom. It was based on the thesis that a non-profit organization could not sue for libel because a corporation could base a libel suit only on the grounds of pecuniary loss. The essence of the newspaper argument was crystal clear: you can print anything you want if you can't be sued. The Court thought otherwise, ruling that charitable and religious organizations do have property rights. "Their usefulness depends largely upon their reputation for honesty, fair dealing and altruistic effort to improve social conditions. The respondent depends entirely upon voluntary contributions for its support. The number and amount of such contributions would necessarily be affected by the publication of false and malicious articles to the effect that it engaged in illegal and reprehensible conduct in the management of its affairs."[1]

It is noteworthy that the New York Court did find fiscal grounds for sustaining a libel finding against the *Evening Graphic*. The Massachusetts Court, in *Finnish Temperance Society v. Socialistic Publishing Company*[2] went farther and found them unnecessary. It recognized that if a benevolent, charitable, or religious corporation had to prove special damages to support a libel action, it might "easily become the prey of the libeller, who remains immune, because not being connected with mercantile transactions or monetary profit, or gain, or loss of any sort, it cannot be injured." The Finnish Temperance Society was certainly not designed to make money and it certainly did not do so. But injury can be suffered, in the view of the Massachusetts Court, to nerves other than the fiscal.

If not in any sense a money making concern, the plaintiff, a citizen of this commonwealth, is promoting an enterprise, or engaged in an occupation recognized, fostered, and protected by our laws. And unless the present action can be maintained, the wrong practiced upon it, and the injury sustained, cannot be redressed; it is remediless. We are accordingly of the opinion, that the plaintiff even if insensible to mental suffering and distress as ordinarily understood, is entitled to general damages, the amount of which assessed by the judge is not as a matter of law shown to be erroneous.

Both cases have an historic importance in the law because they paved the way for an acceptance of the principle that there can be grounds for the sustaining of actions for group libel other than fiscal loss. The really important contemporary, or nearly contemporary,

---

[1] *New York Society for the Suppression of Vice v. McFadden Publications, Inc.*, 260 N.Y. 167.
[2] 238 Mass. 345.

developments in the area of group libel are pointed toward by the *Society for the Suppression of Vice* and the *Finnish Temperance Society* cases.

Having said this, one must add that it is impossible to classify and codify the actions that have taken place in the area of group libel so as to present a consistent picture. There have been cases bearing the superficial earmarks of group libel cases that were nothing of the sort. An obvious example is the very important case treated under the head of Prior Restraint, the 1931 case of *Near v. Minnesota*. The case was occasioned by the publication of a scurrilous anti-Semitic sheet but the point at issue in the case was the right of the state to rid itself of a nuisance of this sort by prior restraint. There have been cases in which group libel actions have been sustained on grounds at least analogous to those of criminal libel and sometimes identical with it. For example, in the case of *People v. Eastman*,[1] a case which arose from the publication of a pamphlet almost uniquely enriched by that sort of lurid eloquence in which anti-Catholicism meets and matches the best that anti-Semitism can afford, the Court held that a civil action for libel could not be sustained but a criminal action could. The Court stated, "The foundation of the theory on which libel is made a crime is that by provoking passions of persons libeled, it excites them to violence and a breach of the peace. Therefore, a criminal prosecution can be sustained where no civil action would lie, as for instance in this very case, where the libel is against a class. . . ." Massachusetts wrote this principle into law: "Whoever publishes any false written or printed material with intent to maliciously promote hatred of any group of persons in the commonwealth because of race, color or religion shall be guilty of libel and shall be punished by a fine of not more than one thousand dollars or by imprisonment for not more than one year, or both." Specific limitations were written into the law. The defendant was permitted the twin defenses of privileged publication and non-malicious intent. Furthermore, only the attorney general or the district attorney for the area in which the alleged libel was published could enter an action, not the group which considered itself libeled.

There has been, then, some revival of the ancient concept of criminal libel under the guise of group libel. There has not been sufficient revival, however, to indicate anything resembling a definite

[1] 188 N.Y. 480

trend. The same state of New York which accepted the thesis that group libel can be prosecuted on the grounds historically reserved for criminal libel reversed the *Eastman* finding in the case of *People v. Edmundston,*[1] in which the Jewish people were the butt of the usual treatment accorded by those who hate them. What trend there has been is a by-product of the civil rights movement.

The Massachusetts statute punishes group libel in and of itself, without regard for its effects, if the libel is based on religious or racial obloquy. Illinois adopted a similar statute and under it arose the often cited case of *Beauharnais v. Illinois.* Illinois had a statute forbidding the distribution of printed material which traced lack of virtue in groups to their race, color, or religion, thereby exposing them to contempt and giving rise to the danger of violence and disorder. One Beauharnais, analyzing the shortcomings of the blacks of Chicago, in terms of "encroachment, harassments, and invasion of white people" and denouncing their "rapes, robberies, knives, guns, and marijuana" fell afoul of this law. His case came to the United States Supreme Court in 1952 and the Court upheld the Illinois statute.

Justice Frankfurter wrote the Court decision. He pointed out that every state has laws punishing the libel of individuals. He added that there are types of epithet for which no constitutional protection has ever been claimed: "Resort to epithets and personal abuse is not in any proper sense communication of information or opinion safeguarded by the Constitution, and its punishment as a criminal act would raise no question under that instrument." Such were the epithets involved in this case, and the Court extended the libel principle as applied to individuals as applicable to groups. After establishing that the Fourteenth Amendment does not prevent states from punishing such libels, Justice Frankfurter proceeded to establish a link between personal and group libel: "But if an utterance directed at an individual may be the object of criminal sanctions, we cannot deny to a State power to punish the same utterance directed at a defined group, unless we can say that this is a wilful and purposeless restriction unrelated to the peace and well-being of the State." He then pointed out that Illinois had a rich experience with race riots and maintained for the Court that the state had a right to take measures appropriate to prevent the fanning of such disorders

[1] 168 N.Y. Misc. 141.

by the publication of racist attacks. Naturally the Court was quite aware that the "clear and present danger" test might well be called for in such matters, and in his conclusion he contended that just as the clear-and-present-danger test does not apply to obscene publications, neither should it apply to group libel.

The *Beauharnais* case represents the high-water mark in American jurisprudence where group libel grounded on racial or religious bigotry is concerned. There have been other group libel cases in which injury without racial or religious overtones was charged to aspects of the human psyche other than the instinct for enrichment. For example, there was *Fowler v. Curtis Publishing Company*.[1] A cab driver of Washington, D.C., took umbrage at the way he and his fellows had been handled in a magazine article, and in the name of his fifty-nine associates and himself brought suit against the publisher. He lost. The court held,

> . . . in case of a defamatory publication directed against a class, without in any way identifying any specific individual, no individual member of the group has any redress. The reason for this rule is that ordinarily a defamatory statement relating to a group as a whole does not necessarily apply to every single member. A minority not intended to be castigated has no legal cause for complaint. The only exception involves cases in which the phraseology of a defamatory publication directed at a small group is such as to apply to every member of the class without exception.

Group libel of the latter sort has been sustained as grounds for successful action. An example came in 1958 when *True Magazine* had to pay for the privilege of attributing the 1956 national football championship won by the University of Oklahoma team to an inspiration derived from drugs rather than to the native derring-do of the Sooners.

The concept of group libel is a tenuous one at the best, for the reason stated in the *Fowler* case. Its original and indeed its abiding usefulness is to be found in the field of corporation law, since the libel of a corporation can work a grave financial injury upon the object of attack. This truth is more important today than ever, with our contemporary preoccupation with ecology, food purity, and the

[1] 78 F. Supp. 303.

like. The corporation is fully entitled to the protection of the libel law, but the protection of the libel law is powerless against the impact of the truth. If a corporation does offend against the public safety and welfare, it is a public service to point out the fact in print and a service that can be performed with total legal safety. *Consumer Reports* performs it all the time.

The usefulness of the group libel concept elsewhere is dubious at the best. The libel of a race or a religion falls of its own weight, and is invariably the work of a crank whose scurrilous little sheet would pass unnoticed if the legal spotlight did not illuminate its distorted darkness. If such a publication actually poses a clear and present danger of public disorder, there are ample laws on the books with which to handle the situation. The sort of legislation under which *Beauharnais* arose was well intentioned, but it is not without significance that the law itself was repealed a few years later.

It is a mathematical principle that the larger the group libeled, the more diluted the libel itself. As the *Fowler* decision indicated, when a libel is subdivided among fifty-nine cab drivers, it is diluted out of existence. The libel of the Oklahoma football team presents an example of group libel that could be sustained as applicable to all the members of the group without implying any fiscal injury to them, but examples of that sort are excessively hard to find.

On the other hand, the sort of libel directed at a group sufficiently small to be sustained as an actionable matter usually can be resolved into a set of individual libels. Philip Wittenberg[1] cites a good example in *De Hoyos v. Thornton*.[2] The village of Monticello, New York, had a mayor for its 4000 inhabitants, and three village trustees. A local resident opined in the public press that the acquisition of property for a community hall was another example of taxpayer bloodletting which would end only when men of brains and sense ran the village and not persons "dictated to by gansters or Chambers of Commerce." One court found the article non-libelous since it did not identify the mayor and trustees, but a higher court disagreed. It held that it would not have been libelous to say that the only four persons who could possibly be the objects of attack were extravagant and injudicious in their use of public funds. It went farther, and held that it was not libelous to say that they were influenced by Cham-

[1] *Dangerous Words*, New York: Columbia University Press, 1947; p. 228.
[2] 259 N.Y. App. Div. 1.

bers of Commerce. But *gangsters* was another matter. Compensatory damages followed as a matter of course. Technically the action in *De Hoyos* was one of group libel, but it was group libel only because the group was so small that each individual in it was clearly identified and personally libeled.

The application of the principle to the libel of a corporation is clear enough. If it is the action of the corporation as a corporation that is libeled, and if the libel works fiscal injury, an action for group libel that seeks compensatory damages is most certainly justified and the legal machinery that operates in such a case should be kept in good working order. On the other hand, if it is the directors or other officers of the corporation who are libeled, even as a group, the libel usually can be resolved into a set of individual libels and handled accordingly. Elsewhere the reasonable basis for actions involving group libel is extremely difficult to establish. Either the group libeled is sufficiently small to resolve the group libel into a set of individual libels, as in the case of the town fathers of Monticello, or it is sufficiently large for the diluted libel to drift off into thin air, as in the case of the cab drivers of Washington.

LIBEL IS A FACT

There are two statements from the Supreme Court bench which America would do well to ponder. One was the statement made by Justice Goldberg in his concurring opinion in the New York Time Rule case: "In my view, the First and Fourteenth Amendmeents to the Constitution afford to the citizen and to the press an absolute, unconditional privilege to criticize official conduct despite the harm which may flow from excesses and abuses." The second is the statement made by Justice Black in connection with the decisions in the *Walker* and *Butts* cases: "I think it is time for this Court to abandon *New York Times v. Sullivan* and adopt the rule to the effect that the First Amendment was intended to leave the press free from the harassment of libel judgments."

We have here two degrees of absolutism voiced by members of the highest tribunal in American law. There is an implicit limitation to the absolutism of Justice Goldberg. The absolute, unconditional privilege for which he pleads extends only to official conduct, by which he meant the conduct of public officials acting in their public capacity. Presumably by the "harm which may flow from excesses and abuses" he meant the harm resulting from malice and the reckless disregard of truth. In his concept there should be no check to the voice of malice and falsehood so long as it limits itself to the official acts of the public servant. Justice Goldberg's thesis is that within the limited area to which he restricted his absolutism, the truth has the best chance to be heard if every utterance is free from any danger of limitation or retaliation.

Obviously no case can be made out in morality for the equality of truth and falsehood, honest intention and malicious. Can a case that is pragmatically convincing be made out? Justice Goldberg would grant unlimited freedom of criticism to citizen and press within a limited area, on the thesis that truth would thus prevail. But what about those who work within that area? With total freedom the citizen and press might well be fearless, but what about the public official? Would he work with total dedication to the right course of action as he sees it, knowing that he is permitted no legal defense against malicious and false attack? Would the citizen whose public spirit might induce him to take a sensitive appointment in the public service take it if he knew his motives and his actions could be libeled with impunity by every blatherskite with access to a ballpoint pen? Would we get good government by opening its servants to every vicious assault perverse ingenuity and malicious envy can conjure out of the blackness of a worthless human heart? There is more than one case that can be made out of Justice Goldberg's thesis, and it is far from obvious that his is the only one.

If we find it difficult to make out a case for Justice Goldberg's thesis, no case that can stand the test of American principles can be made out for Justice Black's. In the first place, it is the function of the Supreme Court to interpret what is already in the Constitution, not to read meanings into it. If the Constitution means what the New York Times Rule holds it to mean, that is what it means until it is amended by the process which the Constitution itself provides. The Supreme Court certainly can be in error and can correct its errors, but it is the process of amendment and not the passage of time that changes the intent of the Constitution. Furthermore, it is totally against both the letter and spirit of the Constitution to abandon the principle incorporated into the Fourteenth Amendment and applied thereafter in so many aspects of American life, the principle that every American citizen has the constitutional right to the due process of the law. The Constitution provides a solemn guarantee for the freedom of the press, but freedom is not uncontrolled license. The principle that the American press is a free press responsible for what it prints is so written into the fabric of American legal history and so consonant with the basic spirit of American life that any distortion of it by a legally and historically unwarranted reading of the First Amendment could be even a perilous thing.

It is a fact, to be sure, that the libel suit can be a most troublesome plague to the press. It can be instituted for a range of reasons extending from the most thoroughly justified through the possibly warranted toward and beyond the dubiously justified to the totally groundless case and the case opened with intent to blackmail. Defense can be costly, is usually time consuming, and at the best is a nuisance. And yet, to paraphrase Justice Goldberg, the Fourteenth Amendment does afford the citizen the privilege of suing the press for libel despite the harm which may flow from excesses and abuses. If that right did not exist and the right of the free press were made an absolute, the right to one's good name would be denied in the very area in which a man's good name can be most effectively assailed.

It would be a grave mistake to imagine that the press is at the mercy of the person who files a libel action. The ancient, all-pervading principle that the defendant is innocent until proven guilty holds in libel actions quite as truly as in criminal cases. The great burden of proof rests on the plaintiff. Furthermore, a libel in and of itself is merely a published statement about an identified person which makes the reader think worse of him. The person libeled cannot collect if the libel is true or if there is a defense in libel law for the publishing of the statement. Such defenses exist in abundance. One of the best studies of this subject is *Libel*[1] by Robert H. Phelps, a veteran newspaper man, and E. Douglas Hamilton, a New York lawyer with wide experience in libel suits. The authors list eight complete defenses in libel actions against the press: the statute of limitations, the privilege of a participant, the truth, the privilege of reporting, the New York Times Rule, fair comment and criticism, consent or authorization, and self-defense or the right of reply. One might add that there are in existence some very practical handbooks of libel law to guide the unwary through the verbal thickets.

There is a quite different sort of problem present in the matter of

[1] New York: The Macmillan Company, 1966.

malice. Legal malice is a technicality: it means merely that the defendant committed the offense. Actual malice is a matter of intent and must be proved by the plaintiff. If he succeeds he may recover special damages to the extent of his financial loss through the malicious libel. Proof of the amount of loss rests on the plaintiff. If the plaintiff has suffered injury through a libel for which there is no defense, he may collect compensatory damages for the injury done his reputation, his mental and emotional pain resulting from the slight upon his honor, and in the case of a corporation the general injury done its business. Obviously there is no yardstick by which compensatory damages can be measured, and here the judgment of the jury is the deciding factor. It is important that the jury have two distinct points on which to pass judgment: was the malice of the libel deliberate and what were its injurious results?

As a result of the New York Times Rule malice toward a private citizen is one thing to establish, malice toward a public official something quite different in the establishing, although it may well be precisely the same thing in reality. Malice manifested toward a public official in upbraiding him for his official acts can be proved only if the official can prove that the offending publication knew that the charges made were false but made them anyway, or if it were reckless in its disregard for their truth or falsity. Since there were alleged false statements in the ad which led to the Rule, and since it was claimed that their falsity could be established by the news columns of *The Times* itself, obviously in the view of the Court reckless disregard of the truth goes far beyond ordinary failure to observe proper care in determining it. This point was made explicit in the *Garrison* case which was decided on the Rule. The Court stated, "The test which we laid down in *New York Times* is not keyed to ordinary care; defeasance of the privilege is conditioned, not on mere negligence, but on reckless disregard for the truth." The conclusion is inescapable. Under the New York Times Rule, a public official can successfully sue for a libel directed at his official acts only if he can prove that a deliberate and serious lie was told about them with the malicious intent to do him grave injury. The press is hardly in dire straits when it faces a libel suit by a public official. The sort of straits in which a public official finds himself when a publication hates him is a different matter.

A private citizen is in a better position than a public official where libel suits are concerned, but as always the proof of libel for which special or compensatory damages may be awarded rests squarely upon him. He may be able to prove a deliberate attempt to destroy his reputation or his means of livelihood; repetition of the printed libel and refusal to print a retraction when its falsity is demonstrated may be evidence of that. He may be able to prove that the publication was grossly negligent in seeking out the truth. Failure to seek out his side of the story may be evidence of that. There is a third type of damages, punitive damages, that may be awarded to a plaintiff who has convinced a jury that he has been the victim of actual malice. As the term indicates, they are intended as punishment and bear no relationship to the financial loss suffered by the libeled party and while they may be heart balm for the sufferer, they are intended as gall and wormwood for the culprit. Even when actual malice has been proved, the law in many states forbids the exaction of punitive damages if the publisher convicted of the libel has a change of heart and publishes a retraction.

The law of libel is one of the most ancient constructions in Western civilization. Its final roots are the final roots of law itself, the substitution of orderly and objective processes by society for the code of personal vengeance. The supreme achievement of ancient tragic literature, the *Oresteia,* has as its theme that substitution which may well be considered man's first upward stage on the Bright Angel Trail which leads from the canyon of savagery to the level of civilization. The code of personal vengeance was long adhered to, nor is it entirely abandoned yet. It is the code of gangland, where belief in capital punishment is unquestioned and gangland executions the undeviating rule. Given a veneer of civilization it became the code of the duel, with all the meticulous conventions that partially masked the law of personal vengeance out of which the duel grew. The law of libel was the orderly and objective process society contrived whereby a person's honor might be vindicated without the shedding of blood. The law of libel is a mark of civilization, one of the stages achieved by man as he civilizes himself. Ancient Rome, with its instinct for law, had libel law before it knew the Caesars. As England slowly rose above the Dark Ages it marked its growth, among other ways, by achieving a libel law. It was older still among the Salian Franks who established themselves on the Ijssel River in the Netherlands and there achieved a rude culture and with it Salic Law. By Salic Law to call a man a hare and be unable to use the defense of truth cost three shillings, to call a woman a harlot and not substantiate the charge cost forty-five shillings. This was libel law, and the fact that it cost fifteen times as much to libel the honesty of a woman as to impugn the courage of a man supports the claim that the Roman historian Tacitus made for the honor paid to chastity among the ancient Germans.

In short, libel law is one of the hallmarks of civilization and libel law as we have it in the English-speaking world is the end product of over two millennia of growth. So long as men quarrel, quarrels must be adjudicated and libel law is one of the means to that end. Entirely adequate bulwarks have been built into libel law to protect the freedom of the press, and indeed the most important twentieth-century development in American libel law, the New York Times Rule, could readily change that freedom into license where the official acts of public officials are concerned. There is a genuine danger here to the processes of good government, and it may threaten those processes all the way from Grover's Corner, where the weekly newspaper rides herd on the selectmen, to the national capital itself. There is no right that citizens have more precious than the right to their good name, "the immediate jewel of their souls." The law of libel is a mighty equalizer when that good name is threatened by a public voice to which the citizen has no means of public answer. It is one of the rights of American citizenship to be jealously guarded, just as jealously as the freedom of the press itself.

Part IV

PRIVACY

"See here!" an outraged bystander exclaimed as Henry Higgins recorded the varied indignities his subjects inflict on the King's English. "What call have you to know about people what never offered to meddle with you?" But the outrage Eliza Doolittle felt was tinged with fear. "Oh, sir, don't let him charge me. You dunno what it means to me. They'll take away my character and drive me on the streets for speaking to gentlemen." In the reaction of outrage and the reaction of fear to an unexpected and unwarranted invasion of privacy as depicted by Shaw in his *Pygmalion* may be found the total case for privacy as the human race has instinctively upheld it through the ages.

Privacy is the inalienable right of the individual to hold inviolate the fortress of self, lowering the drawbridge of communication with others when he chooses, staying secure within the moat of isolation when he desires. Privacy, like beauty, is its own excuse for being, a basic axiom of the human condition which needs no defense for its existence and towers above the need of proof for its validity. There is no possible answer to the question of the outraged bystander. What call indeed did Henry Higgins have to meddle with people that never offered to meddle with him? The claim to privacy is so native to human nature that its reason for being is implicit in the very fact of the human state itself.

Privacy, nevertheless, is invaded. It may be invaded through curiosity, either the amateur curiosity of the busybody or the professional curiosity of the news gatherer. It may be invaded by the criminal who is intent on robbery. It may be the privacy of the suspect invaded by the police intent on the apprehension of a criminal. To call the last instance an invasion of privacy should be a misnomer, and would be if certain court attitudes and decisions did not invite it. In the last analysis, the total case for legitimate privacy is contained within the viewpoints of the two characters in *Pygmalion,* or if one prefers, in *My Fair Lady.* Our real concern is with the bystander who is indignant when his privacy is invaded and with Eliza who is fearful, but we cannot entirely ignore the criminal and the policeman. We may start with the bystander, whose case finds its historic expression in an essay by Louis Brandeis and Samuel Warren.

BRANDEIS AND WARREN

Samuel D. Warren was the law partner of Louis D. Brandeis, with offices on Devonshire Street in Boston and a law practice that in 1890 was burgeoning into something very substantial. Its growth was not impeded by the social prominence of attorney Warren, who came from the top echelon of Boston society. When his daughter was married, the Boston press gave the event the sort of intimate and detailed coverage best calculated to arouse the resentment of a naturally reserved and dignified Boston family. Warren was outraged, and his partner was outraged for him. The result was a series of colloquies between the partners. The impudence of the press in its disregard for human dignity had to be curbed. What basis could be found on which a legal case for privacy might rest? The result of the colloquies was the best known essay ever written on the subject of privacy and a document with which every modern discussion of privacy concerns itself, the essay called "The Right to Privacy" which appeared in the *Harvard Law Review* on December 15, 1890.

Brandeis and Warren certainly did not invent privacy nor discover it, and in a sense they did not contrive the grounds on which it might rest in law. Rather they made explicit and logical the reason for its existence which man had intuitively perceived from the start. Previously the case for privacy had been couched in terms more poetic than legalistic. Consider Sir Edward Coke maintaining before the King's Bench in 1605 that "the house of every one is to him as his castle and fortress, as well for his defense against injury and violence as for his repose." Or Lord Chatham proclaiming with even greater eloquence in 1766, "The poorest man may, in his cottage, bid defiance to all the forces of the Crown. It may be frail; its roof may shake; the wind may blow through it; the storm may enter, but the King of England may not enter; all his forces dare not cross the threshold of the ruined tenement." Time passed and the King of England still was unable to enter, but the prying reporter could and somewhat later the wire tapper. It was the former that outraged the bystander, and the metaphorical latter whom Eliza feared.

THE ROYAL ETCHINGS

Before considering the Brandeis-Warren article, we have some ground to clear. It is fundamental that privacy is not identical with either secrecy or autonomy. Privacy is the withdrawal of oneself from the view of others, secrecy the concealment of something from the knowledge of others, autonomy the governance of oneself without interference by others. One may seek privacy to keep inviolate one's private affairs, to avoid undesired publicity, to shun the misrepresentation of one's beliefs or attitudes, to protect one's name and position from exploitation, and no doubt for other reasons as well. But one's right to do these things has its own limitations. It is limited by the legitimate public interest in one's activities when they affect the public interest in either a constructive or destructive sense. The bystander has no overriding right to his privacy if he is a public figure whose thoughts, words, and actions do have an influence on the public weal, and the felon has no right to privacy as he concocts his felonious plans.

Of what, then, does this right to privacy consist, if there is such a right, and where are the boundary lines of privacy to be drawn in the case of the public personage whose activities affect the public welfare in a constructive sense? Brandeis and Warren found a clue in the most unexpected place, Windsor Castle. Queen Victoria and Prince Albert had their modest pretensions to artistic gifts, and they had done some etchings. They had done them for their own enjoyment, and they wished to share their innocent pleasure with some intimate friends. They gave them to an engraver and from his hands they fell into the hands of a man named Strange, who knew a very good thing when he saw it. He issued a catalogue, in which the etchings were praised in terms that might lead one to think that her Majesty and the royal consort were pseudonyms for Rembrandt van Rijn, and undertook to offer them for sale. There followed the case of *Prince Albert v. Strange*[1] in which the entrepreneur was soundly routed. Vice Chancellor Knight Bruce based his decision partly on the obvious grounds of property rights but also on grounds more philosophic, the right to privacy even in that English home to which privacy was most foreign. He called the intended publication "an intrusion not alone in breach of conventional rules, but offensive to that inbred sense of propriety natural to every man—if intrusion, indeed, fitly describes a sordid spying into the privacy of domestic life—into the home (a word hitherto sacred among us), the home of a family whose life and conduct form an acknowledged title, though

[1] 2 De Gex & Sm. 652 (1849)

not their only unquestionable title, to the most marked respect in this country." Thus it was established that if the King of England could not violate the cottage of the common Englishman, neither could the common Englishman violate the royal residence. There is privacy even in palaces, and not all royal acts belong to the public domain. That and not the more obvious and more easily defensible right to private property was the real foundation of the verdict.

GODKIN ON PROPERTY

Brandeis and Warren were not the first Americans to become disturbed at the arrogant bad manners of the fin de siècle yellow press. Some months before the appearance of the Brandeis-Warren article E. L. Godkin, editor of the New York *Post* and a civic reformer of distinction, published an article in *Scribner's Magazine* entitled "The Rights of the Citizen—IV. To His Reputation"[1]. He advanced the thesis that the traditional respect accorded to a man's home was symbolic of the implicit human right to privacy, "the outward and visible sign of the law's respect for his personality as an individual, for that kingdom of the mind, that inner world of personal thought and feeling in which every man passes some time, and in which every man who is worth much to himself or others, passes a great deal of time." Godkin had in mind the invasion of the privacy of law abiding citizens, an invasion prompted by curiosity and nothing more. But curiosity was a motivation sufficiently strong to produce a market for its satisfaction, and in that market sensation-seeking newspapers were thriving. This was a fact, he deplored it, and felt powerless in the face of it. If the invasion of privacy resulted in libel, there were laws to cover the situation, but the libel law was no protection of privacy itself. Godkin questioned the likelihood of a jury awarding special damages to one whose privacy had been invaded unless libel resulted, and he thought that the only protection the public had was the generation of a public opposition to invasion of personal privacy by the press. He had no confidence that such an opposition could be created. People were too curious.

[1] *Scribner's Magazine*, VIII (1890), 58 ff.

"THE RIGHT TO PRIVACY"

In a way the Brandeis-Warren article was an attempt to supply the legal protection for privacy of which Godkin despaired. It started with the truism that law exists to protect person and property. Initially it protected property in the literal, physical sense. But the concept of property was deepened and refined with the passing of time. It came to be accepted that people have property rights in their good names and reputations, and hence arose the law of libel. By the law of libel mental and emotional protection was added to physical protection. But technology was posing new threats and new needs. The authors stated, "Instantaneous photographs and newspaper enterprise have invaded the sacred precincts of private and domestic life; and numerous mechanical devices threaten to make good the prediction that 'what is whispered in the closet shall be proclaimed from the housetops.' "[1] By 1890 the instantaneous photograph, or "snapshot," had largely replaced the posed photograph which alone had been technically possible some years before. It was proving itself a most useful tool for yellow journalism.

As technology advanced, the human spirit perforce retreated. "The intensity and complexity of life, attendant upon advancing civilization, have rendered necessary some retreat from the world, and man, under the refining influence of culture, has become more sensitive to publicity, so that solitude and privacy have become more essential to the individual; but modern enterprise and invention have, through invasions upon his privacy, subjected him to mental pain and distress, far greater than could be inflicted by mere bodily injury."[2] The purpose of the essay was to determine if a principle could be found in law that would protect people like the Warrens from the indignities imposed upon them by the journalistic Paul Prys of Boston when their daughter was married.

There was really nothing in the libel law on which they could lean. The laws against defamation concern the injury done to a person's reputation and deal with his material well being, as the very term *damages* attests. They found a better precedent for the principle they sought in common law copyright which protects artistic productions prior to publication. The analogy was far from perfect, since such productions have material value, but as the authors said,

---

[1] Adam Carlyle Breckenridge, *The Right to Privacy,* University of Nebraska Press, 1970, p. 134. "The Right to Privacy" by Brandeis and Warren is printed as an Appendix to this volume.
[2] *Ibid.,* p. 135.

"where the value of the production is found not in the right to take the profits arising from publication, but in the peace of mind or the relief afforded by the ability to prevent any publication at all, it is difficult to regard the right as one of property, in the common acceptance of that term."[1]

THE ROYAL PRECEDENT

This was the consideration which made the case of the royal British etchings a useful precedent. The royal family certainly did not wish to bar their publication because it feared financial loss. Its case was based on common law copyright as a legal principle, but its motive was the protection of that privacy in which the royal family had indulged its artistic enterprise. The British Court recognized this fact, and Vice Chancellor Bruce made a recognition of it the most telling part of the decision. Brandeis and Warren considered this as they did other and hypothetical applications of the privacy motivation possible in common law copyright. Their conclusion followed: "These considerations lead to the conclusion that the protection afforded to thoughts, sentiments, and emotions, expressed through the medium of writing or of the arts, so far as it consists in preventing publication, is merely an instance of the enforcement of the more general right of the individual to be let alone. It is like the right not to be assaulted or beaten, the right not to be imprisoned, the right not to be maliciously prosecuted, the right not to be defamed. In each of these rights, as indeed in all other rights recognized by the law, there inheres the quality of being owned or possessed—and (as that is the distinguishing attribute of property) there may be some propriety in speaking of those rights as property. But, obviously, they bear little resemblance to what is ordinarily comprehended under that term. The principle which protects personal writings and all other personal productions, not against theft and physical appropriation but against publication in any form, is in reality not the principle of private property, but that of an inviolate personality."[2]

Thus what is being protected is not the piece of writing or the piece of art work that the creator does not want published, but the

[1] p. 138
[2] p. 141.

thoughts, emotions, sensations that underlie it. It is the inviolate personality that is protected, and this can manifest itself in a myriad of ways quite unconnected with artistic creativity. "The principle which protects personal writings and any other productions of the intellect or of the emotions, is the right to privacy and the law has no new principle to formulate when it extends this protection to the personal appearance, sayings, acts, and to personal relations, domestic or otherwise. If the invasion of privacy constitutes a legal *injuria*, the elements for demanding redress exist, since already the value of mental sufferings, caused by an act wrongful in itself, is recognized as a basis for compensation."[1]

LEGITIMATE NEWS AND ILLEGITIMATE

At this point the authors reach the obvious parting of the ways between legitimate news gathering and invasion of privacy in the name of curiosity and sensation. Obviously the right of the public to knowledge about what concerns the public interest is paramount to any desire for personal privacy by those legitimately in the public eye. The authors had no desire to make a transcontinental Star Chamber out of American life, and they recognized that one cannot be a luminary and escape the light shed by one's position and achievements. "The general object in view is to protect the privacy of private life, and to whatever degree and in whatever connection a man's life has ceased to be private, before the publication under consideration has been made, to that extent the protection is to be withdrawn. Since, then, the propriety of publishing the very same facts may depend wholly upon the person concerning whom they are published, no fixed formula can be used to prohibit obnoxious publications."[2]

Their proposed legal remedy was simple and the same in all cases, an action of tort for damages. Substantial compensation is allowed for injury to feelings in cases of libel. The precedent could be useful for cases of unwarranted invasion of privacy. The protection of society is achieved only through the protection of the individual. "The common law has always recognized a man's house as his castle, impregnable, often, even to its own officers engaged in the execution

of its commands. Shall the courts thus close the front entrance to
constituted authority, and open wide the back door to idle or prurient curiosity?"[1]

Law Has a New Principle

Brandeis and Warren attempted in this essay to do one of the most
difficult and unusual of legal feats, to establish a new principle on
which to erect a legal structure previously without existence. It had
an existence as one of the unreasoned axioms on which human life is
conducted. It had been couched in terms of metaphor and poetry: a
man's house is his castle; the storm may enter, but the King of
England may not enter. It had not been translated into law, in either
the United States or any other Western nation, and by the very
nature of the situation the precedents on which a law of privacy
might be based had to be partial, inferential, and indeed inadequate.
Such a law would have a superficial resemblance to the law of libel,
but when it came to laying a solid foundation for a law of privacy
the resemblance would do more harm than good. Brandeis and
Warren hit upon a better precedent in the common law of copyright, and the interpretation of that sort of copyright in the case of
the royal etchings came as close as anything they could find to give
them a solid foundation on which to build. Even there the precedent
was only partial, since common law copyright commonly concerns
artistic productions and the etchings were such. The nub of the
matter was the transferral of protection from artistic productions
created solely for personal satisfaction to other manifestations of the
human personality: "personal appearance, sayings, acts, and . . .
personal relations, domestic or otherwise," to employ their formulation. It is never easy to hew a path through the wilderness, but it is
trebly difficult when no path has been deemed possible, and even no
wilderness is believed to exist. Brandeis and Warren did it about as
well as it could be done, and the twentieth-century development of
the concept of privacy as it concerns law-abiding citizens has been
largely a series of formulations based upon their reasoning. One
point cannot be emphasized too strongly: the Brandeis-Warren formulation had nothing whatever to do with the matter of privacy
invasion where illegal acts are suspected. The history of that development is a totally different matter, and only incidentally of concern

[1] p. 152

to us. There is a whole library available upon it, with Alan F. Westin's *Privacy and Freedom*[1] probably its most useful volume. Our concern is the innocent bystander whose verbal aberrations are meticulously recorded by the Paul Pry philologist Henry Higgins, whose own predilection for privacy is as pronounced as that of anyone in imaginative literature. We want to know what the bystander wanted to know: "What call have you to know about people what never offered to meddle with you?"

"FLOUR OF THE FAMILY"

The Brandeis-Warren thesis for some time remained simply incredible to the legal profession and the courts. It was an age when rights were vested in property, and property was physical and tangible, vested with a cash value. The concept of libel was accepted, because libel could cause measurable damages that had cash value. That any yardstick could measure damages except the one notched with dollar signs was an idea that made a bloody entrance, as new ideas always must. The result was a number of cases in which the argument that privacy had a measurable value was scoffed at.

The first was an 1891 case that arose in New York, *Schuyler v. Curtis*.[2] It was a curious case, since it involved the precise opposite of defamation. A group of citizens wanted to erect a statue in honor of a locally prominent woman. Her family objected on the grounds that such an act would be an invasion of privacy. A court, possibly as much bewildered by the fact of opposition as by the reason, held that there was no legal precedent for a right of privacy. It is not part of the record that the reasoning of Brandeis and Warren entered the judgment in the case.

The second case was one the significance of which anyone could grasp, and it did have a constructive legislative sequel. Miss Roberson was an unusually attractive girl. A New York milling company understandably felt that her picture on its flour boxes would enhance their attractiveness. Passing over as an inconsequential detail the obtaining of her permission to grace their product, the company proceeded to embellish the boxes with her picture. With the subtlety of humor characteristic of enterprises of this sort her picture bore the caption "Flour of the Family." The result was the 1902 case

[1] New York: Atheneum, 1967.
[2] 15 N.Y. Supp. 787.

Roberson v. Rochester Folding Box Co.[1] Miss Roberson lost, the Court ruling that to give a verdict to her for unpermitted invasion of privacy would flood the Court with "litigation bordering upon the absurd."

The people of New York thought otherwise, and their legislators read their thoughts correctly. The result was a law passed the following year which established privacy as a right. It required the written consent of a person for his name or picture to be used in an advertisement. The New York privacy statute, now New York Civil Rights Law, secs. 50 and 51, drew the necessary distinction between the trade use of a personality and the use of a personality in the dissemination of news. It has left a rather shadowy border zone between the world of news and the world of entertainment, and a number of invasion-of-privacy cases have arisen in this zone. Despite the primacy of New York in recognizing a person's legal right to protect his privacy against commercial invasion, New York courts have consistently tended to interpret news quite freely in a conflict with privacy and to furnish less protection to privacy than is furnished by most states. Incidentally, it was the 1903 statute which established modeling as an occupation with a reality in law.

PRIVACY AND NATURAL LAW

In 1905 Judge Cobb of Georgia suggested in *Pavesich v. New England Life Insurance Co.*[2] a foundation for the right of privacy quite different from that proposed by Brandeis and Warren. In their effort to find a legal foundation for a right the very existence of which had not been recognized, they hit upon the concept of common law copyright as offering the soundest analogy to the right the validity of which they were attempting to establish. Judge Cobb found a very different basis in natural law. He stated in *Pavesich*,

The right of privacy has its foundations in the instincts of nature. It is recognized intuitively, consciousness being witness that can be called to establish its existence. Any person whose intellect is in a normal condition recognizes at once that as to each individual member of society there are matters private and there are matters

[1] 171 N.Y. 538.
[2] 122 Ga. 190, 194.

public so far as the individual is concerned. Each individual as instinctively resents any encroachment by the public upon his rights which are of a private nature as he does the withdrawal of those rights which are of a public nature. A right of privacy in matters purely private is therefore derived from natural law.

In all the realm of philosophy and in all its efforts to explain the state of man in this earthly life there is no question more fundamental than the question of natural law and its corollary, natural rights. Two millennia ago Cicero declared in his *De Legibus*, "The supreme law was born in all the ages, before any law had been written or any state had been established." There are two ultimate explanations of society, the natural law explanation and the contract explanation. Was Cicero right and does society not so much write its basic laws as discover them in the natural order, or was Thomas Henry Huxley right when he declared a century ago, "I say that natural knowledge, in desiring to ascertain the laws of comfort, has been driven to discover those of conduct, and to lay the foundations of a new morality"? As applied specifically to the issue of privacy, is privacy a natural right founded in the natural order and hence inalienable, or is it a legal creation, one of the laws of comfort out of which have grown the laws of conduct and the new morality which Huxley proclaimed?

Like all such ultimate questions, this one has no ultimate answer attainable, short of the resolution of the basic division between the natural law concept and the contract theory of society. Some jurists, however, have held it possible to find the concept of privacy embodied in the American Constitution and particularly in the Bill of Rights, although privacy itself is not an explicit constitutional right. The Bill of Rights provides a ban on the quartering of troops in private homes; it secures persons, houses, papers, and effects from unreasonable search and seizure; it assures the citizen of the right to avoid self-incrimination. These provisions are obviously consistent with such other provisions as the guarantees of free speech, a free press, free assembly, and free worship, but they do not rest upon exactly the same ideological foundation. We drew at the outset a distinction between privacy and autonomy. This is precisely the distinction which exists between the first group of rights and the second. To keep one's house inviolate against the quartering of troops, an archaic proviso, and the illicit invasion of it by law-enforcement authorities as well as the illicit invasion of one's personal sanctuary by forced self-incrimination, still potential menaces, are all based on the axiom that the right of privacy is a natural and inalienable right. On the other hand, to be free to speak one's mind, to print what is in one's mind, to gather as one chooses to share a voice in the common will, to worship God in the manner of one's choice and on the foundation of one's belief are all based on the axiom that the right of autonomy is a natural right inalienable in its nature although subject to proper regulation by society. There is nothing contradictory, of course, in the concepts of privacy and autonomy. It is merely that they are different concepts.

Acceptance of this natural law foundation for privacy is far from universal, and debate about it may be found among both those loosely identified as liberals in the current fashion of the time and those no more concretely identified as conservatives. As an example of the former, one may quote from the two foremost liberals of the Warren Court, Justices Black and Douglas. In the *Griswold* case to which we must presently turn our attention, Justices Black and Douglas were on opposite sides. Justice Douglas held invalid a Connecticut statute forbidding the dissemination of birth-control information even to a married couple. He did so on the grounds that there are "zones of privacy" in the Bill of Rights, and that the Connecticut law "operates directly on an intimate relation of husband and wife . . . a right of privacy older than the Bill of Rights." Justice Black, on the other hand, dissented in favor of the Connecticut statute, finding privacy to be "a broad, abstract and ambiguous concept" and commenting, "I like my privacy as well as the next one, but I am nevertheless compelled to admit that government has a right to invade it unless prohibited by some specific constitutional provision." The relatively conservative Justice Potter Stewart agreed with him: "I can find no such general right of privacy in the Bill of Rights, in any other part of the Constitution, or in any case ever before decided by this Court."

This is said by way of anticipation, since the crux to the current legal concept of privacy can be seen more clearly in *Griswold* than in any other case the Supreme Court has settled. It goes far toward explaining the legal pulling and hauling that has taken place for decades in cases that involve invasion of privacy without libel and without the inflicting of material damages. In the last analysis, one's attitude in this matter depends upon one's acceptance or rejection of the concept of natural law. The balance of evidence seems to the writer to favor the viewpoint that it was accepted by the Founding Fathers, and that to them the other name for natural law was the Will of God. It was unquestionably that to James Madison, who stated explicitly in his *Memorial and Remonstrance Against Religious Assessments,* "Before any man can be considered as a member of Civil Society, he must be considered as a subject of the Governor of the Universe: And if a member of Civil Society, who enters into any subordinate Association, must always do it with a reservation of his duty to the general authority; much more must every man who becomes a member of any particular Civil Society, do it with a saving of his allegiance to the Universal Sovereign."[1] However, the philosophy of the Founding Fathers on this, as on other matters, has customarily received the flattery of adulation more than the flattery of imitation. The debate about the right to privacy continued despite the efforts of New York legislative gallantry to protect "the flour of the family" and Georgian scholarship to follow the Founding Fathers in basing the right of privacy upon a bedrock of natural law philosophy.

WRITER, MUSCIAN, GENIUS

Many centuries before Alexander Pope proclaimed that "The proper study of mankind is man," the creative artist had studied his fellow man and produced the fruits of his studies in every form that art has proven possible. No form has been more amenable to this than fiction. To what extent is the modeling of a character in fiction after a living person an actionable invasion of privacy? That was the question a Florida court was asked to decide in 1944, and its consideration dragged on for years. Miss Zelma Cason of Island Grove, Florida, believed with sound reason that a character in Marjorie Kinna Rawling's novel *Cross Creek* was her fictional self. In a sense she was in the position of the woman for whom the statue was to be erected, since the portrayal was highly favorable. In her judgment her privacy should have been sacrosanct even against a highly favorable invasion, and she went to Court to prove her case. After four-and-a-half years she succeeded, although the success was an artistic rather than financial triumph. When *Cason v. Baskin*[2] finally was

[1] *Letters and Writings of James Madison,* 4 vols., New York, 1884; I, 162–163.
[2] 155 Fla. 198 (1944); 159 Fla. 31 (1947).

settled, Miss Cason got none of the $100,000 for which she sued although she got the verdict. The Court ruled that she had suffered neither mental anguish nor physical impairment through reading about herself in the guise of fiction. The victory, for all that, went to the right of privacy.

If it is an invation of privacy to portray a living person in fiction without his consent, can one write the life of a living public figure without his consent? That was the point at issue in the 1947 case of *Koussevitsky v. Allen.*[1] Serge Koussevitsky was the famed conductor of the world-renowned Boston Symphony Orchestra. Did such fame and renown put his life, so to speak, in the public domain? He believed that it did not, and he sued Moses Smith and his publisher Allen, Towne and Heath when Smith wrote an unauthorized biography. The case proceeded through the customary legalistic ups and downs during the winter of 1947. Koussevitsky got a temporary stay of publication and distribution of the book; then the New York Superior Court denied the publisher's plea that the stay be vacated; on the other hand, it denied an injunction in the suit against the author and publisher. The Appellate Court granted an interim injunction but ultimately denied a permanent injunction. The final viewpoint of the Court was that Koussevitsky was a public figure and as such anyone could write a book about his life and career. It would be otherwise, the lower court ruled and the Appellate Court affirmed, if he were made a figure of fiction. The principle on which the judgment was based was the distinction between news and entertainment. A biography, in the view of the New York courts where treatment of the right to privacy has always been very narrowly interpreted, is news.

What if one was once a public figure and then lost that high estate? The case, a cruel one in the judgment of most compassionate observers, concerned William J. Sidis. Sidis had the kind of youthful genius that crops up now and then, and apparently manifests itself more commonly in mathematics and music than in any other areas of human achievement. William Sidis, who graduated from Harvard College at the age of sixteen, had lectured to the Harvard faculty on

[1] 188 Misc. N.Y. 479; affirmed 272 App. Div. N.Y. 759.

his mathematical concepts prior to graduation. Understandably the loftiest hopes were entertained for the achievements of his mature years, but Sidis was not destined to be the Mozart of mathematics. Instead he was destined to be one of life's misfits and failures, and to be cooped in a hall bedroom somewhere in New York City. There the *New Yorker Magazine* found him and paid him in two articles the bitter salt of its merciless respects. Since his birthday was April 1, one of them was called "April Fool." He sued, and failed to recover. The 1940 case of *Sidis v. New Yorker*[1] is instructive reading for those who think of freedom of the press as an immaculate ideal kept spotless by a profession always guided by the serene, white light of truth. The Court recognized, as it had to, that both articles were merciless in the way they humilated the broken, forgotten genius, but they were "news," and news is sacred, far more sacred than decency or humane feeling.

The three cases are instructive, because all three were decided by courts that had no concept of privacy as a natural right. The Florida Court decided that a novelist has no right to use a living model in fiction because an invasion of privacy in the name of entertainment is illicit. The New York Court decided that a biographer does have the right to do the life of an eminent person because the fact of eminence destroys the claim of privacy and puts his life, so to speak, in the public domain. The other Court, also located in New York, decided that a person once eminent who saw his eminence melt away into the Dead Sea of bitter failure and drab obscurity lost his right to privacy in the hour long ago when his Roman candle cast its brilliant, transitory light. The basis of distinction was not the philosophic one written into what can be considered the privacy clauses of the Bill of Rights, but the legalistic one between fact and fiction. One wonders how the courts would have reacted if Maestro Koussevitsky had contended that a property right innate in his life had been gravely lessened in value when he became the subject of unauthorized literary treatment. He might have contended with some logic that his achievements, the result of massive effort as well as innate powers, gave him some property rights where full-scale biography was concerned.

[1] 133 Fed. 2d 806.

THE GRISWOLD CASE

It is well at this point to examine a case in which the justices of the Supreme Court made specific pronouncements of their views on the nature of privacy and the grounds for its recognition as a protected right. The *Griswold* case was decided in terms of the right to privacy although the point at issue, as is inevitable in a privacy case, was something extraneous to privacy itself. The *Griswold* case did not involve a positive invasion of privacy but rather an oblique denial of it.

Connecticut had a statute barring the dissemination of birth-control information even to married couples. Dr. Charles Lee Buxton and Mrs. Estelle T. Griswold, director of the Connecticut Planned Parenthood League, were the operators of the New Haven Clinic. They came afoul of this statute and the result was the Supreme Court case *Griswold v. Connecticut.*[1] The statute was declared unconstitutional on the grounds that it violated the right of marital privacy. Justice Douglas delivered the Court opinion already quoted in which he spoke of "zones of . . . privacy" created by the First, Third, Fourth, Fifth, and Ninth Amendments and declared that the Connecticut law "operates directly on an intimate relation of husband and wife . . . a right of privacy older than the Bill of Rights." Justice Clark joined in the opinion of Justice Douglas.

A concurring opinion was written by Justice Goldberg, in which Chief Justice Warren and Justice Brennan joined. This opinion relied on the Ninth Amendment as applied to the states by the Fourteenth. The Ninth Amendment states, "The enumeration in the Constitution, of certain rights, shall not be construed to deny or disparage others retained by the people." It was not the contention of Justice Goldberg that the Ninth Amendment was in itself a source of rights independent from the other amendments on which Justice Douglas relied in the Court decision, but rather that it was designed to show, in Justice Goldberg's words, "a belief of the Constitution's authors that fundamental rights exist that are not expressly enumerated in the first eight amendments and an intent that the list of rights included there were not exhaustive." He believed that the right of privacy in marriage was the sort of personal right retained by the people and covered by that blanket amendment the Ninth. Justice

[1] 381 U.S. 479 (1965)

Goldberg's opinion was, of course, a concurring opinion and was designed to make more explicit the significance of one of Justice Douglas's "zones of privacy."

Justices White and Harlan concurred in the Court decision, but their processes of reasoning differed not only between themselves but also from the reasoning of their colleagues in the majority. Justice White considered the moot point to be the relative values of the right of privacy and the protection of the public welfare in the case under consideration. He agreed with the others that the right of privacy in marriage is a fundamental human right, but he contended that the relative importance of that right and the justification proffered by the state of invading it had to be weighed in the balance. He did so, and found the weight of the former preponderant. He held that the state had failed to prove any legitimate social interest served by the legislation and he particularly failed to see how a ban on the use of contraceptives by married couples would aid a policy directed against illicit sexual relations. On this pragmatic basis he held that the statute was a sweeping intrusion of the right to freedom conducted without due process of law, and therefore he joined in the majority decision.

Justice Harlan also concurred in the decision, but he opened a new road of philosophic inquiry. The Court opinion as written by Justice Douglas, concurred in by Justice Clark, and with a specific amplification in terms of the Ninth Amendment accepted by Justices Goldberg and Brennan and Chief Justice Warren depended on what Justice Harlan called "radiations" from the Bill of Rights. His concept would appear to have been that in the last analysis his associates based their case on the right of privacy as one of the rights implicit in the blanket Ninth Amendment and made applicable to the states by the due-process clause of the Fourteenth. To Justice Harlan the concept of due process did not depend upon radiations from the Bill of Rights but rather was a concept contained in what he termed "the concept of ordered liberty." To him the real issue was not whether the Connecticut statute violated "radiations" from the Bill of Rights but rather violated basic values implicit in this concept of ordered liberty. The concept, he held, was attained by use of the "teachings of history, solid recognition of the basic values that underlie our society, and wise appreciation of the great roles that the doctrines of federalism and separation of powers have played in establishing and preserving American freedoms." It would not seem unreasonable to see in Justice Harlan's concept of ordered liberty and its organic growth as society has evolved, an echo of two of the most time-honored and tenaciously held concepts in Western thought, Cicero's "supreme law ... born in all the ages" and Edmund Burke's "The principles that guide us in public and private, as they are not of our devising, but moulded into the nature and essence of things, will endure with the sun and the moon. . . ."

The dissenters were Justices Black and Stewart, Justice Black predictably but Justice Stewart somewhat surprisingly. Justice Black consistently held to a literal and absolutist interpretation of the Bill of Rights. He was willing to concede that there are "guarantees in certain specific constitutional provisions which are designed in part to protect privacy at certain times and places with respect to certain activities." He denied that there is such a thing as a general right to privary or any constitutional provision barring a law that would abridge the privacy of individuals. "I like my privacy as well as the next one, but I am nevertheless compelled to admit that government has a right to invade it unless prohibited by some specific constitutional provision." He took direct issue with Justice Goldberg where the Ninth Amendment was concerned, maintaining that for over a century and a half "no serious suggestion was ever made that the Ninth Amendment, enacted to protect State powers against federal invasion, could be used as a weapon of federal power to prevent state legislatures from passing laws they consider appropriate to govern local affairs." He could see in the Court decision the triumph of the Brandeis-Warren thesis, that privacy should be the basis of a tort claim, and he had the gravest reservations as to the quagmires into which the doctrine of privacy might lead. The viewpoint of Justice Stewart was direct and simple. He considered the Connecticut law silly and incapable of enforcement, but "I can find no such general right of privacy in the Bill of Rights, in any other part of the Constitution, or in any case ever before decided by this Court."

THE NATURAL RIGHT TO PRIVACY

All the philosophic arguments that can be adduced to prove that morals are made by man can never still the instinctive voice deep in the human heart which says that they are not, that right and wrong are objective and eternal, and man cannot change the one into the other. It is the same voice that calls certain rights natural and, because they are natural, inalienable. The man in the street believes in privacy as a natural right, a right as Justice Douglas said "older than the Bill of Rights" and not derived from it. Americans of all shades of political and social belief hailed the *Griswold* verdict as a just one, even Americans opposed in principle to contraception. The fact might not be self-evident even to the tiny minority that reads Supreme Court decisions, but the instinctive agreement of the majority surely would be with Justice Harlan in holding that the right to privacy is "implicit in the concept of ordered liberty."

One should note that only Justice Black held that the right to privacy is not an inalienable right, but one that would have to depend upon the presence of a constitutional provision to protect it. Justice Stewart, the other dissenter, could not find a right to privacy in the Constitution. This is not to say that such a right does not exist. It is to say that it does not exist in the Constitution and therefore it is not within the competence of the Supreme Court to apply as a touchstone for determining the constitutionality of a specific piece of legislation. The real point at issue between Justice Stewart and the majority was not at all the point at issue between Justice Black and the majority. There are many rights, legal as well as moral, that do not depend upon the Constitution but do depend possibly upon state or local statute, possibly upon Justice Harlan's "concept of ordered liberty," possibly upon the latter as implemented by the former.

The real issue would appear to boil down to the meaning of the Ninth Amendment, with its statement that the explicit rights spelled out in the first eight amendments are not the totality of rights possessed by the American people. The Constitution could hardly exist, nor indeed could the United States exist as it is and has been, without the Ninth Amendment. Let us consider the implications of a Bill of Rights without a Ninth Amendment. These and these only would be the rights the people were to have: the right to freedom of religion, speech, press, assembly, and petition; the right to bear arms that there may be a well regulated Militia; the right to freedom from the quartering of troops and to security from unreasonable searches and seizures of their property; the right to protection before the law by the observance of due process in the several aspects of legal procedures. The list is impressive, but a moment's pause shows why it is inadequate. The rights provided by the first eight amendments are rights of the individual against infringement in the matters most

notorious at the period in which the Constitution was written. There
are other rights of comparable importance. What of the right to live
where one chooses? To select one's occupation? Or one's wife? It
might be an interesting exercise in ingenuity to put together as
comprehensive a list as possible, but it would be a pointless one
because success would always be one step ahead. There would
always be another natural right one hadn't thought of. There simply
had to be a Ninth Amendment. The Bill of Rights would be a
potential Bill of Wrongs if there were not. The conclusion, that the
right to privacy is a natural right in which man has an instinctive
belief and therefore is the sort of right referred to by the blanket
Ninth Amendment, is an entirely logical conclusion. Justice Douglas
did well to base the Court opinion in part upon the Ninth Amendment, and Justice Goldberg even better to underline its significance.

The essential meaning of the *Griswold* decision is that there are
certain areas in which Americans may order their lives without
interference by the Federal or state governments. Whether one
bases this belief on natural law as Justice Douglas did, in terms of
ordered liberty as Justice Harlan did, or upon a reading of the
Constitution as did the other concurring justices, *Griswold* affirms
the right of privacy as a right that may be antecedent in certain
areas and in certain respects to the right of the state to regulate
social conduct. One point should be borne in mind before one
contemplates the most obvious and stickiest quagmire into which
the constitutional doctrine of privacy might lead. The *Griswold*
decision was handed down in 1965, one year after the decision in
Heart of Atlanta Motel, Inc. v. United States.[1] This case had established the fact that owners of business establishments have no legal
right to select their clientele on the principle of privacy. The *Griswold* decision placed the concept of privacy on a basis of personal
liberty, not a basis of property ownership.

A June, 1972, decision of the Supreme Court further refined the
doctrine of privacy where the operation of a business establishment
is concerned. Three young men had been handing out pamphlets in
an enclosed shopping mall near Portland, Oregon. They were arrested and their case ultimately came to the Supreme Court. In a
five-to-four decision the Court affirmed that a shopping center has
the right to protect the privacy of its patrons from the annoyance of

[1] 379 U.S. 241.

having pamphlets thrust upon them. There was no breach of the peace involved or charged, and in the absence of what could be an extraneous issue the Court in effect affirmed that in certain areas and certain respects the right of privacy is antecedent to freedom of the press. The freedom to publish is one thing, the freedom to distribute what one publishes in any manner and any place one chooses is another. The former is not impaired when the latter is regulated, and the Court quite justly ruled that there is no First Amendment violation present in a local regulation which in no way interferes with freedom of the press to distribute its productions through "adequate alternative avenues of communication." Although the decision was hailed as one favoring property rights, in its essence it was a decision that upheld the right of the shopper to protection from annoyance. That is one aspect of the right to privacy, just as the right of a married couple to seek the medical advice they desire is another. One of the great problems in establishing as a legal principle the right of privacy is that the specific cases which establish it are inevitably contained within the framework of something else. It may be the right to seek specific medical advice, as in the Connecticut case, or the right to protect one's patrons from annoyance, as in the Oregon case. Beneath the tangible and specific lies the philosophical, and to that we must turn our attention since there and there alone may be found the true basis for the right to privacy.

PRIVACY AND AUTONOMY

Before philosophy may speak, however, there is an important question still unanswered. It is obvious that the use of privacy can well be a matter of social concern. When Justice Stewart could not find a right to privacy in the Constitution, there was more than a legalistic quibble in his mind. Again and again privacy and autonomy are treated as if they were perfect synonyms. A moment's thought will make it clear that they are not, and that only confusion can result if they are equated. Privacy is the withdrawal of oneself from the view of others. Autonomy is the governance of oneself without interference by others. What one does in privacy is done by the exercise of autonomy, and what one does autonomously may be a matter of social concern whether done in privacy or not. If one withdraws into fortress self to write poetry, it is one thing. If one withdraws to manufacture bombs for subsequent planting in public buildings, it is another. Privacy is a natural right, but autonomy is not. One has to be an anarchist to believe that autonomy is a natural right.

The question is the degree and manner by which society can regulate the use of autonomy with respect to the right of privacy. That is the real point at issue in the series of court cases involving wire tapping and the use of electronic listening devices, along with lie-testing machines and other paraphernalia for the detection of crime. Privacy is not synonymous with autonomy nor is it synonymous with secrecy. Secrecy, to repeat our definition, is the concealment of something from the knowledge of others. A criminal wishes privacy so that he may have autonomous control of the resulting secrecy for the concocting of whatever villainy he has in mind to perform.

When the law-enforcement officer taps the wire or places the listening device, his presumptive objective is not to violate the privacy of the suspect. It is to penetrate the secrecy and learn how the suspect is employing his autonomy. There is a long series of court cases in which the rights of suspects., mainly under the Fourth Amendment, have been spelled out under the challenge of a steadily burgeoning set of interceptive devices and interrogative techniques. This series is not our concern, since implicit in our subject is the concept of the citizen as law abiding and of the press and media in general as worthy of the same accolade. The press, radio, and television have an excellent record of non-involvement in the use of this expanding set of interceptive and interrogative machines. At times, however, they have been a bit hysterical in their confusion of the right of privacy with the utilization of secrecy and autonomy. The average citizen is in much greater danger of being mugged by the criminal than in having his telephone tapped by the police, and there are few invasions of privacy more upsetting than the breaking into one's home and the entering and pillaging of it by a thief. Furthermore, there is no historical evidence that any "police state" has ever resulted from the use of "police state methods," as Professor Ernest van den Haag has pointed out in his cogent essay "On Privacy,"[1] if by police state one has in mind such a state as Nazi Germany or Communist Russia. Revolutionists, not policemen, create police states.

Not merely can privacy be confused with autonomy and secrecy,

[1] In J. Roland Pennock and John W. Chapman, *Privacy*, Nomos XIII, Yearbook of the American Society for Political and Legal Philosophy, New York: Atherton Press, 1971.

but the limitation of all three can be confused with lack of human feeling. In *Miranda v. Arizona*[1] the Supreme Court held that the police must supply counsel for a suspect even if he does not ask for it and must notify him that he need not make statements. This, according to one professor of law, "gave the poor, unskilled criminals what mafiosi . . . had all along—the means to exercise their constitutional right to keep silent and talk to a lawyer. . . . Rich, sophisticated criminals [do not] deserve a better chance than poor, ignorant criminals."[2] The point is of importance only as an illustration of how the American sense of fair play can get out of hand when common sense does not rule it. No criminal deserves any chance to escape. The law exists to protect the orderly processes of society, not to make a ball game of them. What is more, the poor, ignorant criminal is a much greater threat to the average citizen than the rich, sophisticated one. Average citizens are slugged, stabbed, and shot by poor, ignorant criminals. Rich, sophisticated criminals usually prey on the rich and sophisticated, ordinarily do not use violence, and prey on the average citizen mainly when he strays into the moral twilight zone in which rich, sophisticated criminals batten.

All this, however, is really beside the point. Privacy is not synonymous with secrecy and autonomy. Privacy is a natural right, secrecy and autonomy are not. Privacy is a state of being, secrecy and autonomy involve the employment of that state of being. Whether one believes, as the writer does, that the higher the crime rate the greater the latitude the law-enforcement powers should have in combating it, or whether one believes that there are constitutional principles implicit chiefly in the Fourth Amendment that permanently and specifically limit that latitude, the fact that emerges from any consideration about the subject is that the whole business of wire tapping and its like is not a violation of privacy but an investigation of the employment of autonomy in a state of secrecy, a very different thing indeed.

NEWS AND NOT NEWS

Once it is established that privacy is neither secrecy nor autonomy and that the relationship between the press and the citizen intent on preserving his privacy is poles apart from the relationship between

---

[1] 384 U.S. 436 (1966)
[2] Yale Professor of Law, Joseph W. Bishop, Jr., *New York Times Magazine*, September 7, 1969.

the police and the criminal intent on preserving his secrecy, one may attempt the task of defining the natural limits which the citizen has a right to defend and across which the press should not transgress.

In the first place, it is obviously not the same set of limits for all men. The lives of some men are public by their nature. They may have entered public life by the elective process, or they may have accepted appointive positions of distinction and importance. By that act they have sacrificed privacy entirely where their public acts are concerned, and indeed privacy to the extent that their private lives have a bearing upon their public conduct. The line of demarcation between what is private and what is not private in the lives of public figures cannot be drawn in any generalized fashion that gives the reassuring sense of reliability, and by any criterion its limits are narrow. The principle involved, however, is clear. Anyone who becomes a public figure in this sense voluntarily accepts the limitations on his privacy which follow inevitably upon the decision he has made. The public welfare transcends his private comfort, and the public interest in his public acts and the aspects of his life which are reflected in those acts is legitimate. Its satisfaction by the press is also legitimate and necessary.

In the second place is the person who becomes a public figure by the significance of the position which he holds in the life of his community or state, or in the nation as a whole. At this point one must bear in mind perspective. The selectman or the elected town meeting member in a small town is a semi-public figure in terms of the town, and as such his actions are a source of legitimate interest to the town. That interest may legitimately be satisfied by the weekly paper which keeps the town abreast of local doings. But the fraction of such a person's life which belongs to the public is very much smaller than the fraction of the state or national official's, and the legitimate public interest in his actions is comparably circumscribed. A selectman is a public officer only part of the time, and an elected town meeting member a very small part of the time. Only the comparable fraction of their acts which concern the public weal is outside the veil of privacy. By extension the same concept can be applied to the person who becomes a public figure in the nation as a whole because of the position he holds in its industrial or professional life. He may be president of a great corporation, or a great university, or a great labor union, or he may be a high prelate in a church, or he may have won high distinction in the arts, or in sports.

The very fact that the list is so lacking in any common denominator and so obviously incomplete, stresses what is really the common denominator, the fact of public interest in achievements that have won public recognition. There is certainly a legitimate public interest in the achievements that have won public acclaim and the satisfaction of that interest by the press is entirely legitimate. But the private lives of such people do not have the bearing on the public welfare that the private lives of public figures in the political sense may have, even the private lives of those who hold as modest a position in the realm of politics as the selectman or the elected town meeting member. It is proper that public figures in this sense should enjoy the degree of privacy that they choose to enjoy for those aspects of their lives that are not vested with a legitimate public interest. There are others for whom such privacy is not valuable nor desired. This is true of entertainers whether in the arts or in athletics. There are still others to whom the limelight is cherished for its own sweet sake. There are presidents of great corporations and great labor unions of this propensity, and presidents of great universities. It is rumored that there are even high prelates of this sort.

In the third place is the person who is catapulted into the news by no prior intent on his own part. To categorize such persons is utterly impossible. On the local scene he may be the victim of a tragic accident or vicious crime. On the state and national scene his transient fame may be the result of any quirk in life which produces a result beyond ordinary expectation and fraught with more than ordinary interest. The person caught in a cave whose extrication becomes a continuing life drama for press and television is as good an example as any, but examples are limited only by the capacity of the individual to imagine them and the capacity of life itself to outdo any individual's imagination. Such persons are for the hour central figures on the stage of life, and the eyes of the state or nation are fascinated by them. What fascinates the state or nation is legitimate news, and its coverage is a legitimate press function. Such persons, however, have a natural privacy greater than that of the elected or appointed official, or the person whose state in life keeps him permanently in the public eye, and when they cease to be news all their right to privacy returns.

This division into categories of prominence may perhaps furnish a reasonably satisfactory guide to the necessary distinction to be drawn between news and no news if persons permanently or temporarily in the limelight are to have their proper degree of privacy which is the natural right of every human being. Let us consider first the person who voluntarily enters public life and inferentially the limelight by becoming a successful candidate for public office or accepting a sensitive and important appointive position in the public service. Ever since the disappearance of the concept of seditious libel his official acts and attitudes have been considered proper subject matter for press examination and judgment. As we saw in the process of examining the libel concept, one of the prime motives behind the freedom-of-the-press clause in the First Amendment was the elimination of the sort of screen by which official acts and attitudes could be masked by the protective device of seditious libel. The question no longer concerns the right of the press to examine and criticize the acts of public officials. It now concerns the limitations which justice, truth, and decency impose upon such examination and criticism under the blanket grant of investigative and critical powers called the New York Times Rule. It is well for those who think that justice, truth, and decency are axioms in terms of which the media act, as indeed in the great majority of cases they are, to bear in mind that there have been jurists on the Supreme Court bench who have sincerely held that they need not be, who have held that the news media should be exempt from libel suits. Lord Acton was not the first to note that absolute power corrupts absolutely, nor has the principle become obsolete in the twentieth century. One may again quote Chief Justice Warren who numbered among his colleagues those who held to absolutism as the proper basis for the publishing industry: "Freedom of the press under the First Amendment does not include absolute license to destroy lives or careers." The most that one can say, in terms of the New York Times Rule, is that public officials are also human beings, that they do not relinquish their natural rights by assuming public office, that they are entitled to justice, truth, and decency as are other people, that there are private aspects to their lives as well as public, and add the pious hope that juries and courts will be less reckless in their determination of what constitutes a reckless disregard of truth than some members of the United States Supreme Court have been in the tenor of their arbitrary theories of press freedom.

In the second category are those who are public figures by virtue of the position that they hold in the life of the community, state, or nation. The extension of the New York Times Rule to them was a perilous extension, and the outcome of the Butts case, while satisfactory in itself, should constitute a solemn warning of what may happen if the Rule is applied without the governing control of justice, truth, and decency. Wallace Butts got justice and vindication, but he got it by a perilously narrow margin and to get it he had to go to the Supreme Court and the Supreme Court had to do something it is not designed to do. It had to act as the jury of the last resort on the facts of a case. When the implications of a decision lead to a situation of that sort, the justice and wisdom of the Rule itself are open to the gravest question.

The Butts case brings up the question of the extent to which a person in the public eye must have his life subjected to public scrutiny in the name of public curiosity. Those old enough to remember Colonel Charles A. Lindbergh's magnificent 1927 solo flight across the Atlantic recall as well its outrageous aftermath. Month after month his every action was viewed and recorded that the insatiable maw of public curiosity might have fodder, his every step shadowed, his every hour haunted in what to him must have been a torture comparable to anything torture by the water drop could produce. But is the every action, every step, every hour of any man, no matter how great and justified his distinction, "news" in any valid sense of the term? Why should the concept of news be prostituted to the level of curiosity mongering and the press debased to the function of the village gossip?

Consider, as another instructive and this time contemporary example, the case of Mrs. Onassis and her shadow the photographer. Mrs. Onassis is one of the most glamorous and publicized women of the modern age, and that there be a great public interest in her is inevitable. But is it "news" in any justifiable meaning of the word when she takes a walk with her children? Is it "news" when she does that or any of the other acts that comprise the daily actions of every man and woman in America? Mrs. Onassis did a service to everyone in the public eye as well as a service to herself when she underwent the distasteful ordeal of a court trial to gain a permanent injunction against the photographer from dogging her and her children and taking their pictures at every opportunity.

And yet, what made necessary a court injunction against the invasion of her privacy? Obviously, the photographer whose "occupation" was taking her picture would have been out of work if he could not sell his pictures to publications that batten on the public

curiosity about persons like Mrs. Onassis. Ultimately the fault rests
with that substantial fraction of the public whose curiosity, to judge
by her case and the case of Colonel Lindbergh, must be insatiable.
The real question should be, what is there sacrosanct about that kind
of public curiosity that it must be satisfied at any cost in comfort and
convenience, not to say sheer freedom to move and act like an
ordinary human being, of persons like Mrs. Onassis? And the media
themselves might examine their consciences on this score. Is it really
true that everything such a person as Mrs. Onassis does is news? If it
is, then what is news and why does it have a constitutional protection? Obviously Mrs. Onassis has done things that are news in an
entirely valid sense, but walking down the street with her children is
not one of them. The media can hardly have it both ways. The
media can hardly proclaim their constitutional right as guardians of
the truth that makes men free and then make that high and noble
responsibility a protective cover for pandering for a price to the
vulgar and stupid curiosity of vulgar and stupid people about persons in the public eye. That sort of pandering should be reserved for
the public figures who can profit by it and want it. Many entertainers do, many sports figures do, and some other people in a position to
exact it do. By all means let them have it, and leave the rest of the
world of distinction alone in the routine of ordinary private life.

Mrs. Onassis walking down the street with her children is one
form of not-news. There is another, the sort of stale news that is
merely entertainment in disguise. The *New Yorker* articles on Sidis
are examples of entertainment disguised as news. William J. Sidis
had passed so long and so completely out of the news in any
legitimate sense that he must have been a discovery to the average
reader of the *New Yorker* articles about him. There is something not
particularly attractive about human nature that delights in the fall of
the once high and mighty. There was an entire branch of literature
in the Middle Ages devoted to the Fall of Princes. Once William
Sidis was a prince of the intellect; then he became a sad, frustrated
commoner. For all his youthful promise he is now no better than I
am, if indeed as good, the reader thinks. The reader who thinks in
that fashion places a low premium on himself, and so does the
magazine that makes a dollar out of that reader's sad, frustrated ego.

The conclusion is not too obscure in principle, however desperately difficult to apply in practice. The claim to privacy is implicit in
the human condition. Privacy is a natural right, an inalienable right,

one of the rights not enumerated in the Bill of Rights but recognized by the Ninth Amendment. To say that a right is inalienable, however, is not to say that it is absolute. The more the acts of a person impinge upon the public weal, the less right he has to privacy. The right of a public official is less than the right of a public personage, and the right of a public personage is less than the right of an average citizen. But everyone up to and including the President of the United States has an inalienable right to privacy in those aspects of his life which do not impinge upon the public weal. There is a natural public interest in all aspects of the lives of public figures, and a reasonable satisfaction of that interest by the media can be achieved within the reasonable bounds set by decency, good taste, and an awareness that every human being has an ultimate fortress of self which no other human being has a right to assault.

It is not the constitutionally protected function of the press to pander to vulgar curiosity. If everything Mrs. Onassis does is news, then there is no such thing as news since news by its nature should transcend the ordinary, expected, and inevitable. Enough happens in life that does transcend the ordinary, expected, and inevitable to fill the relatively few columns in the newspapers that are devoted to news in the strict sense, and the relatively few minutes of radio and television time dedicated to it. An unjustifiable assault upon privacy in defiance of decency and good taste should be grounds for a civil suit, as Brandeis and Warren argued many years ago.

Part V

MORAL CLIMATE

Of all the areas in which the rights of a free press and the rights of the free citizen are in potential or actual conflict, that of moral climate is the most difficult to define and the most difficult to maintain by legal means. Indeed, it can be maintained by explicit legal means only to a severely limited degree, and the real problem is to maintain it within a peaceable framework. Every society has a moral climate. It changes and shifts as the accepted values and prevailing attitudes of society change and shift, and the forms it can assume are protean. No approach to the study of a society casts quite as much light upon it as the study of what its moral climate permits and what it prohibits, and the one is as revealing as the other.

The tendency today is to think of moral climate in terms of sex. This would have bewildered a man of the Middle Ages, who thought of moral climate in terms of theology. Medieval literature is quite urbane on the subject of sex, and one imagines that the Canterbury pilgrims would be at least as much amused by the titillation of the modern undergraduate when the Miller's Tale first bursts upon him as they would be by the tale itself. One should recall that the Miller's ribaldry was delivered in the presence of the elegant Prioress, the idealistic Knight, and the saintly Parson as well as to its presumptive audience, the Miller's sociological comrades in arms, the Pardoner, the Summoner, and the Wife of Bath. Chaucer does not record that the more erudite, refined, and moral members of the company left Harry Bailly's group to join some properly conducted tour to Canterbury, operated by the medieval equivalent of Thomas Cook and Sons.

That does not mean that the Canterbury pilgrims would have listened with complacence to a tale told by a Lollard and illustrative of the dangerous nonsense of John Wycliffe or the even more subversive doctrines being brewed in Bohemia by John Huss and the Hussites. That would be heresy, or at least open to the charge of heresy, and so matter to be referred with the appropriate mixture of reverence and repugnance to proper authority. The *Canterbury Tales* abounds in ribaldry and differs from other collections of its age only in being vastly better written and more entertaining, but no tale contains so much as a smidgen of heresy. The moral climate of the age would not allow it, and Geoffrey Chaucer was too solid a member of the contemporary Establishment to risk offense to that moral climate, even if his proclivities lay in that direction. One should add, to keep the record balanced as well as straight, that Chaucer did write a *Retraction* of his ribald writing before he died.

It is sometimes said that censorship began with printing. This is, of course, true in the literal meaning of the word but the Roman poet Ovid, who did transgress the moral climate of his age, had ample opportunity for the rest of his life to ponder the significance of violating the moral climate and evoking the retaliation of censorship as he eked out his days in bleak barbarism north of the Black Sea. The literary career of the world's final authority on the art of love makes it clear that his offense had nothing to do with sex. Neither had it anything to do with heresy, a concept that would have been incomprehensible in the age of Augustus. It had to do with an offense to moral climate far more widespread and enduring in human history than offense to purity or theology, the offense of lese majesty.

In most periods of the Christian era the moral climate has been quite tolerant of literary lightheartedness toward sex, tight lipped toward heresy, and adamant against that denigration of sovereignty called lese majesty, which can run the gamut from unseemly jocosity about the world's high and mighty to downright treason against them. We have already seen that behind the guarantees of the First Amendment was a struggle to break the iron bonds of seditious libel, that aspect of moral climate which made it smack of treason to criticize any aspect of government or the governor. Early eighteenth-century England would tolerate bawdy comedy very nicely and remained blandly indifferent toward heresy, but the moral climate suddenly grew ominously frosty at the hint of lese majesty. Much of the history of the later eighteenth century, written in the lives and subsequent influence of men like Fox and Burke and in the careers of Jefferson, Madison, and Hamilton, concerns the struggle to change the moral climate where the expression of political belief was concerned and to open the minds of men to new political, social, and economic ideas. The giants of the century would deem the literary treatment of sex appropriate enough for a Drury Lane diversion and were Olympian in their indifference to heresy. Their pens were dedicated to what in the eighteenth-century view really mattered, and the final outcome was the Declaration of Independence and the American Constitution.

The tendency to call suppression of the literary treatment of sex Puritanism is decried by those who admire the wonderfully steadfast qualities of the Puritans at their best. It has, furthermore, all the shortcomings of partial metaphor, but there is a certain justification for it. The moral climate of Puritanism, in both England and America, was repressive of heresy to a degree beyond the Middle Ages, highly censorious of sex, but utterly permissive of lese majesty. Discussion of pulpit dogma was rigidly controlled, imaginative forays into the literary depiction of love and dalliance austerely circumscribed, but jeremiads of denunciation of the political regime poured from the Puritan press. The Puritans had their moral climate quite as truly as the Romans of the Age of Augustus, the English of the Middle Ages, the Renaissance, or the eighteenth century, or the Americans of the last third of the twentieth. A Puritan might print what he would about the king but not about consubstantiation, and relatively little about his imaginary neighbor and his wife.

By and large twentieth-century America inherited the Puritan tradition as modified during the nineteenth century, partly by the melting of that part of Puritanism which had been ideological ice, partly by the impact of industrialism, the frontier tradition, and the influx of people from lands in which Puritanism had no hold, and partly by the slow attrition of time. Unmodified Puritanism is a desperately difficult moral posture to maintain. For most of the twentieth century the moral climate has been increasingly hospitable to heresy, broadly tolerant of lese majesty, and unsure of itself about sex, in both literature and life. On the last pair of points the situation as we enter the fourth quarter of the century is considerably looser than it used to be.

We have, of course, a moral climate quite as truly as any other age, and it is merely that aspect of our Puritan inheritance which makes us equate moral climate with attitude toward sex that makes us think our moral climate relaxed and permissive. There is a sense in which it is, and a sense in which it is not. It is certainly far more relaxed and permissive toward sex, in literature and life, than it has been since the eighteenth century in England. This age, however, has an austerity toward certain kinds of heresy that rivals anything Fear God Barebones conjured up in the heyday of the ducking stool.

The current pattern of heresy is rooted in humanism rather than theology, and its preoccupation is race. One may print anything one likes about God, very nearly anything one likes about one's fellow man's social or political convictions, and certainly next to anything one likes about the use, misuse, and abuse of the human body, but that does not mean one can print anything one likes about minority groups of the currently favored sort. Minority groups not currently favored are not minority groups but ethnic groups, and they are fair game. This is not to be considered a plea in the name of freedom of speech and of the press for the verbal abuse of minority groups, or indeed of ethnic groups, or one may go the whole way and say of WASPS. It is merely to point out that the moral climate of the present day is not more permissive than the moral climate of previous periods. It is merely more permissive of different things. We are latitudinarian toward religious heresy, but Puritanic toward racial heresy. We luxuriate in lese majesty where our own government is concerned, but we are circumspect in the printed attitudes allowed toward certain foreign governments. It is far from good form to say a bad word about Israel or a good word about South Africa. The truce on religious acrimony which was one of the few beneficial by-products of the ecumenical movement seems to be loosening at the seams, and the moral climate especially toward anti-Catholic utterance is considerably freer than it was a few years ago, although it is far from having regained the absolute freedom of the nineteenth century. The spirit of Thomas Jefferson and James Madison still lives, and so does the spirit of Savonarola and John Knox. Every age has its heresy and every age burns its heretics at least at the metaphoric stake.

It is necessary to say all this, digression from our theme though it obviously is, because the current tendency to equate moral climate with attitude toward sex and to view freedom of thought and action as a self-justifying absolute has to be cut down to size before its permissible limits can be suggested. It is necessary for a reason still more commanding. The moral climate of an age in which men have a fair degree of freedom is never brought into being by legislation nor perpetuated by court action. It is a spontaneous product of the age itself, and the enactment and interpretation of legislation is the result and not the cause of the spirit of the age. If the sort of ignominy inflicted on the black race by the old-fashioned minstrel show and the kind of radio humor that depended on the tired old joke of the black man terrified of haunts and spectral visitants are not permitted by the moral climate of the times, it is not because they have been made illegal but because the moral climate of our day has made them intolerable.

The conclusion follows. Control of freedom of speech and of the press is not an evil in itself, and no age really thinks it such. It is an evil when it represses what should not be repressed, a good when it represses what should. Ages differ in their concepts of what should be repressed and what should not, but no age ever really believes in freedom of expression as an uncontrolled absolute. Every age has a moral climate, in some respects permissive, in some respects austere, and every age is determined to maintain its moral climate in the face of those who call for change until their numbers become so many and their power so great that the moral climate is changed and a new standard of permissiveness and of inhibition is established. The real objective of statesmanship in this regard is to limit what is banned to what has no conceivable intrinsic justification for expression, what in a current phrase is utterly without redeeming social value. The real tragedy of the repression of heresy, lese majesty, and sex expression has been that thought with an intrinsic justification for expression, thought with a social value, has so often been suppressed. The principle follows that if one must err, one should err on the side of expression. But there is a principle antecedent even to this. It is the duty of statesmanship, within the limits of human achievement, not to err at all. One may start, then, with the sort of expression that has no intrinsic justification for expression and is totally without conceivable social value. One starts with pornography, and with the understanding that it is not easy to define and with the further understanding that the real problem may be to expand and not to limit the definition.

THE HICKLIN RULE

In 1709 an English justice was presented with a conundrum. A man had been indicted for printing a book called *The Fifteen Plagues of a Maidenhead.* The justice faced the sixteenth plague: what to do about it? It was not a libel, since a libel must attack some individual or the government. It was certainly bawdy stuff, "stuff not fit to be mentioned publicly." But the justice was forced to add: "There is no law to punish it: I wish there were: but we cannot make law. It indeed tends to the corruption of good manners, but that is not sufficient for us to punish."[1] In 1709 England had just turned the corner from the seventeenth century, the century with the most

[1] *Regina V. Read,* 11 Mod. Rep. 142.

austere climate toward heresy in all English history, but England had no anti-pornography law.

In 1724 the English Attorney General attempted to discover one imbedded in existing statutes. A bookseller named Edmund Curll had been arrested for printing *Venus in the Cloister, or, The Nun in Her Smock*. As the title indicates, the volume was a deft blend of two hardy perennials, pornography and anti-Catholicism. The Court agreed that Curll was a criminal, wicked fellow (*homo iniquus et sceleratus*), but the law punishes a man for committing a crime, not for being a criminal type. The Attorney General argued that to corrupt the morals of the King's subjects was a breaking of the peace of the realm and therefore an offense at common law. The Lord Chief Justice was both impressed and perplexed. He found the argument of the Attorney General intellectually attractive but legally thin. Curll was found guilty, but given no sentence. Two years later he was again in trouble over his *The Case of Seduction; translated from the French* (translation from the French has always been an English guarantee of high quality pornography). Nothing particular happened. Curll finally landed in the nets of the law in 1739, when he published some political pamphlets of a Jacobite taint. That was seditious libel, a real crime.

Through the eighteenth century the moral climate of England remained glacial toward lese majesty, benign toward heresy, but increasingly disturbed about sex. This disturbance took specific form in 1802 when the Methodists formed the Society for the Suppression of Vice. Its objectives are instructive for the light they shed on the moral climate as the nineteenth century started: to prevent a profanation of the Lord's Day, prosecute blasphemy, suppress blasphemous publications, stop trade in obscene books, and close bawdy houses. Blasphemy is not heresy and it is a fair guess that to the Society blasphemy really was the sort of lurid profanity that relies for its main impact on the use of the divine name, but blasphemous publications can be a somewhat different matter. Blasphemy in print has a way of fusing with heresy. The main drive was against blasphemy during the first quarter century of its existence, but the Society also concerned itself, to general public approval, with the problem of obscene books. Finally, in 1857, Parliament passed the Obscene Publications Act, a measure that aimed at stifling pornography by the simple expedient of confiscating and destroying obscene books. Ten years later it came to the test.

A pamphlet was printed entitled *The Confessional Unmasked.* This anonymous work purported to be an exposé of the Catholic confessional, which was depicted as an instrumentality for the intimate and detailed investigation of illicit sex acts not for their elimination, or at least purification, but for their expansion and development. It blended the time-honored ingredients of the particularly British sort of pornography already mentioned: anti-Catholicism and obscenity. The former, presumably, served a social purpose and the latter sold the book. A metal broker of Wolverhampton named Henry Scott, a man apparently of dedicated Protestant convictions and more than adequately insulated from a sense of humor, honestly considered it a suitable vehicle to further the work of the Protestant Electoral Union and at his own expense mailed out some 200 copies of it. He was arrested for distributing an obscene work in violation of the Obscene Publications Act.

The justices of Westminster found the book guilty but not Scott. The Recorder, Benjamin Hicklin, gave the ruling that although the book itself was obscene Scott's motives in distributing it were innocent. The Catholics of England appealed the finding and the result was *Regina v. Hicklin.*[1] The higher Court concerned itself less with the guilt of Scott, whose guilt all appear to have accepted as the technical guilt of a well-meaning man amateurish in both theology and politics, than it did with the guilt of the printer. His defense was essentially that of Scott: the laudable, or at least innocent, motivation for the publication of an obscene book cancels the obscenity. The Court ruled otherwise, and Lord Chief Justice Cockburn handed down the decision which is known alternately as the Hicklin Rule and the Cockburn Rule: "The test of obscenity is this, whether the tendency of the matter charged as obscenity is to deprave and corrupt those whose minds are open to such immoral influences and into whose hands a publication of this sort may fall."

For decades this was the Rule followed by courts in England and America, and consequently its historic significance to our subject is substantial. Three points must be borne in mind, since these are the three points that will be blunted and even broken in subsequent decisions. The first is that under the Hicklin Rule the motive of publication is not a factor, nor is the possibility of social value. The

[1] *Law Reports 3 Court of Queen's Bench 360.* The findings have been reprinted in *The Hicklin Case,* London, 1937.

mists of history shroud the motivation of the original author and to
some extent the printer, but there is no reasonable doubt about
Scott's motives in distributing the pamphlet. He saw it serving two
social purposes of high value, the unmasking of Catholic hypocrisy
and immorality, and the promotion of stalwart Protestants to public
office. One may accept or reject the actual values involved, but one
can hardly deny that Scott intended to perform a socially valuable
act.

The second point to bear in mind is that a work is to be considered obscene if it tends to corrupt minds open to such immoral
influences. One might be shocked to the depths of one's soul, as
Henry Scott was, by the unmasking of popish perfidy and that shock
obliterate the possibility of any other reaction to the pamphlet. Or,
to take the reaction of the average modern reader, one might expect
a curiosity aroused by this revelation of religious fires now burned
out, or perhaps a pensive if passing thought to their now inexplicable
intensity, and possibly a wonder if there are other fires of the same
intensity burning elsewhere in the ideological woodlands. By the
Rule it was not the reaction of the average man nor the reaction of
the enthusiast Scott that mattered. It was the reaction of those who
might be corrupted by a reading. The Court believed that there
were such, and one is privileged to believe that the Court was right.

The third point concerns the distribution of the pamphlet. One
may safely assume that Scott intended to distribute it to those who
would learn from it the lesson he believed it taught. Such people
would not be harmed by a reading, and indeed would be benefited
as would the nation if they went out and voted for the candidates of
the Protestant Electoral Union. But once a book is published it is
public beyond recall and chance rules its destiny. It was not the
intended reader who mattered, nor the average reader, but the
accidental reader. If the book came by accident into the hands of
one corruptible, it fell beneath the ban.

The Hicklin Rule has passed into limbo, yet the significance of the
Rule is not exclusively historical. It did provide the basis for court
decisions in England and America for many decades, and it would
not be unfair to say that even now a kind of sub-conscious awareness
of its thesis can be present in the minds of judges and jurymen. The
issue of social significance has been made important in later decisions and the issue of the average man's reaction all-important. The
curious thing is that the third point, the one that concerns the

distribution of the pamphlet and the hands into which it may by accident fall, has returned in new and disturbing form. There are thousands of books on the library shelves from which one may choose, but only a few television channels. The accidental viewer may pose a far graver problem than the accidental reader ever could. The Hicklin Rule has passed into limbo, but limbo is not a permanent state.

THE COMPROMISE BETWEEN CANDOR AND SHAME

The attrition of the Hicking Rule was gradual, as the attrition of long-established rules tends to be. It may be said to have started in 1913 in *United States v. Kennerley*.[1] Daniel Carsin Goodman wrote a novel called *Hagar Revelly*. It is the story of a young woman of New York, sensuous, fond of pleasure, impulsive, living in poverty and indeed squalor. Her virtue is subject to both assault and conquest. After various adventures outside marriage she enters a loveless union and faces at the end a future not essentially different from the one she faced when the story started. Technically it is a novel of manners, a collateral descendant by a rather tenuous line of Stephen Crane's *Maggie: A Girl of the Streets*. The book was sent through the mails, a criminal prosecution followed, and the case came before Judge Learned Hand.

Judge Hand, who never forgot that although he was one of the most distinguished jurists in America he was the judge of a lower court and had a tongue-in-the-cheek way of expressing his humility, referred to the Hicklin Rule and stated that its test had so long been accepted in the Federal courts that he could not disregard it. He added the hope that it would not be improper for him to express the belief that the mid-Victorian standard for novels was not consonant with current understanding and morality, and then expressed the view which ultimately would form the background against which the Roth Rule would be constructed:

I question whether in the end men will regard that as obscene which is honestly relevant to the adequate expression of innocent ideas, and whether they will not believe that truth and beauty are too precious to society at large to be mutilated in the interests of those

---

[1] 209 Fed. 119, Southern District of New York.

most likely to pervert them to base uses. Indeed, it seems hardly likely that we are even today so lukewarm in our interest in letters of serious discussion as to be content to reduce our treatment of sex to the standard of a child's library in the supposed interest of a salacious few, or that shame will for long prevent us from adequate portrayal of some of the most serious and beautiful sides of human nature.

Thus Judge Hand recognized that there is such a thing as pornography, but also that there is such a thing as the frank, honest, open, and unashamed portrayal of human motives, aspirations, limitations, illusions and delusions, all comprising human life. He was not empowered by his position to reject the Hicklin Rule and indeed he passed his judgment in *Kennerley* in accordance with it, but he did lay down the principle that many years later the United States Supreme Court accepted as the intent of the Constitution:

... if the time is not yet when men think innocent all that which is honestly germane to a pure subject, however little it may mince its words, still I scarcely think that they would forbid all which might corrupt the most corruptible, or that society is prepared to accept for its own limitations those which may perhaps be necessary to the weakest of its members. If there be no abstract definition, such as I have suggested, should not the word 'obscene' be allowed to indicate the present critical point in the compromise between candor and shame at which the community may have arrived here and now?

ONE BOOK CALLED *ULYSSES*

The critical point between candor and shame was reached from the side of candor in 1933. James Joyce's *Ulysses* was published in Paris in 1922. It is a microscopic examination of one day in the external and even more the internal lives of two Dubliners and is marked in parts, as the *Oxford Companion to English Literature* puts it, "by eccentricities of form (economy of punctuation, ellipses of words, &c.), an utter frankness of language, and a realism that spares the reader neither the sordid nor the indecent. It has, however, been regarded by some intellectuals as the most important novel of modern times." Before it was published in book form it was serialized in *The Little Review* with the resultant arrest and fining of the editor.

After 1922 it was smuggled into the United States in substantial numbers and quite widely circulated. One might say, parentheti- cally, that a conscientious reading of *Ulysses* is probably the most difficult way of becoming corrupted that literature affords, and that the chief evil resulting from the smuggling was the loss of royalties to Joyce on some 30,000 copies of the book. In 1933 Random House challenged a seizure of copies by customs officials and the case came before Federal Judge John M. Woolsey.[1]

Judge Woolsey accepted as a legal definition of *obscene:* "tending to stir the sex impulses or to lead to sexually impure and lustful thoughts. . . ." By the Hicklin Rule this meant to stir such thoughts and impulses in any person into whose hands a book might fall. At this point Judge Woolsey departed from *Hicklin* and moved into the legal ground prepared twenty years before by Judge Hand. He stated, "Whether a particular book would tend to excite such impul- ses and thoughts must be tested by the court's opinion as to its effect on a person with average sex instincts—what the French would call *l'homme moyen sensuel*—who plays, in this branch of legal inquiry, the same role of hypothetical reagent as does the 'reasonable man' in the law of torts, and 'the man learned in the art' on questions of invention in patent law." On the principle that it is the average man whose susceptibility is the test and with the belief that *Ulysses* is "a sincere and serious attempt to devise a new literary method for the observation and description of mankind," he ruled that the book was not obscene and might be imported into the country.

The most important part of the *Ulysses* decision is the fact that the reaction of the average person and not that of the most suscepti- ble person provides the norm. One of the most important of the other norms which Judge Woolsey undertook to establish harkened back to the point at issue in *Hicklin:* does the motive of the writer, publisher, and distributor count? *The Confessional Unmasked* was distributed, at least, by a man whose motives may have been mis- guided and benighted, but were above moral reproach. What about the motives of the writer? Granted the moral climate of the age in which it was written and granted that he believed that what he wrote was true, the writer's motives might have been quite as pure as those of Henry Scott. Judge Woolsey ruled that a book can be deemed obscene only if it can be proved that it is intended to be

[1] *United States v. One Book Called "Ulysses,"* 5 Fed. Supp. 182.

obscene, that the motive of the writer was pornographic. By that test, in part, Joyce's *Ulysses* was cleared. There is a second aspect of the ruling of comparable importance. Under the Hicklin Rule the legal custom had been to cite chapter and verse, and that meant quite literal and limited chapter and verse, as grounds for the charge of obscenity. Thus, in the very decision which undermined the Hicklin Rule, Judge Hand cited pages 169 and 170 of *Hagar Revelly* as possibly obscene. An essential part of the *Ulysses* finding was the contention that the proper test for obscenity is the dominant effect of the entire book and that in determining this effect, the relevancy of the objectionable part to the theme had to be taken into consideration. Thus from the *Ulysses* case emerged at least the potentiality of a principle quite different from the Hicklin Rule: the motive of the writer, the nature of his theme, the relationship of the part suspect to the whole, the dominant effect of the book, and the reaction to it of the average reader provide the proper criteria for the determination of obscenity. Thus Judge Woolsey would effect the compromise between candor and shame at which the community had arrived.

THE ROTH RULE

The point at issue in *Hicklin, Kennerley,* and *Ulysses* was the nature of obscenity and the identity of its presumptive victim. The issue of the constitutionality of a ban on obscene publication was raised in 1948 when Edmund Wilson's *Memoirs of Hecate County,* or more accurately one story in it, was charged with being obscene. The case finally came to the Supreme Court on the sole issue of the constitutional guarantee of freedom of the press. The Court was evenly divided and the result of *Doubleday & Co. v. New York*[1] was in effect an unsettled issue.

An attempt was made the following year in a Pennsylvania court to settle the issue on the clear-and-present-danger principle. In *Commonwealth v. Gordon*[2] Judge Curtis Bok ruled that a statute penalizing obscenity was applicable "where there is a reasonable and demonstrable cause to believe that a crime or misdemeanor has been committed or is about to be committed as the perceptible result of the publication and distribution of the writing in question;

[1] 335 U.S. 48.
[2] 66 Pa. D. and C. 101

the opinion of anyone that a tendency thereto exists or that such a result is self-evident is insufficient and irrelevant. The causal connection between the book and the criminal behaviour must appear beyond a reasonable doubt." This criterion was upheld as the guiding norm the following year when the case was appealed to the Superior Court of Pennsylvania.

Hecate County and *Gordon* in their several ways evaded the real issue where obscenity is concerned. Do the American people have the constitutional right to live in the moral climate of their choice? The issue was left up in the air in the case involving *Hecate County* and was not made the criterion at all in *Gordon,* where the imminence of overt criminal action was made the test after the analogy of the already established test for the criminality of seditious utterance. It was not until 1957 that the constitutionality of anti-obscenity laws was confirmed by the Supreme Court and the applicability of the clear-and-present-danger principle to the issue of obscenity was denied.

Samuel Roth was a New York seller of books, photographs, and magazines. A New York court convicted him of violating the Federal obscenity statute by mailing an obscene book. It is alleged that the experience was not a new one. Terrence J. Murphy states[1] that between 1928 and 1955 Roth had been in court at least ten times on obscenity charges, had been found guilty or pleaded guilty seven times, and that his business had elicited from postal authorities at least six fraud orders, nine fictitious orders, and eleven unlawful orders against the various trade names he used. He reached legal fame along with David S. Alberts of Los Angeles, who as proprietor of the Male Merchandise Mart, a mail-order house, handled such male merchandise as *The Prostitute and Her Lover, The Love Affair of a Priest and a Nun, Male Homosexuals Tell Their Stories,* and *The Picture of Conjugal Love.* Roth entered the marble halls of the Supreme Court to test the constitutionality of the Federal obscenity statute, Alberts the applicability to his case of the due-process clause. Behind both cases was that decision of far-reaching importance which concerned the issue of racial defamation and tested it by the powers of the state to apply prior restraint, the *Near* case. The various strands were woven together in the Roth-Alberts case. Is an anti-obscenity statute constitutional? Does the confiscation of

[1] *Censorship: Government and Obscenity,* Baltimore, 1963, p. 21.

allegedly obscene material violate the due-process clause? Is the clear-and-present-danger test applicable to obscenity? Is the suppression of obscene publications an unconstitutional exercise of prior restraint? Other strands not previously mentioned were woven in as well. Are anti-obscenity statutes so vague that the difficulty of understanding their applicability induces a violation of due process? Is the power to punish obscenity solely a state power and therefore the Federal anti-obscenity statute a violation of the Ninth and Tenth Amendments? All these issues either were raised in the twin cases or were so clearly implicit in them that they had to be settled.

The Supreme Court upheld the conviction of both men, Justice William J. Brennan writing the decision. After pointing out the issues he stated, ". . . it is apparent that the unconditional phrasing of the First Amendment was not intended to protect every utterance. This phrasing did not prevent this Court from concluding that libelous utterances are not within the area of constitutionally protected speech. . . . At the time of the adoption of the First Amendment, obscenity law was not as fully developed as libel law, but there is sufficiently contemporaneous evidence to show that obscenity, too, was outside the protection intended for speech and press."

The conclusion of the Court that the First Amendment did not protect obscene utterance took care of the directly related issues of the confiscation and the suppression of obscene material. Passing to the issue presented by the clear-and-present-danger test, Justice Brennan quoted from the Court decision in *Beauharnais:* "Libelous utterances not being within the area of constitutionally protected speech, it is unnecessary, either for us or for the State courts, to consider the issues behind the phrase 'clear and present danger.' Certainly no one would contend that obscene speech, for example, may be punished only upon a showing of such circumstances. Libel, as we have seen, is in the same class."

Justice Brennan turned his attention later in the decision to the issue of vagueness in anti-obscenity statutes and the possible violation of due process to which such vagueness may lead. He recognized that the problem is a real one but added, "The Court, however, has consistently held that lack of precision is not itself offensive to the requirements of due process" and proceeded to quote *United States v. Petrillo,*[1] "The Constitution does not require impossible

[1] 332 U.S. 1.

standards"; all it requires is that the language "conveys sufficiently definite warning as to the proscribed conduct when measured by common understanding and practices. . . ."

To this point Justice Brennan was clearing away in the name of the Court the obscuring underbrush which had grown up around the issue of obscenity. Anti-obscenity statutes did not violate the freedom-of-speech clause of the First Amendment nor the due-process clause of the Fourteenth, nor did a Federal statute of the sort run afoul of the Ninth and Tenth Amendments. The main point, however, remained unreached. Where is the line to be drawn between what may legally be banned as obscene and what may not, and since there must be a subjective test as well as an objective test in such matters, by what reader's subjective reaction is the matter to be decided? The Court proceeded to disavow the Hicklin Rule. The legal test was not the obscenity of isolated passages nor was it the reaction of the most susceptible reader, the former being "unconstitutionally restrictive of the freedoms of speech and press." The latter was ruled out on the implicit basis of *Ulysses* although that decision was not named: "On the other hand, the substituted standard provides safeguards adequate to withstand the charge of constitutional infirmity." What, then, is printable? Justice Brennan proceeded to define what is printable under the First Amendment guarantee of a free press:

The protection given speech and press was fashioned to assure unfettered interchange of ideas for the bringing about of political and social changes desired by the people. . . . All ideas having even the slightest redeeming social importance—unorthodox ideas, controversial ideas, even ideas hateful to the prevailing climate of opinion—have the full protection of the guaranties, unless excludable because they encroach upon the limited area of more important interests. But implicit in the history of the First Amendment is the rejection of obscenity as utterly without redeeming social importance.

He then indicated that not only does every state in the union have an anti-obscenity law, but that there is an international agreement among fifty nations to control obscene publications. The conclusion of the Court was totally uncompromising: "We hold that obscenity is not within the area of constitutionally protected speech or press."

The Court was not unanimous in *Roth.* Justices Douglas and Black dissented, with Justice Douglas writing the dissent. They took their stand simply and solely upon the clear-and-present-danger test. As Justice Douglas expressed his viewpoint and that of Justice Black: "To allow the state to step in and punish mere speech or publication that the judge or the jury thinks has an undesirable impact on thoughts but that is not shown to be a part of unlawful action is drastically to curtail the First Amendment." In an uncompromising denial of the right of the community to maintain the morale climate of its choice he stated, "The legality of the publication in this country should never be allowed to turn either on the purity of thought which it instills in the mind of the reader or on the degree to which it offends the community conscience."

ROTH REFINED AND EXPLICATED

Every Supreme Court case concerning obscenity since *Roth* has been a commentary on *Roth.* Each has made its contribution, frequently valuable, to the fundamental decision that there is such a thing as obscenity, that it is not exclusively in the eye of the beholder, and that it is outside the legal pale. *Roth* was barely history when *Butler v. Michigan*[1] reached the Supreme Court. John H. Griffin had written a paperback novel called *The Devil Rides Outside.* It was sold to a minor, and a Michigan statute held that anyone selling a book with obscene and immoral descriptions "tending to incite minors to violent or depraved or immoral acts, manifestly tending to the corruption of the morals of youth," was guilty of a misdemeanor.[2] A unanimous Court held the statute a violation of due process since it used state powers to protect the morals of youth in an "arbitrary and oppressive" way when it made the moral criterion of a book its effect upon children. *Butler* reinforced the rejection of *Hicklin,* which started with *Kennerley,* was strengthened by *Ulysses,* and presumably finalized by *Roth.* To be legal, an anti-obscenity statute must be defined in terms of the average adult.

The constitutionality of the Federal anti-obscenity statute had been upheld by *Roth,* but an important question had been left unanswered. Who has the right to decide what is to be barred from

---
[1] 352 U.S. 380.
[2] Penal Code, Pub. Acts 1931, No. 328, Sec. 343, as amended by Pub. Acts 1953, No. 74.

the mails on the grounds of obscenity? That question was answered in a Federal court when Judge Frederick van Pelt Bryan opened the mails to D. H. Lawrence's novel *Lady Chatterley's Lover.* Postmaster General Arthur E. Summerfield had ruled that the book was unmailable for reasons of obscenity. The decision of Judge Bryan, which was not contested to the Supreme Court, was that the Postmaster General could only apply the current legal standard for obscenity and that his decision was subject to court review. Judge Bryan's definition of the current legal standard of obscenity is as follows: "The material must also exceed the limits of tolerance imposed by current standards of the community with respect to freedom of expression in matters concerning sex and sex relations. Moreover, a book is not to be judged by excerpts or individual passages but must be judged as a whole," an obvious acceptance of the Roth Rule.

The critical point between candor and shame had been reached from the side of candor in 1933 by the *Ulysses* decision. There is a sense, although a less clear one, in which it might be said to have been reached from the side of shame in the 1959 case of *Smith v. California.*[1] Eleasar Smith ran a bookstore in Los Angeles. He was convicted in municipal court of violating a city ordinance relative to the sale of obscene material. He appealed and at the heart of his appeal was the issue of *scienter,* the question of the knowledge of the seller of what is in the merchandise he sells. To what extent is it practical or reasonable to expect a bookseller to know the contents of the multitude of books upon his shelves, a multitude that changes weekly as new books steadily roll off the presses? Eleasar Smith appealed his conviction and the case ultimately reached the Supreme Court.

Justice Brennan wrote the Court decision. It dealt basically with the concept of *scienter.* Since the Los Angeles statute ignored the element of *scienter,* a bookseller would be held responsible under it for the possession of obscene material whether he knew it was obscene or not. Consequently the Court feared that booksellers would be so wary of handling any printed material which was suspect that their wariness would inhibit constitutionally protected rights of the press. The case was sent back to the California Court for action in accordance with the Supreme Court ruling that a

[1] 361 U.S. 147.

bookseller must have some *scienter* to be legally responsible under an anti-obscenity law for the sale of obscene material. Precisely how much knowledge he must have the Court did not state, nor probably in fairness could it state. California could handle the factual aspects of the case of Eleasar Smith, but the legal principle that *scienter* must be a factor in a valid conviction for the sale of obscene literature was established by the case.

The Smith decision of 1959 helped to define the legal limits of knowledge necessary for a licit conviction for the sale of obscene material. The *Bantam Books* decision of 1963 defined with greater clarity than it had been defined before the boundary that prior restraint on the distribution of allegedly obscene material could not pass. The case in question was *Bantam Books v. Sullivan*.[1] The Rhode Island legislature had set up a commission to "educate the public about obscene literature and material manifestly tending to corrupt youth." The Commission notified the distributors of magazines and books what publications did so. The Commission and Max Silverstein & Sons, distributors of Bantam Books for Rhode Island, worked harmoniously for some time, the Commission notifying Silverstein of the books that imperilled youth and on receipt of this information Silverstein stopping their circulation. The arrangement was challenged and the case ultimately reached the Supreme Court.

One should observe that no actual censorship had taken place, but one would be naive not to note also that there was a threat of censorship implicit in the action of the Commission and a realistic acceptance of that threat and avoidance of its consequences by Max Silverstein & Sons. The Supreme Court held that the threat of censorship by those in a position to make such threats effective was in effect censorship of a sort that violated the First Amendment. The Court decision, which was written by Justice Brennan, states, "What Rhode Island has done, in fact, has been to subject the distribution of publications to a system of prior administrative restraints, since the Commission is not a judicial body and its decisions to list particular publications as objectionable do not follow judicial determinations that such publications may lawfully be banned. Any system of prior restraints of expression comes to this Court bearing a heavy presumption against its constitutional validity."

Roth has been further refined and explicated by two 1966 Supreme Court decisions, *Michkin* and *Ginzburg*. Michkin was a New

[1] 372 U.S. 58

York publisher of tracts admittedly "sadistic and masochistic." He was arrested and convicted of selling obscene material, and his case ultimately reached the Supreme Court under the title *Michkin v. New York*.[1] The Roth Rule had accepted the viewpoint of Judge Woolsey in *Ulysses*, that the person whose susceptibility was the norm in a case of obscenity was the average man, the person with average sex instincts, "what the French would call *l'homme moyen sensuel*." Michkin dealt in specialized material for perverts, material that would leave the average man thoroughly disgusted, one might imagine, but certainly not sexually disturbed. The Court ruled that if a publication is intended for sexual deviants and appeals to their prurient interests, it is obscene and subject to anti-obscenity laws even if its intended effect is totally lost upon the average man.

Michkin obviously depended for success upon a distortion of the clear intent of the Roth Rule, but *Ginzburg v. United States*[2] was a more nearly clear test of the norm set up by the Rule. Ralph Ginzburg had been convicted of sending three obscene publications through the mail, a hard cover magazine of expensive format called *Eros*, a bi-weekly news letter entitled *Liaison*, and a shorter publication with the presumably self-defining title *The Housewife's Handbook of Selective Promiscuity*. The Roth Rule for the guidance of a trial judge and jury was "whether to the average person, applying contemporary community standards, the dominant theme of the material taken as a whole appeals to prurient interest." What if an objective examination of the material leaves the issue in doubt? The Court ruling in *Ginzburg* was that then the publisher's intent could be taken into consideration. If the publisher tried to "titillate the public's sexual interest," his advertisement could be taken "at its face value" and the publication declared obscene. Thus to the objective criterion based on the material itself which had been established in *Roth* there was added in *Ginzburg* the framework of production, sales, and publicity. Justice Brennan stated in the Court decision, "We agree that the question of obscenity may include consideration of the setting in which the publications were presented as an aid to determining the question of obscenity, and assume without deciding that the prosecution could not have succeeded otherwise. . . . We view the publications against a background of commercial exploitation of erotica solely for the sake of their prurient appeal. The record in that regard amply supports the

[1] 383 U.S. 502
[2] 383 U.S. 463.

decision of the trial judge that the mailing of all three publications offended the statute." The Court further stated, "Where the purveyor's sole emphasis is on the sexually provocative aspects of his publications, that fact may be decisive in the determination of obscenity. Certainly in a prosecution which, as here, does not necessarily imply suppression of the materials involved, the fact that they originate or are used as a subject of pandering is relevant to the application of the *Roth* test."

The current status of the Roth Rule may be considered established by *Ginzburg*. And yet, to call a status current is not to call it final. There was dissent from *Ginzburg*, by Justice Black in the form predictable in the light of his absolutist position toward the Bill of Rights, but also by Justice Potter Stewart. Justice Stewart dissented partly on the grounds that "commercial exploitation," "pandering," and "titillation" are not criminal offenses nor are they capable of the exact definition that could make them such. His basic dissent, however, was based on a belief that the Court was itself violating the Constitution in denying Ginzburg First Amendment protection. "For the First Amendment protects us all with an even hand. It applies to Ralph Ginzburg with no less completeness than to G. P. Putnam Sons. In upholding and enforcing the Bill of Rights, this Court has no power to pick or to choose. When we lose sight of that fixed star of constitutional adjudication, we lose our way. For then we forsake a government of law and are left with government by Big Brother." The dissent by a justice whose opinions in general are so balanced and far-sighted as those of Justice Stewart, coupled with the fact that fourteen separate opinions were filed in *Mishkin, Ginzburg,* and an obscenity case that originated in Massachusetts and concerned the eighteenth-century novel usually referred to as *Fanny Hill,*[1] indicates that the current status of the Roth Rule may not be the final status. On the other hand, it may be, because much careful thought has gone into its formulation and refinement, and the test of time has been applied to it with good effect. Its present status may now be defined.

THE ROTH RULE TODAY

It is the law of the land, confirmed by Supreme Court decisions, that there is such a thing as pornography and that its publication and

---

[1] *A Book Named "John Cleland's Memoirs of a Woman of Pleasure" v. Massachusetts,* 383 U.S. 413 (1966).

distribution are punishable by the laws of the several states and by a Federal anti-obscenity statute. It is currently fashionable to call it hard-core pornography. Pornography is hard to define, and no one has attempted to set up an objective standard for testing the hardness of its core. One definition with the merit of epigrammatic succinctness is that of a Methodist clergyman of England: "pornography is sex out of all context except that of sensational enjoyment."[1] Whether this definition, for all its merit, it really adequate for the last quarter of the twentieth century must presently be considered. The average man, whose role in determining pornography has received the highest formal recognition, probably would be satisfied with the viewpoint of Huntington Cairns, general counsel of the National Gallery of Art, special legal adviser to the Secretary of the Treasury on censorship questions pertaining to the Customs Bureau, and the man whom that eloquent exponent of free speech Zechariah Chafee called "the ideal censor"[2]: "There is no difficulty in distinguishing between books the impulse behind which is literary and those whose impulse is pornography. Any man with a modicum of literary knowledge can do so without hesitation."[3] If there is no difficulty in spotting it, it is hard-core pornography even if it cannot be defined.

Most of the problem involved in the suppression of pornography has been caused by publications in which the writing accused of obscenity has been incidental to something else, most frequently but by no means exclusively to the depiction of sordid aspects of life at the lower social levels done in the literary tradition of naturalism. At this point we see why *Hagar Revelly* fell into the toils, and possibly *Ulysses*, though hardly *Lady Chatterley's Lover*. We also see why "Banned in Boston" was once as useful an advertising slogan as "I'd walk a mile for a Camel." By and large books written in the tradition of naturalism do have ideas of redeeming social importance, and some novels of the sort have had ideas of great value. The point which Justice Brennan stressed in *Roth* is a vital one, and to protect books highly offensive to the good taste of the average man may be an entirely valid application of the First Amendment. To say this is not to say that the average man may not quite understandably find

---

[1] Donald Soper, in C. H. Ralph, Ed., *Does Pornography Matter?* London, 1961, p. 42
[2] *Government and Mass Communications*, I, 269.
[3] "Freedom of Expression in Literature," *Annals of the American Academy of Political and Social Science*, vol. 200 (Nov. 1938), p. 87.

certain books with redeeming social value highly offensive. There is certainly no reason in a nation that also protects free speech that people should not dislike them, denounce them, not read them, and keep their children from reading them. The one thing they should not do is suppress them.

Next to the criterion of the possession of ideas the criterion of greatest importance confirmed by *Roth* is the reaction of the average man as the basis for a decision about pornography. It would be a great mistake to think that the Hicklin Rule is dead merely because it has been declared unconstitutional. Every time a person says that a particular publication should not be allowed to exist because it might fall into the hands of children he is affirming his belief in the Hicklin Rule. The Hicklin Rule lives on in people's minds because it is an entirely natural, normal, admirable, instinctively attractive Rule, since the instinct to protect the young is natural, normal, and admirable. The point to be stressed, however, is that the proper criterion in the world of literature is not the needs of the young, and the law in its impartiality must not make the welfare of the young, nor indeed of any other subdivision of the human community, the sole criterion of legality. If the law must be impartial, however, it does not follow that the individual citizen need be impartial. He is and should be totally free to criticize any publication he considers deserving of criticism, and to denounce the man who wrote it, within the limits of libel law. A book is quite as truly in the public domain as any public personality, and the New York Times Rule is just as valid applied to books as applied to politicians. Furthermore, there is no reason that an individual should not be entirely free to protect anyone under his natural guardianship from a book the reading of which he considers morally pernicious.

The application of this principle where reading in schools, required or permitted, is concerned poses a thorny question, and in view of the length and sharpness of the thorns the writer is not dissatisfied that it lies outside the scope of the present work. This he would say in passing, for what it is worth. It seems to him tenable that persons legally and morally responsibile for the academic curriculum have as much right to discourage and forbid the reading of certain books as a part of the curriculum as they have to encourage or require it. It seems to him defensible that the reading which comprises the curriculum should be consistent with the moral climate of the community as determined by its general attitude and should not include books which, in the words of Judge Bryan as he opened the mails to *Lady Chatterley's Lover,* "exceed the limits of tolerance imposed by current standards of the community with respect to freedom of expression in matters concerning sex and sex relations." Any individual parent who believes that his child will benefit from the reading of such books has the right, and the responsibility inherent in it, to encourage him to read them, but he should not be allowed to impose his judgment on the community by an abuse of the injunctive process. All too often actual freedom is destroyed in the name of theoretical freedom. Again and again, in the opinion of critics of the Warren Court, the Supreme Court has done precisely that. In the ultimate reduction of the criticism to which the Warren era in the Court has been subjected, the essence of the criticism has really been that the rights of the average man have been curtailed to strengthen the rights of the man who deviates from the average, the freedom of the religious curtailed for the sake of the anti-religious, the law abiding for the sake of the criminal. Justice after justice has proclaimed that the rights of the foes of religion, the foes of society, the deviates from what is generally accepted and respected must be protected, as indeed they should be. They should not be protected, however, at the expense of the rights of the religious, the law abiding, the conformists. Liberty should never be destroyed in the name of liberty, freedoms curtailed in the name of freedom. That this has been done by the Warren Court is the heart of the criticism directed at it, the heart of the demand that the Supreme Court be made once more representative of the American people as a whole. On the principle that the majority also has rights and the judgment of the average man is the valid judgment by which pornography should be tested, the time seems ripe to question the current concept of pornography and to see if an expansion of that concept toward which society in general is groping may not be justified. One may reasonably ask if society in America may not be groping toward a concept of pornography already accepted and now unquestioned in other countries.

PORNO-VIOLENCE

It is tenable that the already quoted definition of pornography, "sex out of all context except that of sensational enjoyment," is now inadequate. It is not inadequate, of course, if sex is given the sort of

comprehensive definition contemporary psychiatry substantiates.
Sadism, masochism, the dark allure of violence are rooted in sex, and
although it distorts *sex* out of all the meaning of the word conveys to
the average man to comprehend such aberrations within the term, it
does not distort it out of a meaning accpetable to medical science.
There is abroad in the land what Tom Wolfe has called *porno-
violence*. Sadism, masochism, and mayhem out of all context except
that of sensational enjoyment might just as well be called pornography as not, since nothing is to be gained by inventing a new name
for an old reality. The real nub of the matter, of course, is that
sadism, masochism, and mayhem are much more vividly portrayed
by pictures than by words, and much more vividly portrayed by
moving pictures than by still. Their true home is the motion picture,
whether shown in a motion picture theatre or on a television screen.
Hence they pose a problem far greater today than in the past.

We had occasion earlier to draw the distinction between the
problem of a fair trial in a tragedy that has aroused a legitimate
intense public interest like the assassination of President Kennedy
and in a tragedy in which the interest was artificially manufactured
like the murder of Marilyn Sheppard. There is, perhaps, a parallel
distinction between the scene of violence in a news presentation on
television and the scene of violence in a motion picture. The difference between the two is an obvious one. There is also a difference,
all but the most naive believe, between a genuine scene of violence
in a TV news program and a manufactured one. If it is cynical to
believe that the violence in TV news films on occasion breaks out
only after the camera has been properly focused and the floodlights
turned on, all one can say is that the cynics of America are numbered by the millions.

The problem here is an extremely difficult one to solve, and the
difficulty certainly is not lessened by the fact that it must be solved
within a constitutional framework. Paul Weber's contention has won
wide acceptance that the television coverage of war scenes, race
riots, and violence of every other form and degree has contributed
its share to that perversion within the individual observer which
Wolfe called porno-violence. As Weber puts it, television violence
"fantasizes the desire, present deep in every man, for easy, violent,

but forbidden, solutions to complex problems."[1] If Wolfe is right in saying that the desire for the quick and violent solution is present deep in every man, and modern psychiatry bears him out, then in this matter the most susceptible is Everyman and the Hicklin and Roth Rules coalesce. It is not a new thesis that the repeated sight of simulated brutality, like the repeated sight of real brutality, tends to brutalize the observer and make him gradually less sensitive and possibly at the end insensitive to what brutality is really like.

There is no question that the American people as a whole favor anti-pornography laws; recent Harris and Gallup polls have shown an overwhelming support of them. The problem becomes more acute where porno-violence is concerned, partly because the issue is relatively new and partly because the problem has aspects not present in the pornography of sex. Violence takes place in life, porno-violence takes place in the mind of the beholder. A scene of violence in a news broadcast is a piece of news quite as truly as the description of it in a newspaper story, yet it may carry a message to the deep abysm and dark backwards of the human mind quite as perilous as the worst pornography of the explicit sort. The argument that the printed story may carry the same message has limited validity. The printed word is less vivid than the picture, and very much less vivid than the moving picture. What, then, can be done about it?

First, the distinction must be borne in mind between fiction and fact, between the moving picture as the term is ordinarily understood and the news story. Porno-violence in a moving picture is artificially contrived by the very nature of a moving picture, by the difference between fiction and fact. Second, many believe in the distinction between the spontaneous and the contrived recording of violence in a news broadcast. Even in the case of the spontaneous recording, the very limitations of television as a medium must not be forgotten. A policeman uses violence on a protesting student, or a protesting student uses violence on a policeman. The fact is filmed and transmitted from coast to coast. There may have been a hundred other policemen present and five hundred other protesting students, none employing violence and therefore not photogenic. The fact that violence was extremely sporadic may be part of the

---

[1] Quoted in David Manning White and Richard Averson, *Sight, Sound, and Society: Motion Pictures and Television in America*, Boston: Beacon Press, 1968, p. 236.

story as recorded in the newspaper, but it is not part of the story as shown on television. The violent moment is the entire story where the television episode is concerned. The result is the distortion of truth that vividness achieves at the expense of comprehensive accuracy. Television by its nature inclines to vividness rather than to comprehensive accuracy. In addition, since the voice of cynicism is so common in this matter that it must be listened to, one should refer at least in passing to the myriads of cynics who maintain that the violent policeman has appeared on the TV screen out of all statistical proportion to the violent student.

There is, then, a discernible gradation in justification where television violence is concerned. Its justification is greater in the honestly filmed news story than in the slanted one, and greater in any news story than in a fictional TV entertainment. It is by no means a clear-cut matter that its justification is greater in programs for adults than in programs for children, if the psychological case against porno-violence is sound. In any event, there is no dearth of violence in children's programs. One study of one hundred hours of children's programs revealed twelve murders, sixteen gun fights, twenty-one shootings, twenty-one other incidents involving guns, fifteen fist fights, fifteen sluggings, three successful and one unsuccessful suicides, and a potpourri of violence harder to classify, such as a raving maniac loose on a plane and a man ground beneath a horse's hooves.[1]

The defense is sometimes offered that this diet of violence does not adversely affect the normal child, just as the argument is sometimes advanced that capital punishment bore most heavily upon the poor and ignorant. Capital punishment did not bear most heavily upon the poor and ignorant. It bore most heavily on those found guilty of first-degree murder. The fact that many of them were poor and ignorant is of no consequence unless one can prove that they murdered because they were poor and ignorant. Most poor, unlettered people are perfectly law abiding and respectable. The real truth is that capital punishment bore most heavily on the poor, ignorant, frustrated, over-aggressive psychotics who moved from the violence of fantasy into the violence of reality. Crime statistics too well known for needed repetition prove that the peril from such psychotics is greater than ever before in American history, and every

[1] Wilbur Schramm, Jack Lyle, and Edwin B. Parker, *Television in the Lives of Our Children*, Stanford University Press, 1961, pp. 139-140.

American city dweller knows it without statistics. It is the poor, ignorant psychotic who crushes the skull of the innocent citizen on the darkened street of the American city, not the clever, sophisticated criminal who preys on the wealthy. The poor, ignorant psychotic is the real peril to the average man.

To how many such psychotics has the porno-violence of television and the motion picture been a training school? It is absurd to think that the final downfall of the villain in a movie, with the trite "crime does not pay" message it connotes, in any way affects the psychotic who is watching the picture to see how it is done. No criminal envisages failure as the result of his crime. He does not intend to make the mistake his model made. Nor does it help to say that violent crime has roots far deeper than those which may extend into the soil of television and the moving picture. Of course there are roots in the mental inheritance of the criminal and the environment in which he has lived, but TV violence can feed a diet of porno-violence to the psychotic until malignancy bursts what has inhibited it and physical violence breaks out. Wilbur Schramm and his associates asked one hundred young prisoners in a Chicago jail what turned them to crime. The conclusion of the investigators was, "TV, pornography, and movies play a distinct role in the creation of the anti-social behavior in susceptible teen-agers."[1] The criminals said that TV, movies, radio, and pornography played a part in turning them to crime. They should know.

HEADQUARTERS DETECTIVE

The suggestion that the concept of pornography be expanded to include masochism, sadism, and mayhem is a relatively new one and in this country has received relatively little legal testing. The one test it has received in the Supreme Court it failed. In 1941 New York, which had had a law on the books for some time aimed at curbing "bloodshed, lust, or crime" stories, revised the law and began to enforce it. A man was arrested for selling a magazine called *Headquarters Detective,* and it was charged that stories therein were brewed from these illegal ingredients. He was found guilty, his conviction was upheld by the New York Court of Appeals, the case

[1] *Ibid.,* p. 302.

went to the United States Supreme Court, and in 1948 the Supreme Court reversed the decision of the New York courts.[1]

Justice Reed wrote the majority verdict. The Court held the New York statute unconstitutional on three grounds: it was too vague, it violated the due-process clause, and to classify accounts of bloodshed and lust as obscene meant fashioning an "expanded concept of indecency and obscenity." Justices Frankfurter, Jackson, and Burton dissented. They stressed the fact that many states had anti-obscenity statutes of the New York type and held that a certain indefiniteness in their phraseology was inevitable. They believed that their colleagues were confusing "want of certainty as to the outcome of different prosecutions for similar conduct, with want of definiteness in what the law prohibits." Justice Frankfurter held that it was within the competence of a legislature to strike a balance between a narrowness which makes a law easy to circumvent and a vagueness which makes it impossible to know what is forbidden. He believed that the Court was reading its own psychological convictions into the law, and its own concepts of criminology, and was taking away from the elected representatives of the people the right to judge the causes of the crimes they are required to prevent. He wrote, "The essence of the Court's decision is that it gives publications which have 'nothing of any possible value to society' constitutional protection but denies to the States the power to prevent the grave evils to which, in their rational judgment, such publications give rise." In effect, the Supreme Court did not explicitly restrain all legal control of the instrumentalities of porno-violence, but it did make more austere requirements for any statute designed for that end. One might add that "void for vagueness" is a device that neatly sidesteps the real issue, the legal validity of the purpose for which a statute has been adopted and the legal validity of a statute of its sort as a means of fulfilling that purpose.

The *Headquarters Detective* case should not be considered the last word on the subject. For one thing, the Supreme Court has frequently demonstrated its own capacity to double back on its tracks and to dart off on ideological tangents. It should be noted that even Chief Justice Warren was capable of saying, "It is the manner

[1] The New York case is 294 N.Y. 545, 550 (1945); the Supreme Court case is 333 U.S. 503 (1948).

of use that should determine obscenity. It is the conduct of the individual that should be judged, not the quality of art or literature."[1] If the Court should ever go so far as to accept as valid this viewpoint, then the establishment of the concept of porno-violence as falling under the ban on pornography might not be difficult. It is far from certain, however, that it ever would do so, or indeed should do so. Porno-violence, to be sure, is something that takes place in the mind of the beholder, but there is an objective reality that causes it and it is the objective reality that should be judged. It would seem not impossible, after another quarter century of sadism, masochism, and mayhem on television and an indeterminate number of sacrificed lives, that a statute could be written against porno-violence sufficiently exact in terminology to meet the Court requirements. Nine years after this case, Justice Brennan in the course of the Court decision in *Roth* came to grips with the contention that terms of obscenity statutes are too imprecise in the standards of guilt they set up to stand the test of the due-process clause. After pointing out that the Court has frequently recognized this fact, he added, "The Court, however, has consistently held that lack of precision is not itself offensive to the requirements of due process," and he cited *United States v. Petrillo:*[2] "The constitution does not require impossible standards"; all that is required is that the language "conveys sufficiently definite warning as to the prescribed conduct when measured by common understanding and practices. . . ." The Court viewpoint in *Roth* was reasonable and practical. Statutes can be written with sufficient definiteness, if *Roth* is to be believed, to stand the due-process test if law-enforcement authorities follow the more than ample guidelines laid down for them in a series of decisions that harkens back to *Miranda* and beyond. Thus two of the three objections of the Court majority in *Headquarters Detective* can on the basis of *Roth* be met successfully. The third objection was that a statute banning the fictional presentation of porno-violence involved an "expanded concept of indecency and obscenity." To that charge the proponents of such a statute can only plead guilty. That is precisely what they are trying to do.

[1] *Kingsley Books v. Brown*, 354 U.S. 436 (1957). *Kingsley Books* was an obscenity case which hinged on the issue of prior restraint.
[2] *United States v. Petrillo*, 332 U.S. 1.

THE MORAL CLIMATE ABROAD

America is not unique in being concerned about the area of conflict between the rights of a free press and the right of the people to the moral climate of their choice. Other nations, no less dedicated than America is to the general principle of freedom and its specific application to the press, have faced up to the problem and have not hesitated to curb porno-violence in print. The crudely drawn and cheaply printed cartoons of sadism, masochism, and mayhem known by some verbal aberration as comic books have been a problem abroad and a problem solved by summary action. Canada banned them in 1949, New Zealand and Australia in 1954. In 1955 Great Britain banned horror comics and thereafter sharpened its anti-obscenity law. No evidence has been forthcoming that freedom in any true sense has thereby been curtailed in the Commonwealth. The 1959 Obscene Publications Act of Great Britain defined obscene materials by the generic description, "such as tend to deprave." The Federal law of Australia forbids the importation of published material which "unduly emphasizes matters of sex or crime." New South Wales expanded the definition of *obscene* in these terms: "Without prejudice to the generality of the meaning of the word 'obscene' any publication or advertisement shall be deemed to be obscene if it unduly emphasizes matters of sex, crimes of violence, gross cruelty or horror." New Zealand has an Indecent Publications Act which makes it an offense to publish anything that "unduly emphasizes matters of sex, horror, crime, cruelty or violence." Nor is this attitude toward porno-violence limited to the British Commonwealth. France, a nation at least as committed as we are to the ideal of freedom and a nation with a glowing record of tolerance for published ideas of the most unorthodox sort, has a positively Puritanic anti-obscenity law governing publications for the young. Such publications "must not contain any section or insertions presenting under a favorable light banditry, falsehood, theft, laziness, cowardice, hatred, debauchery, or any acts classified as crimes or misdemeanors or of a nature demoralizing to childhood or youth."[1]

It is well not to get this matter out of perspective, or to permit it to be twisted out of perspective. There have been witch hunts against books considered unorthodox by whatever may be the stan-

[1] Loi No. 49-956 of July 16, 1949. There is an excellent survey of anti-obscenity laws abroad in Terrence J. Murphy, *Censorship: Government and Obscenity*, Baltimore: Helicon Press, 1963.

dards of orthodoxy held by the witch hunters. The English-speaking world has an intermittent penchant for such hunts, and the United States has not been behind the rest of the Anglo-Saxon brotherhood in this regard. A particularly silly one was conducted over a generation ago in Boston, but before long it died of that very principle of self-destruction which is innate in all movements of its sort. As a matter of fact, only two novels by serious authors have been tested for obscenity in Federal courts in the last forty years, James Joyce's *Ulysses* and D. H. Lawrence's *Lady Chatterley's Lover*, and both passed the test. There simply is no evidence that the laws against pornography pose a serious threat to serious writing, and there is even less ground for dread that similar laws against porno-violence would menace the sort of visual drama that should be free. Our courts are not so benighted as to confuse macabre horror on television with Shakespeare's *Titus Andronicus*.

It might even be plausibly argued that those most devoted to freedom in the abstract and to freedom concretely to be realized in the arts could find logical grounds for a vigorous defense of anti-pornography statutes. If the instinct of the witch hunter is to ban the book, the instinct of the libertarian is to hide behind the courts. The distrust of the people in the mind of the latter is every bit as strong as the distrust of the book in the mind of the former. The Puritan says that the masses must be preserved from pollution by the arts, the libertarian says that the arts must be preserved from pollution by the masses. Neither pays any attention to the possibility that the masses may be quite as capable of knowing good from evil in private life as they are when serving on a jury, and that the private lives of most adults are very little influenced by the arts in any form. It is the fashion with some to say that no one was ever injured by reading a book. One can say that if one is willing to support the corollary that no one was ever helped by reading a book. Neither statement is tenable. Lives have been formed and transformed by the reading of books, and lives have been deformed. The essential purpose of the anti-obscenity statute is to eliminate from circulation that which can only deform and cannot possibly do anything else. That is what is meant by hard-core pornography, and the argument is sound that there is hard-core porno-violence every bit as perilous to those capable of being deformed by it.

There is an admirable piece of reasoning in the Preface to George Bernard Shaw's *The Shewing-Up of Blanco Posnet* in the passage called "The Necessity of Immoral Plays." Shaw explains that he is a specialist in heretical and immoral plays. "Whatever is contrary to established manners and customs is immoral. An immoral act or doctrine is not necessarily a sinful one: on the contrary, every advance in thought and conduct is by definition immoral until it has converted the majority." This is the essential argument for the publication of whatever may contain ideas of conceivable even if far from obvious value. But does that mean that nothing in the theatre should be censored? In Shaw's view, the theatre should not be censored but the theatre should be judged.

A magistrate has laws to administer: a censor has nothing but his own opinion. A judge leaves the question of guilt to the jury: the Censor is jury and judge as well as lawgiver.... The law may be only the intolerance of the community; but it is a defined and limited intolerance.... In short, no man is lawfully at the mercy of the magistrate's personal caprice, prejudice, ignorance, superstition, temper, stupidity, resentment, timidity, ambition, or private conviction. But a playwright's livelihood, his reputation, and his inspiration and mission are at the personal mercy of the Censor. The two do not stand, as the criminal and the judge stand, in the presence of a law that binds them both equally, and was made by neither of them, but by the deliberate collective wisdom of the community.

This is the essential argument for the anti-obscenity law and the determination of its applicability by a jury which embodies, to the extent that such embodiment is attainable in this far from perfect world, the collective wisdom of the community.

The concept that the average citizen is capable of judging morality in the arts is quite as heretical and immoral in late twentieth-century America as it was in early twentieth-century Britain. American liberal thought has been possessed of the conviction that the arts must be protected from the people. As Terrence Murphy puts it, "an unspoken premise of the libertarian position is that the American public can not be trusted to devise reasonable public policies in regard to the arts. Therefore the courts must be persuaded to put the arts beyond the vulgar reach of the masses."[1] This is a strange reversal of the normal position of liberalism where freedom is con-

[1] *Op. cit.*, pp. 120–121.

cerned. Yves Simon put the original truth about liberalism as well as anyone when he said,

At the heart of Liberalism lies an almost religious belief in a kind of Demiurge immanent in the stream of contingent events, or better, identical with the very stream of contingencies. . . . Owing to this benevolent Spirit of Nature, contingency and chance are supposed to result indefectibly in happy achievements. Wrong use of human freedom, in the long run at least, does not matter. Regarding both truth values and economic values, the Liberal confidently relies upon the laissez faire laissez passer system. Liberalism is an optimistic naturalism.[1]

But liberalism has been notably false to its early premises in two primary areas, economics and the arts. Only one who has studied the history of economic thought can appreciate the totality of the about-face liberalism has taken where the doctrine of economic *laissez faire* is concerned. The constant appeal to the courts to protect the arts from the people is a comparable abandonment of artistic *laissez faire.*

There are many reasons for accepting the possible validity of Shaw's heretical and immoral belief in the right of a people to live in the moral climate of their choice and to make that right effective by subjecting possible abuses of it to trial by jury after the analogy of the libel law. The most important set of reasons is bound up with the rationale of freedom itself, and there is no particular need to attempt again what the Founding Fathers did when they wrote the Declaration of Independence. There is a subordinate set of reasons that should appeal to those to whom the arts are precious. The basis of the argument is purely humanistic and it was very well put by one of America's leading humanistic philosophers, Professor William H. Hocking of Harvard:

If I were personally to challenge one product of an uncontrolled liberty more than another, it would be the liberty to degrade, and especially to degrade the arts, which are man's own religion of self-elevation. I confess I am angry with the defilers of this religion, and still more angry when they bleat 'freedom of the press' to cover their

[1] *Nature and Functions of Authority*, New York, 1940, p. 59.

treasons. . . . If we reject the aid of the state as incompetent in these matters, we would seem bound to recognize of this common good we call culture that it is at once peculiarly defenseless against wanton assault by the more brutal individual impulses which still claim freedom. . . .[1]

There is, then, a certain fundamental principle at work in the matter of obscenity just as it is at work in all the issues considered in this book. We started with the axiom that in the ultimate sense the only inalienable right not subject to limitation or control by society is the right of the individual to live a life of virtue. The rights we commonly and properly call inalienable such as the immortal three of the Declaration of Independence are in the nature of definitions of that right. The rights enshrined in the Bill of Rights are inalienable in the same sense, the conditions which expedite the living by the individual of the life of virtue and therefore antecedent to man-made statutes which, at the most, lay down the ground rules under which such rights are to be maintained. The right to the truth is a right inalienable from the right to live the life of virtue, and freedom of thought, speech, press, and religion are definitions and exemplifications of the right to truth. They are inalienable viewed as definitions and exemplifications, but once they are treated as absolutes having existence apart from the right to truth which is one of the necessary conditions for the life of virtue, their real significance is destroyed and they can be distorted into vehicles of error and tyranny.

America has never known a more eloquent exponent of free speech than Zechariah Chafee. He said,

. . . it is useless to define free speech by talk about rights. . . . To find the boundary line in any right, we must get behind rules to human facts. In our problem, we must regard the desires and needs of the individual human who wants to speak and those of the great groups of human beings among whom he speaks. That is, in technical language, there are individual interests and social interests, which must be balanced against each other, if they conflict, in order to determine which interest shall be sacrificed under the circumstances. . . . It must never be forgotten that the balancing cannot be properly done unless all the interests involved are ade-

[1] *Freedom of the Press*, Chicago, 1947, p. 48.

*quately ascertained, and the great evil about all this talk about rights
is that each side is so busy denying the other's claim to rights that it
entirely overlooks the human desires and needs behind that claim.*[1]

Even the right to truth is not inalienable at the expense of other
rights. As Chafee points out, there is also the right to the preservation of order, the right of the young to proper training, the right of
the citizen to protection against external aggression. "Unlimited
discussion sometimes interferes with these purposes, which must
then be balanced against freedom of speech, but freedom of speech
ought to weigh very heavily on the scale. . . ."[2] This is the test by
which freedom of the press and the other media is to be determined
and the reason that freedom of the press, like every other freedom
named in the Bill of Rights, is not an absolute but a relative to be
considered in terms of all the other rights enumerated. The right of
the citizen to protection against aggression carries as its corollary the
duty of the government to exercise prior restraint on the issuance of
news when such issuance would endanger the citizen's safety. The
right of the citizen to a fair trial carries as its corollary the duty of
the government to maintain an atmosphere in which a fair trial is
possible and to regulate media treatment of the case in such a way as
to preserve that atmosphere. The right of the citizen to his good
name is the justification of the libel laws and the curb upon press
freedom they connote. The right of the citizen to proper privacy
carries as its corollary the duty of the press and the other media to
observe propriety in their search for the news and the duty of the
government to translate propriety into law. The right of citizens to
live in the moral climate of their choice derives from the right of the
individual to live the life of virtue.

Some persons who speak with the authority that commands respect believe that today the press faces a challenge as potent in its
way as the very different challenge faced in 1932 when the American press went down to ideological defeat along with Herbert Hoover and the political and social philosophy they shared. Then the
impact of economic depression flattened the castle of cards erected
in the name of economic *laissez faire* and blindly buttressed by a
press oblivious to the way in which the American pulse was beating.
Today, in the view of many, the impact of social *laissez faire* has

[1] *Free Speech in the United States,* 1941, pp. 31–32.
[2] *Ibid.*

caused an all but intolerable disorder in society, and there is a growing tide of resentment, bitterness, and the will to change among citizens of America whose very lives are disordered and even threatened by social excesses at least tolerated, often fostered, and in some cases explicitly caused by press, radio, and television. History repeatedly has taught that just as the consequence of excessive social restraint is not more restraint but the snapping of the bonds of restraint, so the consequence of excessive libertarianism is not more libertarianism but a return to stern, often rigid, sometimes stifling controls. Let enough people become convinced that their safety as American citizens, their right to a fair trial, their right to their good name, their right to personal privacy, and their right to live in an atmosphere of decency, safety, and peace are being endangered by the degree of permissiveness allowed, and the history of libertarianism and its consequences may repeat itself. Unlimited freedom for any instrumentality of society always threatens the stability of society, and society will react to protect its stability. Totally unfettered media could threaten and in the view of many already do threaten the stability of American life. Americans will react to re-establish and strengthen that stability. The lesson should not be lost on the press, radio, and television. Above all it should not be lost upon the press, which is the oldest and still the most important of the media, and the one that reviews the rest. The press is never really free unless it accepts a pattern which protects it from the peril of self-destruction.

INDEX